COMMUNITY PROPERTY LAW IN A MOBILE AMERICA

A Comprehensive Guide for Estate Planners

Brock T. Exline, Alan S. Gassman, Vincent Miranda

AMERICAN BAR ASSOCIATION

Real Property, Trust and Estate Law Section

Cover design by Andrew Alcala

The materials contained herein represent the opinions of the authors and/or the editors and should not be construed to be the views or opinions of the law firms or companies that such persons are in partnership with, associated with, or employed by, nor of the American Bar Association or the Section of Real Property, Trust and Estate Law, unless adopted pursuant to the bylaws of the Association.

Nothing contained in this book is to be considered as the rendering of legal advice for specific cases, and readers are responsible for obtaining such advice from their own legal counsel. This book is intended for educational and informational purposes only.

Printed in the United States of America.

30 29 28 27 26 5 4 3 2 1

ISBN 978-1-63905-796-2

Library of Congress Cataloging-in-Publication Data
Names: Exline, Brock T. author | Gassman, Alan S. author | Miranda, Vincent author
Title: Community property law in a mobile America : a comprehensive guide for estate planners / Brock T. Exline, Alan S. Gassman, Vincent Miranda.
Description: Chicago : American Bar Association, 2026. | Includes bibliographical references and index. | Summary: "This book is intended as a general educational resource for estate planning practitioners and is not intended as a definitive reference for the law of any particular community property estate. Estate planning for clients with community property interests requires more than just an understanding of traditional estate and gift tax principles; it demands fluency in the varying marital property frameworks that exist across the United State and, if planning with international clients, abroad. The rise of the "Community Property Trust" and its development from 1998 to present is examined as well. The authors analyze the planning opportunities these trusts may present, the requirements for their validity and enforceability across jurisdictions that authorize them, and their efficacy in securing the full (or "double") step-up in basis on the death of the first dying spouse under Internal Revenue Code"–Provided by publisher.
Identifiers: LCCN 2026019660 (print) | LCCN 2026019661 (ebook) |
ISBN 9781639057962 paperback | ISBN 9781639057979 epub
Subjects: LCSH: Community property--United States |
Estate planning--United States | Trusts and trustees--United States |
Inheritance and succession--United States | Husband and wife--Property--United States |
Taxation--United States
Classification: LCC KF526.E95 2026 (print) | LCC KF526 (ebook)
LC record available at https://lccn.loc.gov/2026019660
LC ebook record available at https://lccn.loc.gov/2026019661

Discounts are available for books ordered in bulk. Special consideration is given to state bars, CLE programs, and other bar-related organizations. Inquire at Book Publishing, ABA Publishing, American Bar Association, 321 N. Clark Street, Chicago, Illinois 60654-7598.

www.shopABA.org

Contents

Chapter 6: Migratory Spouses and the Permutations of Marital Property 123

Chapter 7: Transmutations of Property 143

Chapter 8: Federal Taxation of Community Property 171

About the Authors

Alan S. Gassman is a board certified Trust and Estates lawyer practicing with Gassman, Denicolo & Ketron, P.A., which he founded in 1987. The firm focuses on the representation of high net worth families, physicians, and business owners and their companies in estate planning, taxation, and business and personal asset structuring.

Mr. Gassman is the lead author of many books, including *Gassman and Markham on Florida and Federal Asset Protection Law, The Estate Planner's Guide to Bankruptcy, Florida Law for Tax, Business & Financial Planning Advisors, Eight Steps to a Proper Florida Trust and Estate Plan, A Practical Guide to Kickback & Self-Referral Laws for Florida Physicians, The Florida Power of Attorney & Incapacity Planning Guide, The Florida Advisor's Guide To Counseling Same Sex Couples, and is co-author of the Legal Guide To NFA Firearms and Gun Trusts,* among others.

Mr. Gassman holds a law degree and a Masters of Law degree (LL.M.) in Taxation from the University of Florida, and a business degree from Rollins College. Mr. Gassman is board certified by the Florida Bar Association in Estate Planning and Trust Law and was inducted into the Estate Planning Hall of Fame Class of 2021 and has received the Accredited Estate Planner Designation from the National Association of Estate Planners & Council (NAEPC). Mr. Gassman has maintained an AV rating from the Martindale-Hubbell for over 20 years and is listed in both Best Lawyers in America and Florida Super Lawyers.

Brock Exline is an Associate Attorney at Gassman, Denicolo & Ketron, P.A., in Clearwater, Florida, where he supports the firm's work providing sophisticated estate and tax planning for high-net-worth individuals and families, closely held business owners, and professionals. He earned his Juris Doctor from Stetson University College of Law and holds an LL.M. in Taxation from the University of Florida Levin College of Law. His practice includes estate planning, probate and trust administration, business planning, and related tax matters. He is a published co-author on trusts and planning topics, including work appearing in The Florida Bar Journal, the Stetson Business Law Review, and Leimberg Information Services. He is admitted to practice law in Florida.

Vincent Miranda is an Associate at Cauthen & Burns, P.A., in Tavares, Florida, where he practices in the areas of estate planning and tax law. He earned his Juris Doctor, cum laude, from Stetson University College of Law and holds an LL.M. in Taxation from the University of Florida. His academic and professional work centers on federal estate and gift taxation, trust taxation, and advanced wealth transfer planning. He is a published author on tax and planning topics, with work appearing in the Stetson Business Law Review. He is admitted to practice law in Florida.

Preface

Disclaimer: *This book is intended as a general educational resource for estate planning practitioners and is not intended as a definitive reference for the law of any particular community property state. Although this book discusses the laws of various community property and separate property states in some detail, those statutes, regulations, and cases are subject to change. Practitioners are reminded to conduct their own independent research in the specific state whose law they are addressing and to consult with local counsel as appropriate before advising clients or preparing documents. Nothing in this book should be construed as legal advice for any specific situation.*

In today's highly mobile society, individuals and families frequently relocate across state and national borders for career opportunities, lifestyle changes, or financial reasons. Estate planning practitioners in noncommunity property states will therefore likely work with clients who have relocated from a community property state, or who have acquired property in a community property jurisdiction at some point during marriage. Effective estate planning for clients with community property interests requires more than just an understanding of traditional estate and gift tax principles; it demands fluency in the varying marital property frameworks that exist across the United States and, if planning with international clients, abroad.

Discussions of community property—and marital property more broadly—often fail to distinguish between outcomes that depend on whether the property is divided because of divorce or because of a spouse's death. While divorce is governed by family law, inheritance law applies to property transfers at death. As a result, the legal framework governing a spouse's property rights shifts depending on whether the marriage ends in divorce or death.

Upon divorce, property division follows either the equitable distribution[1] rules of common law states or the community property rules of community property states. At death, a different set of principles determines the rights of the surviving spouse and other heirs in the decedent's property. Surviving spouses may have marital property rights in common law states, community property entitlements in community property states, or, in some circumstances, community property entitlements in separate property states. Those variations can produce markedly different outcomes that can significantly impact estate planning strategies. Estate planning practitioners must therefore carefully navigate both marital property law and inheritance rights to ensure clients' assets are distributed as intended and that the spouses' financial protections are preserved.

Because community property generally retains its character as such even after a couple moves to a separate property state, estate planners in noncommunity property jurisdictions must understand the complexities of community property law. Importantly, the federal tax law does not create property rights but instead applies federally defined tax consequences to property rights established under state law. As a result, practitioners must carefully navigate varying state property laws, choice-of-law principles, and the corresponding state and federal tax implications when dealing with characterizations of property that are not uniformly respected across the states.

If a married couple does not plan before relocating, the law of their new state of domicile may treat property acquired in their former domicile in unexpected ways. This book frames much of the discussion around six key property outcomes—the ownership and division of community and separate property during marriage, at divorce, and at death—to provide a practical framework estate planners can use with confidence. Through case studies, legal analysis, and planning tools, this book equips practitioners with the knowledge needed to craft estate plans that are both tax efficient and legally sound while accounting for community property issues.

---

[1] "Equitable distribution" is often used interchangeably with "equitable division"; both refer to a system of marital property division at divorce whereby the court has discretion to make a fair, but not necessarily equal, distribution of the marital assets and liabilities between the spouses. Compare TENN. STAT. § 36-4-121(c) (referring to equitable "division") with FLA. STAT. § 61.075 (referring to equitable "distribution").

The rise of the "community property trust" and its development from 1998 to present are examined as well. The authors analyze the planning opportunities these trusts may present, the requirements for their validity and enforceability across jurisdictions that authorize them, and their efficacy in securing the full (or "double") step-up in basis on the death of the first dying spouse under Internal Revenue Code § 1014(b)(6) for assets placed into such trusts.

Since 2020 domestic migration has increased notably. Top destination states have included Texas, Florida, Arizona, and the Carolinas,[2] while states with the highest outbound migration rates have included California and Louisiana, both community property jurisdictions.[3] Understanding how community property functions is therefore becoming an essential competency for practitioners in separate property states.

[2] Jeanne Batalova, *Frequently Requested Statistics on Immigrants and Immigration in the United* States, MIGRATION POL'Y INST. (Mar. 13, 2024), https://www.migrationpolicy.org/article/frequently-requested-statistics-immigrants-and-immigration-united-states-2024.

[3] *Id.*

Chapter 1

Purpose of the Book; Introduction to Community Property

PURPOSE OF THE BOOK

To Clarify State Law Differences, Explain Divergent Outcomes, and Explore the Extent to Which State Law Rights Will Be Respected

At first glance, community property law may seem straightforward when viewed in isolation. Once a practitioner moves beyond theory and compares the community property system with the separate property system in detail, however, the complexity becomes evident.[1] That complexity is amplified by substantial variations among community property jurisdictions and by differing equitable distribution and elective share rules that vary widely among the separate property states.

Distinguishing between separate and community property—or between marital and nonmarital assets—is a highly nuanced and technical process fraught with complexities and pitfalls. The analysis is complicated by the fact that laws differ across the jurisdictions that follow the community

[1] There is also significant variation among the community property laws of the various jurisdictions in which the community property system obtains and variation in the equitable division and elective share laws of the separate property states.

property regime. For example, Texas's community property rules developed from Spanish legal traditions, while Louisiana's stem from French legal traditions, producing divergent outcomes for property ownership and division based on the particular community property state's law governing the acquisition.

As a general matter, the two marital property regimes differ fundamentally. In separate property states (often called common law or noncommunity property states), each spouse generally retains ownership of assets acquired in their own name during marriage unless they agree otherwise, and the concept of "marital property" generally becomes operative only when a divorce petition is filed.[2] By contrast, in community property states, all property acquired during the marriage is presumptively community property except for gifts and inheritances, and each spouse is said to have a presently vested one-half interest in that community property.[3]

What is often missing in the literature on community property for estate planners is a clear explanation of the American choice-of-law principles and the state marital property rules that affect the analysis. For example, whether a separate property state has adopted a version of the Uniform Disposition of Community Property Rights at Death Act (UDCPRDA) will shape the issues that arise when a spouse domiciled in that state dies owning community property. Practitioners must also understand state law rules governing the validity of pre- and postnuptial agreements, transmutation agreements, and gifts of community property to make tax-effective estate planning decisions that achieve their clients' intended results.

To Create a Practical Framework for Estate Planners to Tackle Community Property Issues

More specifically, the marital property rights of spouses under American law can be distinguished between the rules applicable in determining the

---

[2] *See, e.g.*, KAN. STAT. ANN. § 23-2801 (2025); *see* Est. of Lineweaver v. Comm'r, 71 T.C.M. (CCH) 3058 (T.C. 1996) (noting that North Carolina's equitable distribution statute "created a type of deferred community property law system governing marital property in the case of divorce"); John W. Willis, *The Equitable Distribution of Marital Property: Toward a Deferred Community Property System*, 14 FAM. L.Q. 1 (1980).

[3] Comm'r v. Chase Manhattan Bank, 259 F.2d 231 (5th Cir. 1958).

spouses' ownership rights in property (1) during an intact marriage, (2) upon divorce,[4] and (3) upon the death of one spouse.[5] As such there are really three distinct legal frameworks that marital property rights should be categorized within:

1. Property ownership during an intact marriage
2. Property division upon divorce
3. Property division upon the death of a spouse

These legal frameworks apply differently depending on whether the property in question is community property or separate property. To better understand the implications, it is helpful to consider six key scenarios:

- Ownership of community property during an intact marriage
- Division of community property at divorce
- Division of community property upon the death of a spouse
- Ownership of separate property during an intact marriage
- Division of marital property at divorce
- Division of separate property upon the death of a spouse

As discussed in Chapter 3 and 4, the division of community property at divorce and at death is nearly identical because community property jurisdictions treat each spouse's interest in community property as vesting upon the moment an asset is acquired during the marriage. By contrast, separate property jurisdictions treat property acquired by either spouse during the marriage as separate property until a divorce is filed or a spouse dies, at which point the right to have marital property divided equitably vests in the

---

[4] J. Thomas Oldham, *What If the Beckhams Move to L.A. and Divorce? Marital Property Rights of Mobile Spouses When They Divorce in the United States*, 42 FAM. L.Q. 263, 265 (2008) ("Any discussion of the marital property rights of mobile spouses under American law needs to distinguish between the law applicable to determine the spouses' ownership rights in property during an intact marriage and the law applicable to decide their property rights if they divorce.").

[5] *See* BRETT R. TURNER, EQUITABLE DISTRIBUTION OF PROPERTY § 2:5. Turner insightfully distinguishes between these three goals. *See also* Laura A. Rosenbury, *Two Ways to End a Marriage: Divorce or Death*, 2005 UTAH L. REV. 1227 (2005); and Mark A. Cox, *What's Right Is Wrong and What to Do About It After Oldham v. Oldham*, 42 N.M. L. REV. 531, 537 (2012).

parties, or the surviving spouse receives the statutory equivalent of dower or curtesy.[6]

As noted by many scholars, a spouse in most states will stand to receive more if the marriage ends by divorce rather than by death, a particularly counterintuitive result that deserves public policy consideration.[7]

This book clarifies these concepts by systematically examining how marital property rights operate in three legal contexts—during marriage, upon divorce, and at death. By breaking down the treatment of community and separate property in each scenario, and by comparing differences among the community property states themselves, the book provides a structured approach to understanding the legal and financial implications for migratory spouses. A key focus of this book is the comparative analysis of community property and separate property jurisdictions, exploring both the historical evolution of marital property law across the 50 states and surveying the different judicial approaches to resolving community and separate property disputes.

On one level, this book serves as a practical guide for estate planning practitioners working with community property, providing a resource to ensure compliance with community property laws and to predict testamentary outcomes for clients. At the same time, it examines the historical development and theoretical foundations of marital property law in the United States, using that background to evaluate the merits and drawbacks of elective community property legislation as a tool for securing the full step-up in basis under I.R.C. § 1014(b)(6). As a result, some chapters are written as a

---

[6] Kenneth W. Kingma, *Property Division at Divorce or Death for Married Couples Migrating Between Common Law and Community Property States*, 35 ACTEC L.J. 74, 78 (2009); *see also* C.I.R. v. Chase Manhattan Bank, 259 F.2d 231 (5th Cir. 1958), noting that a wife's ownership of one-half community is not analogous to the common law inchoate right of dower, one being a present vested ownership and the other a mere expectancy.

It may be helpful to think of the marital property system in equitable division states as a separate property system with a "deferred community." The "deferred community" arises upon divorce. *See* Est. of Lineweaver v. Comm'r, 71 T.C.M. (CCH) 3058 (T.C. 1996), noting that North Carolina's equitable distribution statute "created a type of deferred community property law system governing marital property in the case of divorce."

[7] Rosenbury, *supra* note 5, at 1227; *see also* Mark A. Cox, *What's Right Is Wrong and What to Do About It After Oldham v. Oldham*, 42 N.M. L. Rev. 531, 537 (2012).

practitioner's handbook, while others adopt a more scholarly, law review–style approach.[8]

To assist readers, the authors will alert them before the more extended and history-focused chapters begin, so that those who prefer to focus on the practical guidance may skip ahead to the applied sections. Specifically, Chapter 2 traces the historical evolution of marital property law in America, and Chapters 8 and 9 unpack the origins of the federal taxation of community property—chapters best reserved for the ultra-curious, the dedicated LLM student, or the scholar determined to understand exactly why we believe that a properly drafted community property trust pursuant to a state's Community Property Trust Act should satisfy § 1014(b)(6).

30,000-FOOT VIEW OF COMMUNITY PROPERTY LAW

Before diving into the rules and exceptions, it is helpful to begin with a few key definitions to establish a clear foundation.

Key Definitions

Community Property Defined. Community property consists of all assets acquired by one or both spouses (other than by gift, bequest, devise, or inheritance) while they reside in a community property jurisdiction.[9] This includes IRAs; assets held in only one spouse's name other than those acquired by gift, bequest, or devise; and the right to receive payment or assets in the future.[10]

Gifts of community property typically require the consent of both spouses, and a gift of community property without dual consent of the

---

[8] Specifically, Chapter 2 (on the history of civil law/common law and community property/community property) and Chapters 8 and 9 (on the efficacy of community property trusts for purposes of obtaining the 1014(b)(6) double step-up in basis, take a more scholarly approach).

[9] Gerry W. Beyer, *Community Property: Tips and Traps for Lawyers in Common Law States,* 47th Annual Notre Dame Tax & Estate Planning Institute, at 1 (Oct. 22, 2021).

[10] *See* IRM 25.18.1.3.10 (Feb. 15, 2005); *see also* 26 U.S.C. § 408(g) (1983) (stating that tax laws apply regardless of whether IRAs are located in, and therefore affected by, community property law jurisdictions).

spouses is voidable by the nonconsenting spouse.[11] As a result, a gift lacking the consent of both spouses will generally be deemed incomplete for purposes of the federal gift tax.[12]

Transmute Defined. To transmute means to change in form, nature, or substance. To transmute property is to convert the character of property into another type of ownership. Property may be transmuted from community property to separate property, or from separate property to community property. Typically, this occurs through the execution of an appropriate document by a married couple. A transmutation agreement may need to be recorded in the public records when dealing with real estate in order for the transmutation to be effective as to third parties.

Mutable Defined. Derived from the Latin root "mut," meaning changeable or having a tendency to change, this concept is reflected in words like commute, immutable, mutability, transmute, permute, and mutate. Mutability is a key aspect of U.S. choice-of-law principles, meaning the legal rules governing a married couple's property can change depending on their place of residence over time.

Commingle Defined. Commingling refers broadly to the mixing of funds belonging to one party with funds belonging to one or more other parties, or to the mixing of funds of one type with funds of another type. In the context of this book, commingling typically refers to the mixing of assets characterized as separate with assets characterized as community, such that the original character of the commingled assets becomes indeterminable. In many states, where marital and nonmarital property, or community and separate property, are commingled, the nonmarital or separate property

---

[11] Beyer, *supra* note 9, at 38 (citing Trimble v. Trimble, 26 P.2d 477 (1933)).

[12] *Id.* (citing Treas. Reg. § 25-2511-2(b)); Harper v. Comm'r, 6 T.C. 230, 238 (1946) (applying California law); Est. of Kelly v. Comm'r, 31 T.C. 493, 502 (1958) (applying Louisiana law). Professor Beyer further provides: "See also, e.g., U.S. v Blanche, 97-1 USTC 88,165, 88,169 (W.D. Tex. 1997) (Texas community property law required spousal consent to transfer community property unless an agent was specifically granted the power to do so under a power of attorney.) Further, the gift will remain incomplete until the nondonor spouse provides his or her consent; the statute of limitations, if any, runs on the right of the nonconsenting spouse to void the gift under applicable state law; or the death of the donor spouse, when one-half of the gift may become complete. Comm'r v. Chase Manhattan Bank, 259 F.2d 231, 260–61 (5th Cir. 1958)."

assets can be transformed into marital or community assets if the original character of the property is not reasonably traceable.[13]

The "Double" or "Full" Step-Up in Basis. The double step-up in basis under I.R.C. § 1014(b)(6) allows for a full step-up in basis to fair market value for community property upon the death of one spouse. Under I.R.C. § 1014(a), when a person inherits property, the property's tax basis is adjusted to its fair market value as of the date of the owner's death. This means that the heir's basis in the inherited property is adjusted to its date of death value, so that any appreciation in value that occurred during the decedent's lifetime is not subject to capital gains tax if sold by the heir.[14] Section 1014(b) lists eight types of property considered to have passed from the decedent for this purpose, including the surviving spouse's one-half share of community property, provided that at least one-half of the total community interest was included in the decedent's gross estate. As a result, the surviving spouse receives a stepped-up basis as to their one-half of the community property, and because this half, along with the decedent's half, are considered to have both been acquired from or to have passed from the decedent for purposes of § 1014(a), both ownership interests in the community property are stepped up to fair market value on the first spouse's death (assuming at least one-half of the whole of the community interest was includible in the decedent's gross estate).

Important Notice for Assets Owned Jointly Before 1977: The Gallenstein Rule

Under the case of *Gallenstein v. United States,*[15] a joint asset or account funded by one spouse after 1955 and before 1977 can receive a full step-up in basis upon the death of the donor spouse. It may be best not to transfer

---

[13] *E.g.*, Dravis v. Dravis, 170 So. 3d 849 (Fla. Dist. Ct. App. 2015). In *Dravis,* cash gifts that a wife's mother gave to the wife during marriage lost their nonmarital character when the gifts were commingled with marital money in a savings account. *Id.*

[14] The tax basis of inherited property may also be "stepped-down" if its fair market value on the date of the decedent's death is lower than the decedent's basis in the property.

[15] Gallenstein v. United States, 975 F.2d 286, 286 (6th Cir. 1992).

such pre-1977 joint assets to a community property trust if the donor spouse has a significantly shorter life expectancy than the other spouse.

Community Property Defined

In the United States, two primary systems govern marital property: the community property system and the separate property system. Throughout this book, separate property states may also be called "common law states" or "noncommunity property states." Unfortunately, the phrase "separate property" is also used within community property jurisdictions to describe an asset that is not community property. Because the same phrase denotes both a marital property regime (the common law regime) and an asset classification (noncommunity property assets in a community property state), readers must rely on context. When precision matters, the authors will use "separate property state" or "noncommunity property state" for the regime and "separate (noncommunity) property" for the asset category within a community property state.

The community property system is presently recognized in nine states, primarily located in the southern and western regions of the U.S.[16] The separate property system is followed in the remaining 41 states and the District of Columbia. Each framework establishes distinct rules for acknowledging a spouse's contributions to assets acquired by one or both spouses during their marriage. These two marital property regimes provide the foundations for the different legal rules that may apply to divide marital assets among the spouses upon divorce or protect the surviving spouse from disinheritance upon the decedent spouse's death.

Eight states and two territories of the United States—Arizona, California, Louisiana, Idaho, Nevada, New Mexico, Texas, Washington, Puerto Rico, and Guam—are considered to be "traditional" community property jurisdictions, because the marital property laws in those jurisdictions have their historical and legal origins in the Spanish, Mexican, or French civil law. By contrast, Wisconsin became a community property state through

[16] There are technically 14 community property states if one includes Alaska, Tennessee, Kentucky, South Dakota, and Florida, by virtue of the community property trust legislation in those states. However, the authors will refer to these latter five states as "community property trust states" throughout the book.

its passage of the Uniform Marital Property Act in 1986.[17] More recently, and as discussed in depth later, Alaska, South Dakota, Kentucky, Tennessee, and Florida have enacted statutes allowing couples to elect into community property treatment for assets placed into a community property trust. A map of the states that recognize some form of community property ownership is provided here:

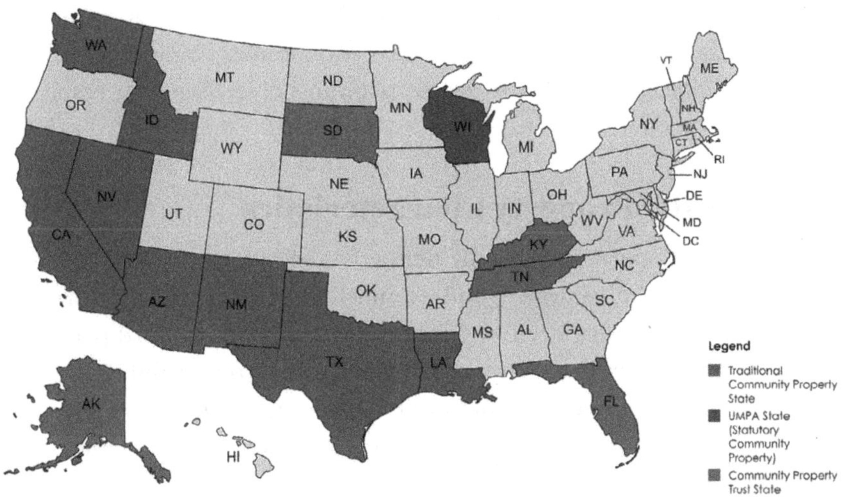

Despite the limited number of states that follow this system, a significant portion of the U.S. population resides in these jurisdictions, which is largely due to the high populations of California and Texas, which together account for nearly 25 percent of the nation's people.[18]

When a married couple acquires property in a community property state, that property generally retains its community property classification

---

[17] *See* Kathy T. Graham, *The Uniform Marital Property Act: A Solution for Common Law Property Systems?*, 48 S. D. L. Rev. 455, 458 (2003). In Rev. Rul. 87-13, the IRS concluded that Wisconsin's Uniform Marital Property Act caused Wisconsin residents to have community property for federal tax purposes even though labeled "marital property" rather than "community property."

[18] Kathy J. Allan, *Property Division Laws in Divorce: 50-State Survey*, Justia (Sep. 22, 2023), https://www.justia.com/family/divorce/dividing-money-and-property/property-division-laws-in-divorce-50-state-survey/.

when the couple later moves to a separate property state.[19] This means many married couples living outside community property jurisdictions may still be subject to community property principles and should take affirmative steps to alter or preserve the character of their assets, depending on whether they want the community property laws of their former domicile or the separate property laws of their new domicile to apply. Many separate property states have statutes requiring their probate courts to recognize the community property rights that spouses bring with them from community property states. However, estate planners should not rely on those statutes alone to achieve their clients' estate planning objectives with respect to community property.

Community Property Characteristics

Community property is generally defined as all assets acquired by either spouse during the marriage while domiciled in a community property state. Any property acquired by gift or inheritance from a third party or as between the spouses themselves remains separate property unless it is commingled or transmuted into community property, and there is a presumption in favor of community property unless evidence proves otherwise.[20] California Family Code § 770 provides a good list of what will generally be considered separate property within a community property regime:

> § 770. (a) Separate property of a married person includes all of the following:
>
> 1. All property owned by the person before marriage.
> 2. All property acquired by the person after marriage by gift, bequest, devise, or descent.

---

[19] 14 A.L.R.3d 404 (1967) ("Whatever may be the underlying theoretical considerations that support it, the proposition that a change of domicil [sic] by a husband and wife from a state in which the community property system obtains to a state in which does not, or vice versa, has no effect on the character, as separate or community, of property acquired prior to the removal or property into which such property can be traced, is almost universally accepted.").

[20] *See, e.g.*, CAL. FAM. CODE § 2581, for the purpose of division of property upon divorce, "property acquired by the parties during marriage in joint form, including property held in tenancy in common, joint tenancy, or tenancy by the entirety, or as community property, is presumed to be community property."

3. The rents, issues, and profits of the property described in this section.

(b) A married person may, without the consent of the person's spouse, convey the person's separate property.

Whether the rents, issues, and profits of separate property are presumed to be community property is an issue that varies among the community property states. California does not presume such income and growth to be community property, whereas Idaho, Louisiana, and Texas start with the presumption that the income and growth on separate property are considered community property. In most states, the starting presumption can be rebutted by direct and positive evidence that the increase was due to community labor, efforts, or funds. For key issues like this one, where there is variance among the community property states, Appendix A provides a very useful state-by-state reference guide that summarizes state law with references to state-specific statutory authority and pertinent case law.

A donor making a gift to a married beneficiary who lives in a community property state should think through *how* the gift is made and *how* it will be held. Although community property states generally treat property received by gift as the recipient spouse's separate property,[21] the intended characterization can be undermined if the asset (or its proceeds) is later commingled or transmuted.[22] All community property states apply a presumption in favor of community property for property acquired during marriage, which may generally be rebutted by evidence establishing the asset's separate character (often by clear and convincing evidence or a

---

[21] *See, e.g.*, CAL. FAM. CODE § 770(a)(2) and TEX. FAM. CODE § 3.001(2).

[22] It is crucial to remember that "in a community property state, title is not determinative of ownership." *See* Thomas M. Featherston, *Separate Property or Community Property: An Introduction to Marital Property Law in the Community Property States* (Am. Bar Ass'n, July 18, 2016), providing that "an asset titled in one spouse's name may be that spouse's separate property or the couple's community property. Property titled in both spouses' names may be community property or the spouses may be tenants in common or joint tenants, each owning an undivided one-half interest as separate property. It is even possible that an asset may be part separate property of each spouse and part their community property, whether title is in one spouse's name or in both of their names." *Id.* For individuals seeking to make a gift that will be excluded from community property and considered the separate property of one spouse, the safest route is to make the gift explicitly to that spouse alone.

preponderance of the evidence, depending on the jurisdiction).[23] In some states, additional or different rules may apply based on the form of title, and the evidentiary review may turn on tracing and documentation. Accordingly, donors may wish to consider whether to structure the transfer (1) to both spouses jointly (if the intent is to benefit the marital community), (2) solely to the intended beneficiary with steps designed to preserve separateness, or (3) to a trust for the benefit of the intended donee that is designed to keep the property separate and reduce the commingling risk.

The foundation of the community property system is the recognition of marriage as an economic partnership, with both spouses sharing in the ownership of property acquired during the marriage other than property received by gift or inheritance. Co-ownership of gains accumulated during marriage is the fundamental principle that underlies community property law.[24]

Each spouse holds an equal, undivided one-half interest in all community property.[25] When one spouse dies, the community dissolves, and the surviving spouse retains outright ownership of their half. As such, a dying spouse has the right to make testamentary disposition of only one-half of the community property, and only that one-half of the property's value is included in the dying spouse's gross estate under I.R.C. § 2033.[26]

The community property systems in Arizona, Idaho, Louisiana, California, New Mexico, Nevada, Texas, Washington, Puerto Rico, and Guam are mandatory, unless residents enter into an agreement that opts them out of the system.[27]

---

[23] *See, e.g.*, Tex. Fam. Code § 3.003. Because the evidentiary burden to rebut the community property presumption varies by jurisdiction and ranges from preponderance to clear and convincing evidence, and in some states turns on specialized title presumptions (notably California), planners should confirm the applicable standard in the beneficiary's state.

[24] William A. Reppy Jr., *Major Events in the Evolution of American Community Property Law and Their Import to Equitable Distribution States*, 23 Fam. L.Q. 163, 163–92 (1989).

[25] M. Read Moore, *Coming Soon to Your State: Community Property*, ST042 ALI-CLE 807 (2012).

[26] *Id.*

[27] *Id.*

Similarly, Wisconsin's Uniform Marital Property Act by default places residents into a community property regime unless the married couple opts out. The automatic application of the community property system in Wisconsin is a critical distinction that places Wisconsin much closer to a traditional community property jurisdiction than the elective community property systems in Alaska, South Dakota, Tennessee, Kentucky, and Florida, where spouses must opt in to the community property regime by signing a community property agreement (for Alaska residents only) or by placing assets under a trust where the trustee or a co-trustee is a resident of the applicable state.[28] Notably, Alaska is the only community property trust state that allows for the creation of community property by simple agreement where both spouses are domiciliaries of the state without the need for placing the property into a trust.[29]

Under the traditional common law marital regime, spouses hold all property individually unless they agree to own it jointly, and courts generally must look to legal title when distributing property in matrimonial

---

[28] *Id.* This is confirmed by IRS Pub. 555, which lists Wisconsin as a community property state. *See also* Rev. Rul. 87-13 ("Unless the rights of the spouses are altered by agreement, the Act automatically vests a 50 percent interest in marital property in each spouse. Under the provisions of the Act, therefore, the rights of spouses in Wisconsin are community property rights.").

[29] *See* Alaska Stat. § 34.77.090. *See also* Shaftel Delman, *Alaska Enacts Elective Community Property System and Creates New Type of Alaska Trust to Obtain Full Stepped-Up Income Tax Basis*, Vol. 15, July 13, 1998. The need to create, fund, and maintain a trust in Tennessee, Kentucky, South Dakota, and Florida represents the least defensible aspect of the elective community property statutes. If a state recognizes community property as a form of ownership, the spouses should not have to avail themselves of a trust in order to be subject to community property principles. For this reason, the authors believe the community property trust states would be well served to amend their statutes to allow couples who reside in those states to elect community property treatment directly by agreement. While we do not believe the requirement of a trust forfeits eligibility for § 1014(b)(6), it undeniably introduces unnecessary complexity and creates avoidable questions about trust administration, for example, whether income distributed from a Florida community property trust to the spouses retains its community property character, particularly where the property used to fund the trust was not community property to begin with, and the trust itself is the mechanism that imparts that character. We discuss the theoretical underpinnings behind this reasoning in Chapters 8 and 9.

actions.[30] By contrast, under the community property system spouses jointly own all property acquired during the marriage, regardless of title, unless they agree to hold it separately.[31] The fact that title is not determinative of ownership in community property states is one of the most critical features of the system.[32]

Community property states typically limit a spouse's ability to sell or gift community property during their lifetime without the other spouse's consent.

The presumption that all property acquired by a married couple is community property (except for gifts or inheritances) can be rebutted with strong evidence to the contrary showing an expression of intent for the property to remain separate or evidence that the property did in fact remain separate, known as "tracing."[33] Simply put, property acquired during the marriage and titled in either or both spouses' names is considered community property unless proven otherwise.[34]

Tenancy by the entireties (TBE) property or joint tenancy with right of survivorship property theoretically cannot coexist with community property due to the survivorship right.[35] However, some community property states have enacted legislation allowing their residents to hold community property with a right of survivorship, as further discussed in Chapter 4.[36]

---

[30] This has changed over time. *See, e.g.*, Kahn v. Kahn, 43 N.Y.2d 203, 371 N.E.2d 809, 401 N.Y.S.2d 47 (1977) (noting that, before New York's passage of an Equitable Distribution Act, New York courts could not distribute spouses' property without regard to legal title). Some common law states now define marital property as all property acquired by either spouse during the marriage, regardless of the form in which title is held. N.Y. Dom. Rel. Law § 236 (McKinney).

[31] *How Does Community Property Law Differ from Common Law Property Concepts?*, 19 Wash. Prac., Fam. & Cmty. Prop. L. § 7:4 (citing Donahue, *What Causes Fundamental Legal Ideas: Marital Property in England and France in the Thirteenth Century*, 78 Mich. L. Rev. 59 (1979)).

[32] *See* Featherston, *supra* note 22.

[33] Read Moore, *supra* note 25.

[34] *Id.*

[35] *Id.*

[36] *See, e.g.*, RCW § 64.88.040; Tex. Est. Code Ann. § 112.051 (West); Nev. Rev. Stat. Ann. § 111.064 (West).

Even among the eight traditional community property states, there is a greater degree of variance with respect to community property law than one might expect.

For example, as mentioned earlier, five community property states—Arizona, New Mexico, Washington, Nevada, and California—hold that income from separate property remains separate property during the marriage. By contrast, Idaho, Texas, and Louisiana treat income generated from separate property during the marriage as community property.[37]

In California, Louisiana, and New Mexico, the same community property rules apply during marriage, at death, and at divorce, so these states treat property consistently regardless of how the marriage ends.[38] Conversely, in the states of Texas, Arizona, Nevada, and Idaho, although separate property is treated the same way during marriage and at death, the approach to community property at divorce differs.[39] With respect to community property at divorce, Texas, Arizona, Nevada, and Idaho consider equitable factors such as need, ability to work, and health, thereby deviating from the strict 50-50 division applied during marriage or at death.[40] Washington takes a minority stance among the community property states that apply equitable factors at divorce: Where the other community property states confirm each spouse's separate property to that spouse and divide only the community estate, Washington authorizes the court to make a just and equitable division of all property before it, community and separate alike.[41]

Additionally, the laws of community property states differ in how they characterize life insurance and employment benefits. For example, California allocates life insurance proceeds between community and separate property in proportion to the nature of the funds used to pay the premiums.[42] In other community property states, whether life insurance is characterized as separate or community property can depend upon whether it is term or whole life insurance.[43]

---

[37] Read Moore, *supra* note 25.

[38] Reppy, *supra* note 24.

[39] *Id.*

[40] *Id.*

[41] *Id.* (citing WASH. REV. CODE § 26.09.080); *see also* Konzen v. Konzen, 103 Wash. 2d 470, 478, 693 P.2d 97, 100, *cert. denied*, 473 U.S. 906 (1985).

[42] Read Moore, *supra* note 25 (citing Biltoft v. Wootten, 157 Cal. Rptr. 581 (Cal. Ct. App. 1979)).

[43] *Id.*

Moreover, where an IRA is subject to community property laws, the rights of a surviving spouse will generally take priority over the rights of the designated IRA beneficiary.[44] The interplay of the community property rules with life insurance, IRAs, and variable annuities is discussed in Chapter 12.

As noted earlier, once property is classified as either community or separate property, it typically retains that status unless affected by two specific situations: commingling and transmutation. Commingling occurs when, in a community property state, separate and community property are mixed such that the separate property and community property portions cannot be clearly identified, causing the entire asset to be deemed community property. This often happens with shared bank accounts or businesses that were initially separate but grow due to the efforts of one or both spouses during the marriage. Transmutation refers to a formal agreement that changes the classification of property from community to separate or vice versa. Most states allow couples to modify property classifications through contracts either before or during marriage, although state laws differ on the formalities required.

While the separate property system stems from the common law, and community property systems generally originated in the civil law, labeling states as "common law" or "civil law" oversimplifies their legal frameworks. Although this distinction may be useful for discussing marital property regimes,[45] it falls short in addressing broader property characterization issues for migratory couples. The common law and civil law traditions as they exist in the United States today are not strictly binary—codification of the law has merged elements of both systems.[46] While the authors may

---

[44] The IRS, in a private letter ruling, concluded that a wife may hold a community property interest in her husband's IRA. PLR 199937055. *See also* https://greenleaf-trust.com/wp-content/uploads/2024/09/IRAs-and-Community-Property.pdf.

[45] A great deal of the literature in this area frequently distinguishes between "common law states" and "community property states."

[46] The historical development of legal systems in regions like Texas and New Mexico illustrates the transition from civil law to common law as the rule of decision. For example, Texas initially operated under a civil law system derived from Mexican and Roman law but later adopted the common law of England as its foundational legal framework, replacing the civil law as the rule of decision. *See* Courand v. Vollmer, 31 Tex. 397 (1868). Similarly New Mexico transitioned from a civil law

use "common law practitioners" or "common law states" as shorthand for individuals in separate property states or the separate property states themselves, we will also briefly explore why this dichotomy is imprecise depending on the context in which it is employed.

The Full Step-Up in Basis for Community Property (I.R.C. § 1014(b)(6))

A key tax benefit unique to community property is the "double step-up" or "full step-up" in basis on the first death of the married couple. The full step-up in basis on the first death is achieved through the operation of I.R.C. § 1014(a) in conjunction with § 1014(b)(6). Generally, when a person dies, assets included in their estate receive a basis equal to their fair market value as of the date of the decedent's death, thereby wiping out the capital gains tax, which is commonly attributable to appreciation (or depreciation recapture) that occurred during the decedent's lifetime for future sales of the property by the heir or devisee.[47] In separate property states, when a spouse dies with jointly owned property, such as a joint tenancy with right of survivorship (JTROS) interest or a TBE interest, only the dying spouse's interest in such property will receive a step-up in basis under § 1014(a).

For example, assume H and W, who are married and reside in Florida, purchase Apple stock for $100 as TBE, and each contributes half of the

---

system to the English common law to harmonize its legal systems with other states in the Union. *See* Beals v. Ares, 25 N.M. 459 (1919). Both Texas and New Mexico follow the civil law marital property regime (community property), but are clearly not pure civil law jurisdictions in modern day. This concept is discussed in more depth in Chapter 2.

[47] I.R.C. § 1014(a)(1) providing: "Except as otherwise provided in this section, the basis of property in the hands of a person acquiring the property from a decedent or to whom the property passed from a decedent shall, if not sold, exchanged, or otherwise disposed of before the decedent's death by such person, be . . . the fair market value of the property at the date of the decedent's death[.]".

By contrast, property transferred by an inter vivos completed gift will generally have the same basis in the hands of the donee as it did in the hands of the donor, known as "carryover basis" (I.R.C. § 1015).

purchase price.[48] Upon the acquisition of the stock, H and W are treated as each having a $50 cost basis in the property.[49] Five years later H dies when the stock has appreciated in value to $1,000. W will receive the property with a $550 basis. This is because upon H's death, H's basis in the property is stepped up from one-half of the initial cost ($50) to one-half of the property's fair market value on H's death ($500) by the operation of § 1014(a). W's basis in her one-half interest in the TBE property remains unchanged because it is not considered to have been "acquired from" or "passed from" a "decedent" under the language of § 1014. W would be subject to capital gains tax on $450 if she were to sell the stock following H's death for $1,000. From this example, one can see that the basis step-up rules with respect to jointly held property in a separate property state operate to eliminate half of the total appreciation in the stock (the one-half of the total appreciation

---

[48] Under the contribution rule of § 2040(a), the entire value of property held jointly with right of survivorship or as TBE is included in the gross estate of the deceased joint tenant unless the surviving tenant can prove they contributed to the property's acquisition with their own funds. *See* I.R.C. § 2040(a) "[t]he value of the gross estate shall include the value of all property to the extent of the interest therein held as joint tenants with right of survivorship by the decedent and any other person, or as tenants by the entirety by the decedent and spouse . . . *except such part thereof as may be shown to have originally belonged to such other person and never to have been received or acquired by the latter from the decedent for less than an adequate and full consideration in money or money's worth: Provided, that where such property or any part thereof, or part of the consideration with which such property was acquired, is shown to have been at any time acquired by such other person from the decedent for less than an adequate and full consideration in money or money's worth, there shall be excepted only such part of the value of such property as is proportionate to the consideration furnished by such other person*" (emphasis added). Clearly, the statute adopts a tracing rule by requiring a determination of whether a contribution to the purchase price by the surviving tenant was from the surviving tenant's own funds. *See* STEPHENS, MAXFIELD, LIND & CALFEE, FEDERAL ESTATE AND GIFT TAXATION § 2040 (Joint Interests) ¶ 4.12, citing Rev. Rul. 78-418, 1978-2 CB 326. Thus, where husband and wife take title to a $100,000 stock as TBE, and husband furnished 100 percent of the purchase price for the stock, husband would include the full value of the stock in his gross estate under § 2040(a).

[49] I.R.C. § 1012.

in the stock attributable to the decedent's one-half interest in the jointly held property).[50]

In community property states, however, both the decedent spouse's and the surviving spouse's one-half interests in assets held jointly as community property receive a new fair market value basis as of the date of the decedent's death, effectively eliminating all built-in gains upon the first death.[51] In the preceding example, if the assets were instead community property, both H's and W's respective initial $50 bases would be stepped up to $500 upon H's death.[52] W would receive the property with a $1,000 basis, equal to its then–fair market value. There would be no capital gains tax on W's subsequent sale of the stock because it was held as community

---

[50] The authors note that § 2040 is complex in its application, and there are many examples in which § 1014 would operate in conjunction with § 2040(a) to provide more or less of a basis adjustment where the joint tenants are not husband and wife, or are husband and wife but have acquired the property prior to 1977, such that the property would not be covered by the qualified joint interest rule of § 2040(b), which includes only one-half of the value of such qualified joint interest in the decedent's gross estate. For example, where the decedent-husband has contributed 100 percent of the funds to the purchase of the jointly held property, and the property was acquired prior to 1977, the entirety of the property would be included in his gross estate, and the property would receive a full basis adjustment as would any other separately owned asset on death. *See* Gallenstein v. U.S., 975 F.2d 286 (6th Cir. 1992). (The full value of property held by spouses in a joint interest with a right of survivorship created before 1977 may be included in the gross estate of the first spouse to die.)

[51] Warning! A step-down in basis also occurs when assets have a basis higher than fair market value before the first death. Those assets may be placed in an irrevocable non-grantor trust so that no step-down occurs on the first death.

[52] *See* I.R.C. § 1014(b)(6) (providing: "[F]or purposes of subsection (a), the following property shall be considered to have been acquired from or to have passed from the decedent: . . . (6) In the case of decedents dying after December 31, 1947, property which represents the surviving spouse's one-half share of community property held by the decedent and the surviving spouse under the community property laws of any State, or possession of the United States or any foreign country, if at least one-half of the whole of the community interest in such property was includible in determining the value of the decedent's gross estate under chapter 11 of subtitle B (section 2001 and following, relating to estate tax) or section 811 of the Internal Revenue Code of 1939.").

property; one-half of the total appreciation attributable to H is eliminated under § 1014(a), and the other half attributable to W is likewise eliminated upon H's death under § 1014(b)(6). This favorable treatment is one of the most significant tax advantages of the community property system.[53]

The obvious allure of a community property trust is the ability to receive a full step-up in basis on the death of the first dying spouse under Internal Revenue Code § 1014(b)(6), which provides that assets owned as community property will receive a new income tax basis equal to their fair market value on the death of the first dying spouse. This "step-up" in basis applies to the full extent of all community property assets, not just to the first dying spouse's interest in community property, regardless of the fact that only one-half of the value of the community property assets is included in the first dying spouse's gross estate for federal estate tax purposes.

In other words, the surviving spouse will receive a step-up in basis for his or her interest in community property *even though* his or her interest is not subject to the federal estate tax system on the first dying spouse's death. This is an incredible advantage provided for community property owners in the Internal Revenue Code, since for federal estate tax purposes the first dying spouse's gross estate typically will include his or her separate property *and* his or her one-half interest in the community property.[54]

Note, however, that the initial enactment of § 1014(b)(6) was not passed with the intent of providing an advantage for community property taxpayers for basis planning, but to remedy a perceived inequality in the federal estate tax, which favored noncommunity property states, as further discussed in Chapter 8.

---

[53] The ultimate utility of the double step-up is discussed in Chapter 10. Section 1014(b)(6) really becomes useful for spouses with large gaps in their respective mortality tables, but query how beneficial the double step-up really is for Bob (81) and Jane (83), who have IRS mortality tables indicating they will die within two years of one another, with Jane outliving Bob by approximately 18 months. Can Jane's heirs not just wait until her death to receive the basis step-up on her one-half of the jointly owned property? Could the spouses have otherwise modified the form of ownership so that Bob owned properties needing the full step-up individually at the time of his death?

[54] 34A Am. Jur. 2d *Federal Taxation* ¶¶ 143,101 & 143,182 (2023).

Intro to Community Property Trusts

The rise of the elective community property trust is one of the most significant developments in modern marital property and income tax planning. Couples in nontraditional community property regimes historically lacked a mechanism to obtain the income tax basis benefits of community property treatment. That changed in 1998, when Alaska enacted the Alaska Community Property Act, which allows residents and nonresidents to opt into community property treatment by entering a community property agreement or establishing a community property trust.

An Alaska community property trust allows married couples to designate property as community property by transferring it into a statutory trust that meets the formal requirements of Alaska Statute § 34.77.100. To qualify, the trust must be signed by both spouses and must have at least one Alaska trustee that is either an individual resident or a qualified trust company. Under Alaska law, each spouse has a vested one-half interest in all community property.[55]

Following Alaska's lead, other states have adopted similar elective community property systems: Tennessee (2010), South Dakota (2016), Kentucky (2020), and Florida (2021). Each statute allows spouses to opt in to community property treatment through a designated "community property trust" or "special spousal trust," generally requiring at least one trustee to be a resident or a corporate fiduciary of the enacting state. These trusts are intended to confer the federal income tax benefits associated with community property, most notably the full step-up in basis at the first death under § 1014(b)(6).

However, federal recognition of these elective community property regimes remains somewhat uncertain; as extensively discussed in Chapter 8, the 1944 Supreme Court case *Commissioner v. Harmon* causes many practitioners concern that a full step-up may not apply on the first death for assets held in community property trusts.[56] Although *Harmon* involved the

---

[55] Alaska Stat. § 34.77.030(c).

[56] As a brief summary of Chapter 8, *Harmon* held that Oklahoma's elective community property statute did not create community property for federal income tax purposes because it functioned only as a contractual reallocation of income rather than a true marital property regime. *Harmon*, however, was decided in the narrow context of the assignment-of-income doctrine and before Congress passed

issue of income splitting rather than basis adjustments, the Internal Revenue Service has cited it in Internal Revenue Manual[57] 25.18.1.2.3 and in IRS Publication 555 to question whether such opt-in trusts will be respected for federal tax purposes.

With the preceding in mind, readers should be cautioned that using a community property trust specifically to secure a full step-up in basis on the first death under § 1014(b)(6) carries some uncertainty as to whether the trust will achieve that outcome. It is worth noting, however, that after polling many practitioners in this area and scouring the case law, there are no known cases or audits in which the assets of a community property trust have been denied the full § 1014(b)(6) basis step-up on the first death.

Practitioners should also be mindful that the effects of a community property trust extend well beyond basis. The transfer of assets to a community property trust may expose the trust property to claims by a divorcing spouse that would otherwise have been treated as nonmarital property or separate property in the event of divorce. Clients considering a community property trust should be counseled on that risk as part of a holistic assessment of the trust's consequences.

Moreover, it is often the experience of the authors that clients wish to transmute out of community property treatment due to the creditor exposure that it causes when compared to other forms of ownership such as tenants by the entireties.

---

the 1948 Revenue Act, which for the first time allowed married couples to file joint returns and effectively permitted all spouses nationwide to split income. In light of these statutory developments, we believe that *Harmon*'s reach is materially limited when evaluating elective community property systems for purposes of § 1014(b)(6). Revenue Ruling 77-359 stands for the proposition that *Harmon*'s influence should be limited to the income-splitting issue; there, the IRS held that a couple cannot convert the income from separate property to community property and split it unless they also change the character of the underlying separate property to community property. Beyer, *supra* note 9, at 50.

[57] The Internal Revenue Manual (IRM) is an interagency document that provides guidance to agents of the IRS and governs the agencies internal operations. The IRM and its provisions are not mandatory on the IRS, are not precedential, and do not have the force and effect of law. *See* King v. Comm'r, T.C. Memo 1992-465 (1992) (citing United States v. Horne, 714 F.2d 206 (1st Cir. 1983); United States v. Will, 671 F.2d 963, 967 (6th Cir. 1982); Vallone v. Comm'r, 88 T.C. 794, 807 (1987)).

Chapter 2

The Evolution of Common and Civil Law in Early America and Its Influence on Modern State Variations in Marital Property Law

Chapters 2 and 3 step into more historical context and what some might find as less practical territory.[1] These chapters provide both the conceptual groundwork for later planning discussions and an intriguing account of how marital property law developed in the United States.

A BRIEF HISTORY OF THE COMMON AND CIVIL LAW TRADITIONS

Globally, legal systems primarily fall into two categories: common law systems and civil law systems. The United States and its territories generally

[1] "Study history, study history. In history lies all the secrets of statecraft."—Winston Churchill, highlighting history as essential for practical governance. https://winstonchurchill.org/resources/speeches/speeches-about-winston-churchill/the-study-of-history-and-the-practice-of-politics/.

follow the common law tradition inherited from England and modified by the social changes that have occurred in the United States since its inception.[2] Under the traditional common law system, the law was generally uncodified, meaning there was no comprehensive compilation of legal rules and statutes, and judicial decisions shaped legal precedent through stare decisis, with those precedents preserved in court records and applied by the presiding judge in each new case.[3]

In contrast, civil law systems, rooted in Roman law and the Corpus Juris Civilis of Emperor Justinian issued between AD 529 and 534, rely on codes of law and certain uncodified traditional legal principles.[4]

Origins of the Common Law

The term "common law" is used in different contexts; in its broadest sense, it denotes the rules and precepts of law in a country, or that body of jurisprudence that is equally applicable everywhere, as distinguished from local laws and rules.[5] More specifically, the common law is the body of legal doctrines and theories that originated, developed, and are applied in England, distinguishing it from Roman law, modern civil law, canon law, and other legal systems.[6] The common law has been widely adopted by nations with Anglo-Saxon legal traditions.[7]

The common law can be traced to England in the Middle Ages. Monarchs consolidated power and established centralized legal institutions. Following the Norman Conquest of 1066, medieval kings introduced new legal

---

[2] With the exceptions of Louisiana, Puerto Rico, and Guam, which are all civil law jurisdictions; *see* John T. Hood Jr., *The History and Development of the Louisiana Civil Code*, 19 La. L. Rev. 18, 25–27 (1958); V. Suarez & Co. v. Dow Brands, Inc., 337 F.3d 1 (1st Cir. 2003) (noting that "Puerto Rico is a civil law jurisdiction and follows the rule of such jurisdictions of heavier reliance on learned commentators than common law jurisdictions"); *see also* IRM 25.18.1.2.2.

[3] *The Common Law and Civil Law Traditions*, UC Berkeley School of Law (Nov. 2017), https://www.law.berkeley.edu/wp-content/uploads/2017/11/Common-LawCivilLawTraditions.pdf.

[4] James Spallino Jr., Esq., 26(3) Ohio Prob. L.J. NL 9.

[5] C.J.S. Common Law § 1.

[6] *Id.*

[7] *Id.*

procedures based on "writs," which were royal orders that provided specific remedies for specific grievances.[8] However, the rigid and highly formalized writ system sometimes failed to deliver justice, leading individuals to appeal directly to the king.[9] This need for flexibility led to the creation of courts of equity, or "chancery" courts, which were overseen by the king's chancellor.[10] These courts applied broader principles of equity in order to achieve just outcomes, drawing from sources such as Roman law and natural law, rather than strictly adhering to common law rules.[11]

Courts of law and courts of equity remained separate until the mid-nineteenth century when the writ system was abolished (though some U.S. states still maintain distinct equity courts).[12] Additionally, certain writs, such as warrants, subpoenas, and habeas corpus, remain integral to modern common law. The writ of habeas corpus, originally a royal order obtained by or on behalf of a prisoner, ensured that detainees could challenge the legality of their imprisonment. This principle emerged alongside the 1215 Magna Carta, which affirmed individual liberties, including the right to a jury trial by one's peers.[13]

Historically, the common law governed all of England, but certain cities and districts maintained unique local customs that diverged from it.[14] These customs, though not universally applicable, were upheld as local privileges and, despite their uncertain origins, were adhered to as the law of each respective city or district.[15] During the Middle Ages, the common

---

8 *The Common Law and Civil Law Traditions,* UC Berkeley School of Law (Nov. 2017), https://www.law.berkeley.edu/wp-content/uploads/2017/11/Common-LawCivilLawTraditions.pdf.

9 *Id.*

10 *Id.*

11 One can already begin to see how the two systems of law are not mutually exclusive; they have been influenced by one another. Each system of the law has found particular legal principles of the other to be useful in the administration of justice in their respective systems.

12 *The Common Law and Civil Law Traditions, supra* note 8.

13 *Id.*

14 *Id.*

15 Joseph T Latronica, J.D., *Maryland Law Encyclopedia,* 5 M.L.E. Common Law § 1 (citing Coomes v. Clements, 4 H. & J. 480, 1819 WL 507 (Md. 1819)).

law therefore coexisted with other legal traditions, including canon law in the church courts, customary law in local jurisdictions, and Roman law in chancery and maritime courts.[16] English jurists of this era took great pride in the distinctiveness of their English legal customs and institutions. This period of legal development "perhaps mixed with envy inspired by the contemporary European movement toward codification" culminated in the first systematic treatise on the English common law: William Blackstone's *Commentaries on the Laws of England (1723–1780).*[17]

Through colonization, the English common law—encompassing principles of both law and equity—became the foundational legal system of the American colonies, at least to the extent that it suited their circumstances.[18] When the colonies declared independence and became states, common law remained the cornerstone of their legal frameworks, subject to necessary modifications.[19]

Yet, the common law is just one form of law and holds no greater significance than statutory law; both equally represent the law of a particular state.[20] The common law is not a universal legal doctrine enforceable across all jurisdictions; rather, each state's common law exists by and through its own authority.

Origins of the Civil Law

The civil law system is the most widely practiced and implemented legal system in the world today.[21] Outside regions historically influenced by British imperialism in the eighteenth and nineteenth centuries, much of the world operates under some form of civil law, or at least under systems that were heavily shaped by civil law principles.[22] This widespread influence can be

---

[16] *The Common Law and Civil Law Traditions, supra* note 8.

[17] *Id.*

[18] *Id.*

[19] *Id.*

[20] 15A C.J.S. Common Law § 2 (citing Copley Press, Inc. v. Superior Court, 39 Cal. 4th 1272, 48 Cal. Rptr. 3d 183, 141 P.3d 288 (2006)).

[21] Wayne R. Barnes, *Contemplating A Civil Law Paradigm for A Future International Commercial Code,* 65 LA. L. REV. 677, 699 (2005).

[22] *Id.*

traced back to the ancient Roman Empire, where the earliest foundations of the system emerged.

The ancient Roman law is considered the backbone of the civil law tradition.[23] One of the first organized collections of Roman law was the Twelve Tables, published in 450 BC, during the early years of the Roman Republic.[24] The Twelve Tables represented Rome's first codified legal system, designed to make legal rules transparent and accessible to all citizens.[25] The principles were physically inscribed onto 12 stone tablets and displayed in the city, ensuring every Roman could know the law that governed them.[26] Even though the physical tablets were destroyed by invading Gauls in 390 BC, the contents survived because Roman citizens had committed the principles to memory.[27] The legacy of the Twelve Tables endured for centuries, influencing Roman legal thinking all the way through to the reforms of Emperor Justinian.

Alongside the Twelve Tables, another key component of Roman law developed—Praetorian law.[28] This body of law emerged from decisions made by magistrates responsible for administering justice. These rulings were not meant to override written law but to interpret and apply it to specific cases. Any lasting influence these rulings had comes not from their authority as precedent (a concept more central to common law systems), but from the strength and reasoning of the legal arguments they presented.[29] To guide the application of law in daily life, Roman magistrates and legal practitioners also relied on the writings of respected legal scholars, known as jurisconsults. These scholars did more than just explain existing laws—they discussed legal principles, proposed solutions to new legal

---

[23] *Id.* at 700 (noting that the civil law system "almost certainly" has its origins in the ancient Roman Empire).

[24] *Id.*

[25] *Id.*

[26] *Id.* at 700–01.

[27] *Id.* at 701.

[28] Hector Reichard Jr., *The Uncommon Law of Puerto Rico,* 10 EXPERIENCE 6 (Fall 1999).

[29] *Id.* at 7–9.

problems, and helped align the written law with evolving cultural and societal values.[30]

This emphasis on codified written law—viewed as the supreme source of legal authority—became a defining feature of the civil law tradition. Judges and magistrates were expected to turn first to the written code, only resorting to their own sense of fairness or equity when the code offered no answer.[31]

A turning point came in AD 533, nearly a thousand years after the Twelve Tables were first published, when Emperor Justinian undertook a sweeping reform and codification of Roman law.[32] Known as the *Corpus Juris Civilis*, Justinian's Code was driven by two main goals. First, Justinian believed Roman law had deteriorated after centuries of conflicting interpretations and corruption, and he wanted to restore it to the clarity and integrity it had during the Republic's early days. Second, the sheer volume of legal texts—rulings, treatises, and commentaries—had created confusion and inconsistency, making it difficult to know what the law actually said. Justinian sought to eliminate these problems by creating a single, comprehensive code that would organize and rationalize the law.[33]

The civil law tradition did not end with Rome, of course. After the fall of the Roman Empire, the tradition of codification and legal systematization carried into the European Renaissance and the formation of modern nation-states. The legal codes developed by these emerging states drew heavily from Roman law, with one of the most famous examples being the *Siete Partidas*, a thirteenth-century legal code compiled under King Alfonso the Wise of Castile.[34] As European nations centralized political power, rulers embraced the role of primary lawmakers, and by the eighteenth century, these older compilations gave way to the creation of national civil codes—establishing the foundation of the modern civil law systems we see today.[35]

---

[30] *Id.*

[31] *Id.*

[32] Wayne R. Barnes, *Contemplating A Civil Law Paradigm for a Future International Commercial Code*, 65 La. L. Rev. 677, 701 (2005).

[33] *Id.*

[34] Reichard, *supra* note 28, at 6, 8 n. (Fall 1999).

[35] *Id.*

Common and Civil Law in America

The legal landscape of the United States is a reflection of its diverse colonial origins, shaped by the settlers who brought with them their own distinct legal traditions. English colonists, settling primarily along the Eastern seaboard, introduced the common law system, which emphasized judicial precedent and individual property ownership. In contrast, Spanish and French settlers in the South and Southwest United States carried with them the civil law tradition, rooted in the Roman and Napoleonic codes, which emphasized codified statutes and community ownership principles.

In the United States, references to the "common law" typically refer to either the common law of England as it existed at the time of our nation's founding or, more commonly, to the modern interpretation and application in contemporary legal disputes. Most states either explicitly adopted English common law and extended its protections to their citizens, or structured their legal systems based on the English common law framework.[36]

The common law system and the civil law system are not mutually exclusive; the two systems have consistently exchanged legal principles and doctrines, influencing each other over time.[37] Each state has its own unique legal character, with a varying degree of influence from both the civil law and the common law.

Contrary to common assumption, the former colonies did not immediately embrace English common law as the foundation for their legal systems. In fact, several colonies explicitly rejected the common law at first, with some even considering the adoption of a civil law framework.[38] Throughout

---

[36] Bethesda Afr. Cemetery Coal. v. Hous. Opportunities Comm'n of Montgomery Cnty., 489 Md. 1, 322 A.3d 681, 690 (2024).

[37] Wayne Barnes, *Hadley v. Baxendale and Other Common Law Borrowings from the Civil Law,* 11 Tex. Wesleyan L. Rev. 627, 638 (2005).

[38] Timothy G. Kearley, *From Rome to the Restatement: S.P. Scott, Fred Blume, Clyde Pharr, and Roman Law in Early Twentieth-Century America,* 108 Law Libr. J. 55 (2016).

the nineteenth century, American jurists involved in the codification movement[39] maintained a fascination with the civil law.[40]

There is no doubt that the legal system of our nation is primarily rooted in a common law heritage, but neither the American federal legal system nor any individual state system is a pure common law system.[41] Indeed, the idea of restating, or "codifying" the law into statutes or code, is itself a civil law concept.[42] Key to understanding the legal landscape of our nation is understanding:

> [t]he fact that the nation has never been a true "common law" legal system does not mean it qualifies as a civil law system . . . [w]hat it does mean is that the American legal system has evolved and matured over the last two centuries to the point that it has become *more like* civil law systems than it is *unlike* them.[43]

---

[39] *Id.* The American Codification Movement was a legal reform effort in the mid-nineteenth century focused on whether the United States should codify its laws, rather than rely on the common law system inherited from England. This period saw intense debates between those who supported codification—arguing it would make laws more accessible, predictable, and democratic—and those who defended the common law as more flexible and adapting to changing circumstances. The movement was largely driven by dissatisfaction with the complexity and inconsistency of the common law, as well as growing anti-English sentiment following the American Revolution and the War of 1812. *See* CHARLES M. COOK, THE AMERICAN CODIFICATION MOVEMENT: A STUDY OF ANTEBELLUM LEGAL REFORM (1981).

[40] Kearley, *supra* note 38, at 67 (noting that many of the original members of the American Law Institute were "familiar with and well disposed toward Roman law and codes," and that many scholars of the time compared the development of the Restatements to the "codification and exposition of Roman law undertaken in the reign of Justinian").

[41] J. Lyn Entrikin, *The Death of the Common Law*, 42 HARV. J.L. & PUB. POL'Y 351, 374–76 (2019) (noting that the Constitution grants plenary lawmaking power to the legislature, not the judiciary).

[42] Wayne Barnes, *Hadley v. Baxendale and Other Common Law Borrowings from the Civil Law*, 11 TEX. WESLEYAN L. REV. 627 (2005) (citing JOHN HENRY MERRYMAN, THE CIVIL LAW TRADITION: AN INTRODUCTION TO THE LEGAL SYSTEMS OF WESTERN EUROPE AND LATIN AMERICA 50–51 (2d ed. 1985)).

[43] Entrikin, *supra* note 41, at 376–77.

The Restatements illustrate how civil law has influenced American jurisprudence; the Restatements—a systematic treatise on the English common law—offer a way of viewing common law through a "civil law lens." Some judges give the Restatements great deference, while others do not recognize their authority.

Louisiana is widely considered to stand alone as the only civil law state in the United States, primarily because it does not apply the doctrine of stare decisis.[44] Even so, courts and scholars observe that Louisiana is more accurately classified as a hybrid system that embodies elements of both civil and common law.[45] Still, Louisiana more closely resembles a pure civil law state than anywhere else in the nation. Unlike the other 49 states and the District of Columbia, Louisiana's primary sources of law are "legislation and custom";[46] the state's constitution, codes, and statutes are the primary sources of law while court decisions serve as secondary sources without the binding precedent of stare decisis.[47]

---

[44] The doctrine of stare decisis provides that courts should honor judicial precedent. Louisiana instead applies the doctrine of *jurisprudence constante. Jurisprudence constante*, unlike stare decisis, "does not contemplate adherence to a principle of law announced and applied on a single occasion in the past" (Bergeron v. Richardson, 2020-01409 (La. 6/30/21), 320 So. 3d 1109, 1115). While a single decision is not binding on other Louisiana courts, when multiple rulings consistently apply the same reasoning, and such rulings create a "constant stream of uniform and homogenous rulings having the same reasoning," then *jurisprudence constante* applies and has considerable persuasive authority. *Id.* (citing James L. Dennis, *Interpretation and Application of the Civil Code and the Evaluation of Judicial Precedent,* 54 LA. L. REV. 1, 15 (1993)). The Louisiana Civil Code makes it clear that the sources of law in Louisiana are "legislation and custom"; the doctrine of *jurisprudence constante* is the judicial recognition of "custom" in Louisiana. *See* LA. CIV. CODE art. 1.

[45] *In re Orso,* 283 F.3d 686, 695 (5th Cir. 2002) (explaining that "[b]ecause Louisiana stands alone among the 50 states as a hybrid Civil Law/common law jurisdiction, its situation is unique[.]"). The fact that the principles of equity and estoppel have been introduced in Louisiana highlight the notion that Louisiana is a civil law state heavily influenced by a common law nation. *See* D. Gruning, *Mapping Society Through Law: Louisiana, Civil Law Recodified,* 19 TUL. EUR. & CIV. L.F. 1, 1–12, 14–20, 31–34, 4 (2004).

[46] LA. CIV. CODE art. 1.

[47] *In re Orso,* 283 F.3d 686, 695 (5th Cir. 2002).

Any effort to classify the different states as either "common law" or "civil law" jurisdictions is likely an oversimplification. The terms are not binary, and scholars have long recognized that traditional classifications obscure complexity.[48] Each of the states has its own unique legal history with varying degrees of influence from the common and civil law systems. Referring to attorneys who practice in noncommunity property states as "common law practitioners" may therefore be somewhat of a misnomer; all community property states other than Louisiana seem properly classified as common law states with a civil law marital property regime. As such, an estate planning attorney in California is properly deemed both a "common law practitioner" and a "community property practitioner." The authors find limited use for the term "common law practitioner" in the context of this discussion.

Civil Law vs. Common Law Property Rights

The two primary distinctions between the common law and the civil law systems lie in the courts' role in shaping the law and their differing approaches to property rights. In common law jurisdictions, judicial decisions serve as the primary legal authority, with statutes and regulations playing a supplementary role. The common law is often referred to as "judge-made" law. The doctrine of stare decisis ensures that court rulings establish binding precedents within jurisdictional limits.[49] In contrast, civil law systems derive their authority from legislation and sometimes other customary or traditional legal principles, rather than judicial interpretations of the law.

Court rulings in civil law jurisdictions do not carry the same precedent-setting weight as they do in common law jurisdictions and instead serve primarily to apply existing law rather than create new legal doctrines. Thus, court decisions in common law states have the force of law, whereas civil law court decisions are merely seen as interpreting the law, with such decisions given no preferential effect.[50] Secondary sources of the law also carry varying degrees of weight in common law and civil law systems. In a civil

---

[48] Entriken, *supra* note 41, at 376.

[49] James Spallino Jr., Esq., *Location, Location, Location: Advising Clients Who Own (or Who Want to Own) Foreign Real Estate,* 26(3) Ohio Prob. L.J. NL 9.

[50] *Id.*

law jurisdiction, a learned professor's opinion of the law will generally have greater weight than the opinion of a judge.[51]

With respect to property rights, the common law focuses on a "bundle of sticks" concept, dividing ownership into various estates with different rights and limitations, while civil law views property ownership rights as a holistic concept with a single, undivided right to the property. Thus, the common law finds more nuance in dividing property interests, while the civil law is more straightforward in defining ownership as a whole.[52]

In civil law, ownership consists of a defined set of rights, specifically, the rights to use the property (*usus*), to enjoy its fruits or profits (*fructus*), and to dispose of it (*abusus*).[53] By contrast, the "bundle of sticks" that make up an individual's interest in property under the common law is less defined.[54] The bundle of sticks concept known to the common law is malleable, meaning that rights may be added or removed by contract, courts, or lawmakers.

Civil law property and common law property are undeniably quite different, but they also share significant similarities.[55] Many common law property doctrines can actually be traced directly back to the civil law.[56] The *Corpus Juris Civilis* laid the groundwork for numerous principles that are still part of American property law today.[57] For instance, in the well-known case of *Pierson v. Post,* the court explicitly referenced the writings of Justinian, along with later civil law scholars such as Pufendorf, Grotius, and Barbeyrac, to resolve the question of whether the person who captures the

---

[51] V. Suarez & Co. v. Dow Brands, Inc., 337 F.3d 1, 7 (1st Cir. 2003) (quoting J.H. Merryman, *The Civil Law Tradition* 56–57 (2d ed. 1985) ("The civil law is a law of the professors. . . . The common law is still a law of the judges.")).

[52] Sally Brown Richardson, *A Tribute to Thanassi: The Influence of Justinian on American Common Law Property,* 78 La. L. Rev. 1111, 1112 (2018).

[53] *Id.*

[54] *Id.; see also* Yun-chien Chang & Henry E. Smith, *The Numerus Clausus Principle, Property Customs, and the Emergence of New Property Forms,* 100 Iowa L. Rev. 2275 (2015).

[55] Brown Richardson, *supra* note 52.

[56] *Id.* at 1112.

[57] *Id.* at 1111.

property becomes its rightful owner.[58] This is just one example of how the civil law has influenced American property law.[59]

Nonetheless, the number of property concepts known to the common law but foreign to the civil law, or vice versa, likely remains greater than any similarities they may share. For example, a fee simple estate, future interests, trusts, the rule against perpetuities, and easements in gross are some examples of property ownership concepts originally unique to the common law. By contrast, usufructuary interests, naked ownership, and the law of obligations are concepts unique to the civil law.

From these two separate systems of law, each with its own distinct rules regarding property ownership, were born two separate ways of viewing marital property rights—the separate property (common law) system and the community property (civil law) system. From jurisdiction to jurisdiction, there is significant variation in the importance of this distinction, particularly when it comes to the spouses' ability to alter the system through agreements before or during marriage, their rights to manage property during the marriage, and how property is divided when the marriage ends.[60] Moreover, the difference between these two systems has become increasingly less clear in recent decades, as further discussed later.[61]

MARITAL PROPERTY IN THE COMMON AND CIVIL LAW TRADITIONS

The concept of "community property," born out of the civil law, treats marriage as a partnership, granting both spouses equal ownership of property acquired during the marriage.[62]

---

[58] *Id.*

[59] Other examples of the civil law concepts of property influencing American property law include servitudes, the doctrine of waste, and copyright law. *See* Brown Richardson, *supra* note 52, at 1113–15.

[60] Charles Donahue Jr., *What Causes Fundamental Legal Ideas? Marital Property in England and France in the Thirteenth Century*, 78(1) MICH. L. REV. (1979).

[61] *Id.*

[62] Judith T. Younger, *Marital Regimes: A Story of Compromise and Demoralization, Together with Criticisms and Suggestions for Reform*, 67 CORNELL L. REV. 45 (Nov. 1981).

In *Commissioner v. Chase Manhattan Bank*, the Fifth Circuit concisely summarized the origins and basic principles of community property:

> The community property system comes from the custom of the women of the Visigoths and other Germanic tribes sharing the fighting and the spoils of war with their men; it owes its strength to the civilized view that marriage is a full partnership. Husband and wife are equal partners. Each has a present, vested half interest in all community property. All property accumulated during marriage is community property, unless it is received by gift, devise, or inheritance. . . . Thus, on death or divorce the community is divided equally. Neither spouse has testamentary disposition over the other's half of the community. The wife has complete testamentary disposition over her half and may leave it even to her paramour.[63]

Under the civil law system, tantamount to a "forced heirship" system, spouses had two kinds of assets: separate assets, owned individually before marriage or acquired after marriage by gift or inheritance, and community assets, acquired during the marriage, excluding gifts or inheritances. Each spouse could devise their one-half of the community assets, and upon a spouse's death the surviving spouse received the other one-half. A spouse's intestate community property and separate property passed to their descendants, ascendants, or collaterals, and only to the surviving spouse if none of those relatives survived. Additionally, the dependent wife received a usufructuary right for life or until remarriage in property inherited by the children, which protected her when the couple had little or no community property.[64]

---

[63] C.I.R. v. Chase Manhattan Bank, 259 F.2d 231 (5th Cir. 1958) (noting that the Visigoths were a Germanic people under the rule of the Roman Empire during late antiquity).

[64] Judith T. Younger, *Marital Regimes: A Story of Compromise and Demoralization, Together with Criticisms and Suggestions for Reform*, 67 CORNELL L. REV. 45 (Nov. 1981).

The Development of the Marital Property Concept in the Common Law

In stark contrast, under the common law system husband and wife were not seen as individuals, but as "one person in law."[65] Upon marriage, a woman became a "feme covert," meaning "a woman under cover" of her husband.[66] Marriage stripped a woman of her capacity to own personal property independently and to manage real estate: Her individual legal identity ceased to exist upon marriage.[67] The merger of a married woman's identity with that of her husband under the laws of the time eliminated the need for any legal framework for property division upon divorce.[68] The common law dealt with the death of a spouse by giving a surviving wife "dower" (a life interest in one-third of the decedent's land) and a surviving husband "curtesy"

---

[65] 1 W. Blackstone, Commentaries pt. 2, at 441 (G. Tucker ed. 1803) ("the very being or legal existence of the woman is suspended during the marriage, or at least is incorporated or consolidated into that of the husband"); 1 W. Blackstone, *Commentaries on the Laws of England* 442 (10th ed. 1787). *But see* Donahue, *supra* note 60, at 59 (noting that "[t]he amorphism 'At English common law the husband and wife were one and that one was husband,' may be amusing, but it is misleading. The fundamental characteristic of the thirteenth century common law of marital property by the time of Bracton was not the unity of husband and wife but their separation. The husband had his lands, the wife hers.").

[66] Judith T. Younger, *Marital Regimes: A Story of Compromise and Demoralization, Together with Criticisms and Suggestions for Reform*, 67 Cornell L. Rev. 45 (Nov. 1981).

[67] *Id.*, citing e.g., Harkins v. Coalter, 2 Port. 463, 473 (Ala. 1835); Fitch v. Ayer, 2 Conn. 143 (1817); Pope v. Tucker, 23 Ga. 484, 487 (1857); Bell v. Bell, 1 Ga. 637, 640 (1846); Skillman v. Skillman, 13 N.J. Eq. 403, 406 (1861); Blanchard v. Blood, 2 Barb. 352, 355 (N.Y. App. Div. 1848); Coleman v. Waples, 1 Del. (1 Harr.) 196, 200 (1833); Cain v. Furlow, 47 Ga. 674, 675 (1873); Herrington v. Herrington, 1 Miss. (1 Walker) 322, 323 (1829); Matthew v. Puffer, 19 N.H. 448, 451 (1849); Lanier v. Ross, 21 N.C. (1 Dev. & Bat. Eq.) 39, 40 (1834).

[68] Kenneth W. Kingma, *Property Division at Divorce or Death for Married Couples Migrating Between Common Law and Community Property States*, 35 ACTEC J. 74 (2009), citing Brett R. Turner, Equitable Distribution of Property § 1.3 n.9 (3d ed. 2005).

(a life estate in all of the decedent's land).[69] The common law rights of dower and curtesy are limited estates in the real property of the spouses, which some states still recognize at common law.[70]

Most noncommunity property states have abolished the common law dower and curtesy in favor of a statutory elective share in either surviving spouse as to both real and personal property.[71]

Suffice it say that the various matrimonial regimes that one may find are essentially adaptations of two fundamental models: community property and separate property. In fact,

---

[69] Curtesy was traditionally only applicable if the marriage produced a child capable of inheriting. *See, e.g.*, Dower and Curtesy, 4 IRM Abr. & Ann. § 5.17.2.7.1.4; DANIEL A. HANLEY, ELECTIVE SHARE, PPC FL-CLE 7-1 (2023). *See also* Donahue, *supra* note 60, for an excellent discussion of the origins of the common law marital property regime.

[70] IRM 5.17.2.7.1.4. Dower and Curtesy.

[71] *Id.* In all but three states (Ohio, Arkansas, and Kentucky), common law dower and curtesy have been abolished in favor of an "elective share," which is a statutory right of dower in either surviving spouse as to both real and personal property. *See* PAULA CLARKSON, DOWER RIGHTS: A RELIC OF THE PAST STILL AFFECTING ESTATE PLANS, May 9, 2025, https://www.mrclawcorp.com/blog/dower-rights-a-relic-of-thc-past-still-affecting-estate-plans/?utm_source=chatgpt.com. Although Georgia has abolished common law dower and curtesy, the state does not have a statutory elective share. Thus, a surviving spouse in Georgia has practically no protection from complete disinheritance. Georgia law does, however, allow for a year's support "in the form of property for their support and maintenance for the period of 12 months from the date of the decedent's death"; this is a transitional allowance intended to protect the family survivors from a reduction in their standard of living while the estate is being settled. The transitional allowance is considered a necessary expense of administration and is prioritized above all other debts of the estate. The property set aside for the year's support may include real property and vests jointly in the surviving spouse and minor children as tenants in common. *See In re* Est. of Sanders, 914 S.E.2d 829 (Ga. App. 2025), citing OCGA § 53-3-1(c). Dower and curtesy rights have no place in a community property system, which already provides for an automatic division of marital property into two equal shares at a spouse's death.

> [t]he concepts of marital and nonmarital property that are employed in most equitable distribution [common law] states are indeed drawn from community property law and in general correspond respectively to community and separate property.[72]

Over the past three centuries, the clear distinctions between these two legal traditions have become blurred. Social changes, primarily driven by the women's rights movement, have provided full recognition of a wife's contributions to marital property, particularly influencing how common law states deal with the property of a married couple. As one scholar has noted, the feminist movement played a large role in the reform of divorce law but largely ignored inheritance law.[73]

The uneven development of divorce and inheritance laws over the past century has resulted in a current legal landscape filled with inconsistencies and hidden dangers for those who are not careful.

The Uniform Marital Property Act (UMPA) and the Uniform Disposition of Community Property Rights at Death Act (UDCPRDA) were promulgated in the early 1970s by the Uniform Law Commission, and marked a shift toward recognizing marriage as a partnership in common law states and respecting the community property rights of spouses who relocated to a common law state. The UMPA acknowledged that both spouses contribute to the partnership and that property acquired during the marriage should be distributed upon dissolution of marriage or death in a manner

---

[72] William A. Reppy Jr., *Major Events in the Evolution of American Community Property Law and Their Import to Equitable Distribution States*, FAM. L.Q. 163, 163–92 (1989) (citing ROBERT J. LEVY, FAMILY LAW QUARTERLY, Volume XXIII, no. 2, at 147 (Summer 1989)). *See also* Nanette K. Laughrey, *Uniform Marital Property Act: A Renewed Commitment to the American Family*, 65(1) NEB. L. REV. art. 5, at 12 (1986) (noting that "at first glance, there seem to be many different matrimonial property regimes in Western societies. A closer examination reveals that these diverse systems are in fact variations on two themes, community property and separate property.").

[73] Laura A. Rosenbury, *Two Ways to End a Marriage: Divorce or Death*, UTAH L. REV. 1227 (2005).

reflecting that principle.[74] The UDCPRDA sought to statutorily preserve the testamentary rights of each spouse in community property that had been brought to a separate property state.

[74] Though only ever adopted by Wisconsin, UMPA created a class of property that belonged to the marriage rather than the individuals. *See* TURNER, *supra* note 68, § 2.5, noting that "Wisconsin's hybrid of community property and equitable distribution law is an excellent overall property division system. Because the various goals of a marital property system do not always agree, there is no discernible reason why the definitions of marital and nonmarital property must be the same for all purposes. Wisconsin's hybrid system addresses both divorce and death in a fair way, by giving each context its own specifically designed subsystem."

Chapter 3

The Equitable Distribution System and the Elective Share

THE EQUITABLE DISTRIBUTION SYSTEM

There are two theories used in the United States for dividing property at divorce: the community property system and the equitable distribution system. A review of the development of equitable distribution across the United States shows that the law governing division of marital property upon divorce often runs parallel in community property and noncommunity property states. This alignment is largely because the shared partnership concept, taken from community property laws, is the root of the principles of equitable distribution now widely adopted among common law states.[1] It is striking that the common law states have so wholeheartedly embraced the idea of marriage as a partnership for purposes of divorce, yet have approached that same idea with far more hesitancy in the context of testamentary disposition.

Moreover, the majority of the community property states no longer *require* an equal division of community property when the marriage ends by divorce.[2] Most community property states follow equitable distribution

[1] GREGORY, THE LAW OF EQUITABLE DISTRIBUTION § 1.02 (1989).

[2] BRETT R. TURNER, EQUITABLE DISTRIBUTION OF PROPERTY § 1:1 (4th ed. 2025).

principles upon divorce. Review Appendix A for a concise state-by-state summary of these rules.

The concept of equitable distribution emerged as a corrective to the traditional title-based property laws of most common law states, which often produced inequality between spouses at divorce. In 1970, the Commissioners on the Uniform State Laws introduced the Uniform Marriage and Divorce Act (UMDA), establishing a framework for classifying property as either (1) marital or (2) separate for purposes of division at divorce. The UMDA became the model for many states adopting the equitable distribution approach. Today, 41 states follow some form of equitable distribution, while the remaining 9 adhere to the community property system. However, as noted earlier and discussed further later, the community property system as traditionally understood implies an equal, not equitable, division of community property at divorce. Nevertheless, the community property regimes currently in force in most of those 9 states have evolved in practice to operate in a manner substantially analogous to the equitable distribution system.

Early American common law on marriage and divorce was largely derived from English common law of the late eighteenth and early nineteenth centuries.

> The oldest traditions of the law were favorable to women as husband and wives enjoyed equal divorce and property rights under Anglo-Saxon law.[3] Following the Norman Conquest, however, the law shifted decisively in favor of husbands. English law conceptualized the marital relationship as a single economic unit, but not as a distinct marital community.

Rather, the wife's legal identity was subsumed into that of her husband, leaving her with no independent legal existence.[4]

Upon marriage, a wife's personal property and possessions became her husband's and, upon his death, passed to his personal representatives.[5] During the marriage, she could not hold property, enter into contracts, make a will, or litigate in her own name.[6] This doctrine of coverture continued to

---

[3] *Id.*, citing Foster Jr., Preface to Baxter, Marital Property v–vi (1973).

[4] *Id.*

[5] *Id.*, citing Clark, The Law of Domestic Relations in the United States § 8.1 at 499 (1987).

[6] *Id.*

dominate English marital property law well into the nineteenth century and was directly incorporated into early American common law.

The doctrine of coverture under early American law foreclosed the need for the development of rules governing the division of property at divorce. Because a married woman lacked an independent legal identity, the law regarded all marital property as belonging exclusively to the husband. From this premise, courts readily concluded that women's property rights were inherently limited and that a wife had no claim to any portion of the marital estate upon dissolution of marriage.[7]

During the nineteenth century, growing criticism of the common law's treatment of married women—particularly the denial of any independent legal identity—gave rise to a reform movement led by women's rights advocates. In response, legislatures across the United States enacted Married Women's Property Acts, which rejected the coverture-based merger of spousal identities and recognized the wife as a distinct legal person. These statutes formally empowered married women to hold legal title to property in their own names. Yet this legal recognition often amounted to little more than a symbolic change, since pervasive social and economic barriers continued to restrict women's participation in the labor market and, in turn, their ability to hold and accumulate property.[8] As a result, most wives remained without significant assets, and societal attitudes continued to assume that property in the husband's name reflected his sole efforts. Because permanent alimony remained available in fault-based divorce proceedings, courts saw little need to develop doctrines of property division. Consequently, by the early twentieth century the prevailing framework was the title theory: Although married women could legally own property, their entitlement upon divorce extended only to assets held in their names.[9]

By the latter part of the nineteenth century, an important departure from the title theory emerged in a group of western jurisdictions that embraced community property principles. Unlike most states, these jurisdictions did not ground their marital laws in the English common law tradition. Louisiana drew its governing rules from the French civil law system, while the seven other states that had once been provinces of Mexico incorporated family law doctrines rooted in Spanish legal tradition.

---

[7] *Id.*

[8] *Id.*

[9] *Id.*

The civil law traditions of France and Spain diverged sharply from the English model. Although all three shared the premise of the unity of the marital partnership, English law vested that unity in the person of the husband, whereas French and Spanish law, drawing on Roman and early Germanic sources, conceptualized the marital community as a distinct legal entity separate from either spouse.[10] Under this framework, husband and wife held equal, undivided interests in the community, and upon divorce or death the assets of the community were, traditionally, divided equally between them.

However, in present day, the majority of community property states have moved away from the strict equal division of community property for purposes of property division at divorce.[11] In Arizona, Idaho, Nevada, Texas, and Washington, community property is divided on an equitable basis at divorce, while California, Louisiana, and New Mexico continue to require an equal division upon divorce.[12]

Presumptions in Equitable Distribution

Within the equitable distribution system, states follow three different approaches to presumptions at divorce. The majority rule applies no presumption: Courts weigh the statutory factors and reach a result without a default assumption of equality. By contrast, several jurisdictions adopt an explicit presumption of equal division; for example, Indiana, New Hampshire, North Carolina, West Virginia, and Wisconsin presume a 50/50 division is equitable, and the spouse seeking more than half bears the burden of showing that an equal division would be unjust. A third group of states rejects a binding presumption but treats equality as the initial reference point. Courts in Ohio, Florida, South Carolina, and Virginia, among others, describe a 50/50 split as the starting point for analysis, allowing departures if the statutory factors clearly favor one spouse. The functional consequence is that, whether labeled a presumption, a starting point, or unstated, trial courts in most jurisdictions tend to divide marital estates equally in longer

---

[10] *Id.*

[11] *Id.* § 2:5.

[12] *Id.* at n.4.

marriages unless the evidence demonstrates a compelling reason to do otherwise.[13]

The key takeaway here is that the division of marital property at divorce is not all that different in community property jurisdictions and noncommunity property jurisdictions. The fundamental difference between community property and equitable distribution states with respect to dividing marital property at divorce is best expressed as follows: The community property rights of spouses are *vested* legal interests acquired during the marriage; by contrast, under the equitable distribution system the marital property rights of the spouses are initially unvested, and vest only if and when a dissolution for divorce proceeding is filed by one of the spouses.[14]

In other words, the concept of "marital property" in noncommunity property states does not even come into existence until such time as a divorce proceeding is initiated by one of the spouses. By contrast, in community property states, all property acquired by either spouse during the marriage does not belong to either spouse individually, "but to a third entity, the marital community."[15]

The authors find it helpful to view noncommunity property states with an equitable distribution system that begins with the presumption or starting point of a 50/50 split of the marital estate at divorce as "separate property states with a deferred community," with such deferred community arising only upon divorce.[16] In this sense, a "deferred community" simply means that although the state does not recognize community property *during* the marriage, it effectively applies a community property presumption at dissolution of marriage by beginning the equitable distribution process with a 50/50 split of the marital property before other rules and factors are applied in the court's determination of what is equitable between the spouses.

---

[13] *Id.* § 8:2.

[14] *Id.* § 2.7.

[15] *Id.* § 2.5.

[16] *See* Est. of Lineweaver v. Comm'r, 71 T.C.M. (CCH) 3058 (T.C. 1996) (noting that North Carolina's equitable distribution statute "created a type of deferred community property law system governing marital property in the case of divorce"); John W. Willis, *The Equitable Distribution of Marital Property: Toward a Deferred Community Property System*, 14 FAM. L.Q. 1 (1980).

THE ELECTIVE SHARE

While the rules for dividing property at divorce have converged over time across the United States, the rules at death remain markedly distinct between community property and noncommunity property states.

Virtually all United States jurisdictions have abolished dower and curtesy in favor of the elective share. Georgia is the only state that does not have a statutory elective share.[17] Therefore, today in the United States, all states except Georgia place restrictions on a person's ability to disinherit a surviving spouse.

Limitations on complete freedom of testation are hardly new; they trace back at least as far as the Code of Hammurabi (around 2084 BC).[18] In early English common law, inheritance rules favored blood relatives rather than surviving spouses—husband and wife were not heirs of one another and therefore could not inherit each other's property.[19] Even so, widows and widowers were not left entirely without protection. The doctrines of dower and curtesy arose in medieval times to provide a lifetime interest in land, serving both to offset the wife's loss of control over her property during marriage and to ensure some measure of support for surviving spouses after title passed to the decedent's heirs.

By the thirteenth century, English common law had formally recognized dower rights, and by the early fifteenth century, it had evolved into a fixed one-third life interest for the wife in the husband's real property at his death. This somewhat arbitrary one-third share was carried forward into early American dower and curtesy laws and still echoes in the structure of many modern elective share statutes.[20] A widow's entitlement, however, was not absolute: It could be forfeited if her husband was convicted of treason or if she herself was guilty of treason, felony, or adultery.[21]

In substance, early concepts of dower resembled modern community property concepts, in that the wife was deemed to hold an interest in any real property acquired by her husband during marriage, notwithstanding

---

[17] Jeffrey N. Pennell, *Minimizing the Surviving Spouse's Elective Share*, 32 U. Miami L. Ctr. Est. Plan. § 904 (1998).

[18] Terry L. Turnipseed, *Community Property v. the Elective Share*, 72 La. L. Rev. 161, 164 (2011).

[19] *Id.*

[20] *Id.*

[21] *Id.*

legal title. The husband could not unilaterally extinguish this right without her consent. If she agreed, however, he could defeat dower through the levy of a fine when conveying land to a third party free of restrictions.[22]

Early English law similarly recognized a husband's rights in his wife's property under the doctrine of curtesy, originally referred to as a tenancy "by the curtesy of England."[23] Unlike dower, which arose automatically in favor of the wife, curtesy required the birth of a child capable of inheriting. Once a child was born, the husband's temporary interest in his wife's inheritable estates became a life estate known as "curtesy initiate," which matured into "curtesy consummate" upon the wife's death. Importantly, the husband's rights extended only to property of which the wife was seized in possession at death, and not to her future or remainder interests.[24]

Curtesy was more expansive than dower in that it gave the husband a life estate in the whole of his wife's qualifying property, rather than a fractional share. Yet it was also more conditional, since the right depended on the birth of a child. Commentators have suggested that this requirement helps explain the social emphasis placed on producing an heir.[25]

In the United States, dower and curtesy concepts were carried into early American law, and eventually evolved into modern elective share statutes. The elective share can thus be understood as the American descendant of these medieval protections, designed to guarantee some measure of economic security for surviving spouses, while balancing that protection against the ideal of testamentary freedom.

Elective share statutes differ significantly from state to state, and have been described as:

> [A] jungle, with hardly two states to be found that are exactly alike, and there exists in reality 50 different schemes most of which, when analyzed, are not built upon a single, adequate interest given the surviving spouse; but instead give her a bit of homestead, a bit of widow's allowance, and in addition a bit of dower or some statutory substitute therefore.[26]

---

[22] *Id.*, citing LEE HOLCOMBE, WIVES & PROPERTY: REFORM OF THE MARRIED WOMEN'S PROPERTY LAW IN NINETEENTH-CENTURY ENGLAND 21 (1983).

[23] *Id.* at 167.

[24] *Id.*

[25] *Id.* at 168.

[26] WILLIAM J. BOWE ET AL., PAGE ON THE LAW OF WILLS § 3.13 (2003).

As its name suggests, the elective share is not automatic; the surviving spouse must either accept the provisions made under the decedent's will or, instead, reject the will and claim the statutory share.[27]

Historically, many states limited the elective share to the decedent's probate estate, usually granting the surviving spouse one-third to one-half of those assets. These statutes, a twentieth-century replacement for dower and curtesy, began with New York's first such law in the 1930s. The probate-only model had the virtue of simplicity: Courts needed only to value the probate estate and apply the statutory fraction without delving into family dynamics or exercising broad discretion. Yet this simplicity came at a cost: The statutes were insensitive to the actual needs of surviving spouses, the nature of their contributions to the marriage, and the reasons behind the decedent's testamentary plan. Because it was easy to avoid probate through trusts and other will substitutes, these statutes were soon criticized as inadequate, and most states moved to broaden the base of assets subject to the elective share.[28]

In response, a number of states expanded the scope of the elective share beyond the probate estate. Following New York's lead, many jurisdictions now apply the elective share to an "augmented estate," which aggregates both probate and certain nonprobate transfers. In theory, this approach better prevents testators from disinheriting a spouse by shifting assets to will substitutes. In practice, however, state definitions of the augmented estate vary dramatically, and gaps remain that allow sophisticated estate planners to minimize or defeat a surviving spouse's rights.[29]

The Uniform Probate Code (UPC) contains the most comprehensive augmented share regime designed to approximate the results one would expect under a community property system.[30] The UPC includes nearly all property owned by either spouse, including premarital property and assets received by gift or inheritance. While this breadth is intended to capture the true economic partnership of marriage, it has been criticized as

---

[27] Turnipseed, *supra* note 18, at 138.

[28] *Id.*

[29] *Id.*

[30] *Id.* (noting that "the goal of the UPC drafters was to approximate as best as possible the division of property at death in a community property jurisdiction").

overinclusive.[31] For example, if the decedent's estate consisted largely of inherited wealth, the surviving spouse's share could be disproportionately inflated, even where the marriage contributed little to the growth of that property. To balance this, the UPC offsets the elective share with the surviving spouse's own wealth, which can sometimes result in no share at all for a wealthy survivor. Perhaps for these reasons, the UPC elective share provisions have been adopted in only a handful of states.[32]

The elective share can be sidestepped fairly easily in some states by transferring assets into certain types of trusts during lifetime. More comprehensive elective share statutes, known as "augmented estate" statutes in some common law jurisdictions, attempt to close this loophole by including lifetime transfers, such as transfers to trusts, in the pool of assets from which the elective share is calculated. Yet even the most carefully drafted elective share statutes remain vulnerable: Offshore trusts can seriously frustrate surviving spousal rights and creditor remedies. This reality underscores a larger structural weakness in the separate property system. While the elective share was originally adopted as a safeguard for surviving spouses, modern wealth planning techniques have made it increasingly ineffective.[33]

"Forced-share law is the law of the second best. It undertakes upon death to correct the failure of a separate-property state to create the appropriate lifetime rights for spouses in each other's earnings."[34] In separate property states, elective share statutes are generally justified by one of three competing theories: the support theory, the marital partnership theory, or the contract theory. At present, however, the statutory landscape reflects a confusing mix of these approaches rather than a coherent guiding principle.[35] The following quote from Professor Jeffrey Pennell best summarizes this confused area of the law:

> As it is, both the policy justifications and the effect of these rules are flawed, confused, or conflicted. To illustrate simply, most statutes cannot even choose whether they are based on a support theory

---

[31] *Id.*

[32] *Id.*

[33] *Id.* at 161.

[34] *Id.*, citing John H. Langbein & Lawrence W. Waggoner, *Redesigning the Spouse's Forced Share*, 22 REAL PROP. PROB. & TR. J. 303, 306 (1987).

[35] *Id.*

> (that is, the surviving spouse should not be left destitute and therefore a ward of the state) or an economic partnership theory (that is, everything acquired by investment or industry by either spouse during the marriage should belong to them equally, as in community property). This easily is shown by the vast divergence in the size of the share from state to state. For example, the surviving spouse's share can range from a low of 0 percent to a high of 50 percent under the new Uniform Probate Code accrual share regime (indicating a marital partnership approach, based on the length of the marriage) but with a support allowance in all cases (the Uniform Probate Code § 2-202(b) Supplemental Elective Share Amount, based on the spouse's other property and property received outside of probate). In some states the share can be as high as 100 percent in certain cases. And those states that still reflect a one-third share presumably are attributable to the dower/curtesy origins of elective share statutes, which arguably are not informed by either the support or the marital partnership theories. . . .
>
> The conflicted underpinnings of these statutes is especially well illustrated by the fact that, in virtually all states, the election is denied if the spouse has died before an election is made. Quaere (sic) how to justify a marital partnership theory underlying these statutes if the surviving spouse's property right substitute is defeated merely by the accident of dying before making the claim. This bespeaks a support theory, but it should not inform an accrual entitlement that increases with the length of the marriage. The conflict also is illustrated almost everywhere by the fact that an election made on behalf of an incapacitated surviving spouse must be justified on the basis of need. Again, if the statutes reflect a marital partnership surrogate for community property, why should need or death of the spouse before completion of the election process be critical at all?[36]

The elective share, while conceived as a modern replacement for dower and curtesy, has never fully lived up to its intended purpose. In theory it exists to balance the ideals of testamentary freedom with the need to

---

[36] Pennell, *supra* note 17, § 904 n.9, citing Thomas Oldham, *Should the Surviving Spouse's Forced Share Be Retained?*, 38 Case W. Res. L. Rev. 223, 224–25 (1987).

protect surviving spouses from disinheritance. In practice, however, it has produced a patchwork of statutory schemes, with each reflecting a different and often conflicting view of marriage. Some statutes rest on a support rationale, others on a partnership rationale, and still others retain remnants of their dower and curtesy origins. The result is an area of law so fragmented that it has been aptly described as a "jungle."

Moreover, the elective share is increasingly ill suited to contemporary wealth planning. Probate-only statutes are easily circumvented, while augmented share regimes vary so widely that even the most robust versions can be defeated by sophisticated or extreme trust planning, such as by transferring assets to an Offshore Asset Protection Trust in a jurisdiction that will not respect U.S. community property (or other) laws. The UPC attempted to approximate the results of community property by creating an augmented estate model, but its complexity and overbreadth have limited its adoption.

What emerges, then, is a system that is both underinclusive and overinclusive: It often fails to provide meaningful protection to those in genuine need, while at the same time awarding disproportionate benefits in cases where the surviving spouse is already independently wealthy, or when there has been a short marriage or a surviving spouse is simply undeserving. This confusion reveals the fundamental weakness of separate property regimes in addressing spousal rights at death. As some commentators have observed, forced or elective-share law is merely "the law of the second best," attempting after death to correct for the absence of true partnership rights during marriage.

The elective share, though designed as a safeguard for surviving spouses, remains a fragmented and often inconsistent body of law. Its statutes reflect competing theories of marriage, retain vestiges of dower and curtesy, and are readily undermined by modern estate planning. While the purpose of this book is not to propose reforms or to rewrite elective share laws, this detour into their history and operation is essential. Any meaningful comparison between the community property and separate property regimes requires first grappling with the complexities of equitable distribution and the elective share. For noncommunity property practitioners, the lesson is clear: One cannot fully appreciate the strengths and shortcomings of the community property system without understanding the separate property regime in all its nuance.

Chapter 4

Understanding Testamentary Disposition of Community Property and the Uniform Disposition of Community Property Rights at Death Act

Upon the death of the first spouse to die, one-half of the aggregate value of all property held as community property belongs to the surviving spouse outright and is not subject to testamentary disposition by the decedent spouse. The decedent may only direct how his or her one-half interest in the community property will pass (as well as any separate property owned or controlled by the decedent), while the surviving spouse retains full ownership of his or her one-half community interest, which becomes that spouse's sole and exclusive property at death.

Note, however, that this general rule is subject to significant exceptions and qualifications arising from federal law, contractual beneficiary designations, and the interaction between state property law and federal distribution and taxation regimes. These issues are discussed in depth in Chapter 12.

Because the law of a decedent's domicile generally controls how property is distributed at death, common law states have enacted special statutes that seek to preserve and classify community property as such when a married couple moves in from a community property jurisdiction.[1] In 1971, the National Conference of Commissioners on Uniform State Laws adopted the Uniform Disposition of Community Property Rights at Death Act.[2] The Uniform Act serves for common law jurisdictions the same function that quasi-community property statutes serve for community property states—it allows the forum state to treat certain out-of-state acquisitions as if they were community property, ensuring fair and consistent division at death or divorce.[3]

Under the Uniform Act, when a married person dies (in a noncommunity property state that has adopted the Act), one-half of the property subject to the Act belongs to the surviving spouse and cannot be disposed of by the decedent's will or by intestacy, while the other half is the decedent's property, subject to testamentary disposition or distribution under state succession law. The Act is generally applicable to a married person's personal or real property that (1) was acquired as community property or (2) was acquired with the rents, issues, or income of, the proceeds from, or in exchange for, derived from, or otherwise traceable to community property under the laws of another jurisdiction.[4]

---

[1] Kenneth W. Kingma, *Property Division at Divorce or Death for Married Couples Migrating Between Common Law and Community Property States*, 35 ACTEC J. 74, 84–85 (2009).

[2] *Id.*, citing Uniform Disposition of Community Property Rights at Death Act (1971), 8A U.L.A. 213 (2003).

[3] *Id.* at 84, providing "[w]hat the Uniform Act is to a common law state, a quasi-community property statute is to a community property state." Quasi-community property is property acquired in a noncommunity property state during marriage that a community property state reclassified as community property at divorce or death because it would have been community property had the couple been domiciled there when it was acquired. Although such property is technically "separate property" under ordinary community property classification rules, many community property states treat it as if it were community property for purposes of division at divorce and, in some states, for purposes of succession at death, to prevent the non-acquiring spouse from being disadvantaged solely because the couple happened to reside in a noncommunity property jurisdiction.

[4] *See, e.g.*, FLA. STAT. § 732.217.

The Uniform Act was designed to prevent a change of domicile from depriving spouses of property rights established under a previous domicile's community property regime.[5] Its narrow purpose is to preserve each spouse's vested one-half interest in property that was community in character before the move, mirroring the traditional rule that the decedent may dispose of only his or her one-half of the community property. By doing so, the Act seeks to ensure continuity of marital property rights, minimizes litigation, and facilitates estate planning for couples migrating between community property and common law jurisdictions that have enacted the Act.

The Prefatory Note to the Uniform Act further provides that:

> [The Act] is intended to have no effect on the rights of creditors who became such before the death of a spouse; neither does it affect the rights of spouses or other persons prior to the death of a spouse. While problems may arise prior to the death of a spouse they are believed to be of relatively less importance than the delineation of dispositive rights (and the correlative effect on planning of estates). The prescription of uniform treatment in other contexts poses somewhat greater difficulties; thus this act is designed solely to cover dispositive rights at death, as an initial step.[6]

Sixteen states have adopted the Uniform Disposition of Community Property Rights at Death Act (UDCPRDA).[7] In 2021, the Uniform Law

---

[5] *Uniform Disposition of Community Property Rights at Death Act*, 1971, With Prefatory Note and Comments, Prefatory Note, providing "Frequently spouses, who have been domiciled in a jurisdiction which has a type of community property regime, move to a jurisdiction which has no such system of marital rights. As a matter of policy, and probably as a matter of constitutional law, the move should not be deemed (in and of itself) to deprive the spouses of any preexisting property rights."

[6] *Uniform Disposition of Community Property Rights at Death Act*, 1971, With Prefatory Note and Comments, Prefatory Note.

[7] These 16 states are as follows: Alaska, Arkansas, Colorado, Connecticut, Florida, Hawaii, Kentucky, Michigan, Minnesota, Montana, New York, North Carolina, Oregon, Utah, Virginia, and Wyoming. Nebraska legislators have recently introduced a bill that would make them the 17th state to adopt the Uniform Disposition of Community Property Rights at Death Act (UDCPRDA). *Community Property Disposition at Death Act*, UNIF. L. COMM'N, https://www.uniformlaws.org/committees/community-home?CommunityKey=425b0732-7ff0-4b28-ada1-fc2b4638f29e (last

Commission promulgated an updated version of the Act, the Uniform Community Property Disposition at Death Act (UCPDDA).[8] Notably, the 1971 UDCPRDA arguably only applied to probate proceedings.[9] The 2021 UCPDDA seeks to broaden the applicability of the Act by making it clearly applicable to nonprobate transfers.[10]

The UCPDDA modernizes definitions to include domestic partners and similar legal relationships capable of acquiring community property, clarifies the treatment of community property trusts, recognizes partial ownership of community property owners, provides explicit procedures for claiming community property rights at the death of a spouse, and expands third-party protections.[11] The UCPDDA has been adopted in only Colorado, Nebraska, Arkansas, North Carolina, and the District of Columbia.[12]

All community property trust states, except South Dakota and Tennessee, have adopted the UDCPRDA. Notably, none of the community property trust states have enacted the UCPDDA. All community property trust states are wise to enact the UCPDDA (2021), or a version thereof. The UCPDDA offers a more comprehensive framework for preserving community property rights at death. By adopting the UCPDDA, the community property trust states could eliminate statutory gaps, and modernize their treatment of community property. This is a particularly wise course of action for an elective community property trust state seeking to have its community property trust legislation respected by the IRS for purposes of the § 1014(b)(6) double step-up in basis.

---

visited July 17, 2023). Note, however, that Colorado, Arkansas, North Carolina, and Nebraska have since updated to the UCPDDA.

[8] *Uniform Community Property Disposition at Death Act,* supra note 7.

[9] Anthony P. Guettler & Patrick J. Lannon, *Florida Uniform Disposition of Community Property Rights at Death Act: Time for an Update?,* Gould Cooksey Fennell (Aug. 31, 2023), https://gouldcooksey.com/blog/florida-uniform-disposition-ofcommunity-property-rights-at-death-act-time-for-an-update/.

[10] *Uniform Community Property Disposition at Death Act, supra* note 7, Prefatory Note. *See also* Guettler & Lannon, *supra* note 9.

[11] *Uniform Community Property Disposition at Death Act, supra* note 7, *see also* Guettler & Lennon, *supra* note 9.

[12] *Uniform Community Property Disposition at Death Act, supra* note 7.

While the Uniform Disposition of Community Property Rights at Death Act (UDCPRDA) (1971) and the less widely adopted Uniform Community Property Disposition at Death Act (UCPDDA) (2021) both represent pragmatic efforts to preserve preexisting community property rights for couples migrating to common law states, neither statute operates as a self-executing community property regime. Each Act addresses only the disposition of property at death; they do not classify, manage, or regulate the property during the spouses' joint lifetimes.

This limitation means that the Act provides no mechanism for maintaining the community character of property after spouses change domicile. For example, if a couple moves from California to Florida in 2025 and continues to maintain a marital domicile in Florida for the next 50 years without taking affirmative steps to segregate or reaffirm the community nature of their assets, the community character of their assets would likely erode over time through commingling, reinvestment, or transmutation. In such a case, absent clear tracing or express agreement, it would be difficult—if not impossible—for the surviving spouse or the estate to establish that the property remaining was "community" at death within the meaning of the Act.[13]

Thus, while the UDCPRDA and the UCPDDA work to preserve dispositive symmetry of community property in noncommunity property states, they fail to provide continuity of classification during the joint lifetime of the spouses while they reside in the noncommunity property state. The Act assumes the continued existence of identifiable community property, but offers no administrative or documentary framework to give guidance as to how to maintain community property status, leaving migrated spouses to be dependent on their own record-keeping and legal counsel if they wish to attempt to preserve community property status over the decades.[14]

---

[13] For instance, if a married couple sells their former California community property home after moving to Florida and uses the sale proceeds (now held in a Florida bank account titled as TBE) to purchase a new residence, the proceeds have effectively been retitled and reinvested under Florida law. Without an agreement preserving their community property status, those funds would almost certainly lose their community character, making it doubtful that the Act would treat the newly acquired Florida property as community property at death.

[14] Note, however, that the UCPDDA, unlike the UDCPRDA, does expressly recognize transmutations and includes sections relating to partition and waiver of

When spouses transfer assets between brokerage accounts or place them into a family limited liability company or other arrangement, the community character can be lost, simply because it becomes difficult or impossible to identify or trace.

A SIMPLE EXAMPLE OF MOVING WITH COMMUNITY PROPERTY

Assume, for example, that Alex and Taylor are domiciled in California (a community property state). Taylor earns $1,000 of wages and uses those wages to buy a brand-new iPhone at the local Verizon store. Taylor decides he does not like the color that he had chosen for his new iPhone. He therefore does not remove the phone from the box or begin using it. Alex and Taylor thereafter move to Florida and establish Florida as their domicile. Shortly after settling down in Florida, Taylor sells his unboxed iPhone on Facebook Marketplace for $1,000 cash. Taylor then goes to the Verizon store in Florida and purchases the color of iPhone he prefers with the $1,000 he received from the Facebook Marketplace buyer. Is the new iPhone that Taylor purchased in Florida considered to be community property?

Under the governing conflict-of-laws principles discussed in Chapter 6, the character of personal property is determined at the time of acquisition under the law of the spouses' marital domicile at that time.[15] While domiciled in California, Taylor earned $1,000 of wages, and because wages earned during marriage in California are community property, the $1,000 earned by Taylor was community property, and the iPhone acquired with those wages was likewise community property.[16]

Alex and Taylor's move to Florida did not alter the character of the property they had acquired in California.[17] Community property neither

---

community property rights. In this regard, the UCPDDA is probably more effective than the UDCPRDA at managing and accounting for the community property during the lifetime of the community.

[15] RESTATEMENT (SECOND) OF CONFLICT OF L. § 258 (1971).

[16] *See, e.g.*, CAL. FAM. CODE § 760.

[17] RESTATEMENT (SECOND) OF CONFLICT OF L. § 259 (1971), providing "a marital property interest in a chattel, or right embodied in a document, which has been acquired by either or both of the spouses, is not affected by the mere removal of

evaporates nor reclassifies itself merely because the couple crosses into a noncommunity property jurisdiction. The first iPhone therefore remained community property in Florida.

When Taylor then sold that unopened iPhone for $1,000, the proceeds of that sale also retained their community character, because community property maintains its character through exchanges so long as the asset remains identifiable and traceable.[18] Here, the entire value of the asset was carried forward in a simple, direct transaction: A $1,000 community property phone was exchanged for $1,000 cash. That cash was then immediately used to purchase a new iPhone.

The second iPhone purchased in Florida is treated as an asset acquired in exchange for existing community property, and therefore it inherits the same community property character. Nothing in the transaction transmuted it, commingled it, or rendered it untraceable. The asset simply changed form.[19]

This example provides a useful illustration of how these principles operate in practice. Chapter 6, however, makes clear that the analysis is not always this straightforward. Although movable property generally retains its character after a change in domicile and through simple, traceable exchanges, courts do not apply these principles uniformly. Outcomes can vary depending on the forum, the context in which the issue arises, and whether the transaction in question occurred before or after the move. In divorce proceedings, for example, many equitable distribution states simply

---

the chattel or document to a second state, whether or not this removal is accompanied by a change of domicil to the other state on the part of one or both of the spouses."

[18] *Id.*, providing "when a chattel or document is taken into a second state and is there exchanged for some other movable or immovable, the spouses acquire the same interests therein as they had in the original chattel or document."

[19] *Id.*, providing "[t]hus, when a husband takes an automobile, which is his alone, from a separate property state to a community property state, and then, having sold the automobile, uses the proceeds to purchase a truck, the truck will be the husband's separate property. On the other hand, if the husband had originally held the automobile in community with his wife and had exchanged it for a truck in a separate property state, the wife's interests in the truck would be the same as those she had previously had in the automobile."

apply forum law (lex fori),[20] and this can result in the court disregarding community property character altogether.[21]

FLORIDA AS A CASE STUDY

Florida's Uniform Disposition of Community Property Rights at Death Act (FUDCPRDA) is contained within Florida Statute §§ 732.216–732.228.[22]

Florida Statute § 732.224 provides that the provisions of the Act do not "affect rights of creditors with respect to property to which [the Act] appl[ies]."[23] There is no inherent change to creditors' rights in community property when a married couple moves to Florida. For example, moving community property from California will not alter a creditor's rights to pursue such assets, unless or until the couple transmutes the property treatment to a protected status, and only then if such transmutation is not a voidable transfer under the Uniform Voidable Transactions Act.

Any property acquired during marriage by a spouse while domiciled in a jurisdiction that permits acquisition of community property is presumed to have been acquired as, or to have become and remained, property governed by the FUDCPRDA. By contrast, real property located in Florida and personal property (wherever located) acquired by a married person while domiciled in a jurisdiction that does not permit community property—and titled in a form creating survivorship rights—is presumed not to be governed by the FUDCPRDA.[24]

The FUDCPRDA "[does] not prevent married couples from severing or altering their interests in property to which [the Act] applies,"[25] but the FUDCPRDA also does not provide a specific form for transmuting or

---

[20] Turner, Equitable Distribution of Property § 3:13 (4th ed. 2025).

[21] *See, e.g.*, Mbatha v. Cutting, 356 Ga. App. 743, 848 S.E.2d 920 (2020).

[22] Florida first enacted the Uniform Disposition of Community Property Rights at Death Act in 1992, underscoring that Florida's engagement with certain community property concepts predates the more recent attention given to Florida community property trusts.

[23] Fla. Stat. § 732.224 (2022).

[24] *Id.* § 732.218.

[25] *Id.* § 732.225.

partitioning property.[26] Oddly, but certainly in the spirit of excluding TBE property and homestead property from the FUDCPRDA, Florida Statute § 732.225 provides that:

> [t]he reinvestment of any property to which these sections apply in real property located in this state which is or becomes real or personal property held by tenants by the entirety or homestead property creates a conclusive presumption that the spouses have agreed to terminate the community property attribute of the property reinvested.[27]

However, this "conclusive presumption" under § 732.225 stands in notable tension with § 736.151 of the Florida Community Property Trust Act, which specifically allows spouses to maintain the community property status of homestead property transferred to a Florida community property trust and even to create community property treatment in homestead property that is acquired subject to such a trust.[28]

Florida Senate Bill 262, filed by Senator Berman in January of 2025, was approved by the governor in June of 2025. The Bill amended portions of the Florida Trust Code, including § 736.151 to add new subsection (3) to confirm that transferring homestead property into a Florida community property trust is not a change of ownership for the purpose of reassessing the value of the homestead property. The Bill is a step forward in creating a coherent and integrated body of community property law in Florida. Notably, the Bill did not amend § 732.225.

---

[26] By contrast, the UCPDDA has a specific section on the form of partition and reclassification of community property. *See* UCPDDA (2021) section 4.

[27] Fla. Stat. § 732.225 (2022).

[28] *Id.* § 736.151. Compare §§ 736.151 and 732.225. On one hand, § 732.225 assumes that reinvestment in a Florida homestead is evidence of an intent to abandon community property principles as to the property reinvested; on the other, § 736.151 assumes that spouses may affirmatively maintain or create community property status in a Florida homestead through the use of a properly drafted trust.

Can a Florida Community Property Trust Hold Homestead Property?

Clearly yes, under Florida Statute § 736.151. The more important question, however, is whether spouses can hold Florida homestead property in a Florida community property trust and have both (1) the homestead designation respected for state law creditor protection and property tax benefits and (2) the community property designation respected by the IRS for federal tax purposes such that the homestead property in the trust will receive a full step-up in basis on the first death under § 1014(b)(6). When answering this question, it is important to remember that state law defines property rights while federal law applies federal tax consequences to those rights.[29]

At first glance, it might be easy to conclude that homestead property subject to the Florida Constitution's devise restrictions cannot coexist with community property, since community property must give each spouse a vested one-half interest capable of testamentary disposition, while Florida homestead law restricts testamentary devise of the homestead in a manner that overrides that freedom typical of a "traditional" community property asset (by requiring a life estate to the surviving spouse with a vested remainder to the descendants in being at the time of the decedent's death, or the surviving spouse may elect to take a 50 percent tenancy-in-common interest along with the surviving descendants in lieu of a life estate).

The apparent "tension" between community property and a forced transfer or default transfer regime is more rhetorical than real. Florida homestead devise restrictions and community property concepts do not occupy the same plane. Community property is an ownership characterization, vesting each spouse with a present, undivided one-half interest; whereas Florida homestead imposes a constitutional death-time limit on disposition.

Other community property jurisdictions illustrate that the two concepts routinely coexist. For example, Texas is a community property state, yet its Constitution provides a homestead regime that functions much like a mandatory survivorship protection: Upon the death of a spouse, the homestead:

> shall not be partitioned among the heirs of the deceased during the lifetime of the surviving husband or wife, or so long as the survivor may elect to use or occupy the same as a homestead.

---

[29] Of course, this is the general rule, but there are exceptions where federal law preempts state law. The most notable of these include bankruptcy, ERISA, etc.

Texas law demonstrates that community property characterization can coexist with a homestead regime that restricts partition and effectively guarantees a surviving spouse a life-estate-like occupancy right, which limits the decedent's practical ability to freely dispose of the residence.

The homestead restriction therefore does not make community property characterization impossible; it caps the decedent's freedom to dispose of whatever interest the decedent owns. In other words, the homestead restriction simply operates as a mandatory succession overlay that can limit testamentary freedom in a manner similar in function to other forced-transfer regimes.

This framing also helps reconcile the statutory tension between Florida Statute § 732.225 and Florida Statute § 736.151. Section 732.225 adopts a default inference within Florida's UDCPRDA scheme that reinvestment of previously acquired community property into Florida homestead or TBE property reflects an intent to terminate UDCPRDA-style community attributes. It is important to take into account the scope of the UDCPRDA, which is properly outlined in Florida Statute § 732.217. Specifically, § 732.217(2)(a) explicitly provides that the act only applies to property that is traceable to community property acquired in a jurisdiction outside of Florida. For this reason, the UDCPRDA does not apply to Florida community property created under a Florida community property trust agreement. The UDCPRDA itself is a limited death-time regime for purposes of handling what happens with community property issues in the Florida probate courts. By contrast, § 736.151 is a deliberate opt-in drafting system designed to let spouses affirmatively elect community property treatment in homestead property through a properly drafted community property trust, and the 2025 amendment confirms that such a transfer is not a change of ownership for homestead reassessment purposes.

In short, Florida's default probate presumption under § 732.225 treats reinvestment of foreign community property into Florida homestead or TBE as conclusive evidence the spouses meant to exit UDCPRDA-style community attributes; the community property trust statute (§ 736.151) supplies an affirmative, written opt-in that points in the other direction. The point of the Florida community property trust is to override the default inference with clear intent. This is one reason why spouses moving from a community property state to Florida should consider the establishment of a new Florida community property trust to avail themselves of the benefits of § 736.151.

The Surviving Spouse's Claim in Community Property Assets

In *Johnson v. Townsend*, the surviving spouse filed a petition to determine and perfect her community property interest in her late husband's estate assets—more than two years after his death. The wife argued that her petition was not a "claim" against the estate within the meaning of §§ 733.702 and 733.710, and therefore not subject to the two-year statutory deadline for filing a creditor claims. She contended that § 732.223 of the FUDCPRDA did not create a filing requirement or refer to creditor claim statutes, but rather limited the personal representative's duty to investigate potential community property. Alternatively, the wife argued that even if her petition constituted a claim, it fell within two recognized exceptions: the common law "trust exception" (asserting that her husband held her one-half community interest in a resulting trust under Texas law) and the lien exception (contending that the vesting of her interest created an equitable lien protected from the limitations period).[30]

Florida's Fourth District Court of Appeal rejected these arguments and affirmed the circuit court's order striking the petition as untimely. The court held that the wife's petition was indeed a "claim" under § 731.201(4), because upon the husband's death, the estate became liable for her one-half community interest, making it a liability of the decedent.[31] Thus, her failure to file within the three-month period under § 733.702 and the two-year repose period under § 733.710 barred her claim. The court further held that neither the common law "trust exception" nor the lien exception applied.[32]

Thus, Florida law will only permit a surviving spouse to successfully assert community property rights against the estate of a deceased spouse if the surviving spouse has filed an appropriate creditor claim within two years of the death of the first dying spouse or within the notice period permitted once a probate has been filed and proper notice has been given, whichever expires first.[33] Community property rights that flow through a

---

[30] Johnson v. Townsend, 259 So. 3d 851 (Fla. 4th DCA 2018).

[31] *Id.* at 857.

[32] *Id.*

[33] Fla. Stat. §§ 733.702(1), 733.710(1); *see* Johnson v. Townsend, 259 So. 3d 851, 853 (Fla. 4th Dist. Ct. App. 2018).

Florida probate estate will be lost if a claim is not made in a timely manner after proper notice has been provided.[34]

In *Johnson v. Townsend,* the wife cited the pre–Probate Code (and pre-FUDCPRDA) 1967 case of *Quintana v. Ordono* as support for her argument that the common law "trust exception" should apply to cause one-half of the property held in her husband's name to be found to be held in a resulting trust for her benefit.[35] The argument was unsuccessful. The court observed that:

> [a]lthough the decedent's possession of the community property in his name may have created a resulting trust . . . upon the decedent's death, his estate became liable to the wife for her community property interest. Thus, upon the decedent's death, the wife's community property interest was a claim which the wife had to pursue.

The holding in *Johnson v. Townsend* would seem to imply that if the wife had timely pursued her community property claim, a resulting trust could have been found in her favor.

Quintana v. Ordono is a good review of the resulting trust remedy discussed in *Johnson v. Townsend,* and reflects how a court in a noncommunity property state that has not yet adopted a version of the UDCPRDA, UCPDDA, or community property trust legislature might analyze these issues.[36] *Quintana* is also a good primer for Chapter 6, which deals more extensively with the issues of property characterization for migratory spouses.

---

[34] Juan C. Antúnez, *A User's Guide to Prosecuting Claims Under Florida's Uniform Disposition of Community Property Rights at Death Act,* Florida Probate + Trust Litigation Blog (Aug. 4, 2020), https://www.flprobatelitigation.com/2020/08/articles/new-probate-cases/marital-agreements-and-spousal/a-users-guide-to-prosecuting-claims-under-floridas-uniform-disposition-of-community-property-rights-at-death-act/; *see also* Johnson v. Townsend, 259 So. 3d 851 (Fla. Dist. Ct. App. 2018). In general, a Florida probate estate creditor has three months after receiving formal notice, or two years if no notice is given, to file claims against the estate. Fla. Stat. §§ 733.702, 733.710. *See also* Alan S. Gassman, Brock Exline & Peter Farrell, *Designing Trust Systems for Florida Residents: Planning Strategies, Things You Should Know, and Traps for the Unwary,* 97(4) Fla. B. J. 28 (July/Aug 2023).

[35] Johnson v. Townsend, 259 So. 3d 851, 855 (Fla. Dist. Ct. App. 2018).

[36] Quintana v. Ordono, 195 So. 2d 577 (Fla. Dist. Ct. App. 1967).

Quintana involved a husband and wife who moved from Cuba to Florida in 1960. Cuba is a community property country.[37] While the couple was residing in Cuba, the husband purchased stock in U.S. companies, which the court found to be community property.[38] After the couple moved to Florida, the husband sold the stock for an $810,000 promissory note, and then died intestate.[39] The children filed an action for a declaratory judgment determining the respective rights of the children and the widow in the note.[40] The court held that the law of the couple's domicile at the time of the acquisition of the property is the law that determines the property interests.[41] Therefore, under the laws of Cuba, the wife had a vested interest in the stock equal to that of her husband.[42] "The interest that vested in the wife was not affected by the subsequent change of domicile from Cuba to Florida in 1960."[43] However, "since the promissory note and contract were acquired while the husband and wife were domicile in Florida, this transaction is controlled by [Florida] law."[44] The court ultimately applied the common law "resulting trust" remedy, concluding that half of the note, or its proceeds, were to be held in a resulting trust for the benefit of the wife, stating as follows:

> Under Florida law, if a portion of the consideration belongs to the wife and title is taken in the husband's name alone, a resulting trust arises in her favor by implication of law to the extent that consideration furnished by her is used. A resulting trust is generally found to exist in transactions affecting community property in noncommunity property states where a husband buys property in his own name. Therefore, while the husband held legal title to the note and contract, he held a one-half interest in trust for his wife.[45]

---

[37] *Id.* at 578.

[38] *Id.* at 579–80.

[39] *Id.*

[40] *Id.* at 578.

[41] *Id.* at 579–80.

[42] *Id.* at 580.

[43] *Id.*

[44] *Id.*

[45] *Id.*

The *Quintana* decision, though predating the FUDCPRDA and the modern UCPDDA, remains instructive. It demonstrates that even in the absence of statutory preservations of community property rights, equitable doctrines may be applicable to achieve substantially similar results. By applying the resulting trust theory, a court can effectively restore the wife's one-half ownership interest in the property. *Johnson v. Townsend* makes clear that, in Florida, this resulting trust status still must be claimed within two years following the date of the decedent's death. Practitioners in all noncommunity property states should assume that a claim to perfect a surviving spouse's interest in community property must be filed within the state's applicable probate claims period.

The *Quintana* case also illustrates how community property retains its character as such when spouses move from a community property state to a noncommunity property state.

COMMUNITY PROPERTY WITH RIGHT OF SURVIVORSHIP (CP-WROS)

Some states have legislation that allows community property to be held with right of survivorship (CP-WROS).[46] With property held as CP-WROS, the spouses retain all the typical rights and obligations of community property during their lifetimes, but upon the death of one spouse, the decedent's one-half share of community property automatically transfers to the survivor, bypassing the probate system while (most likely) preserving the stepped-up fair market value basis for the survivor's own one-half share.[47]

CP-WROS is a relatively modern hybrid that attempts to merge two traditionally incompatible concepts: community property and joint tenancy with right of survivorship. In the community property system, each spouse owns a vested, undivided one-half interest in the property. Neither spouse's half automatically passes to the other at death; it is instead

---

[46] *See, e.g.*, Ariz. Rev. Stat. §§ 33-431.C, 33-431.D; Idaho Code § 15-6-201; Nev. Rev. Stat. Ann. § 111.064.2. Compare N.M. Stat. Ann. §§ 40-3-8.B, 40-3-8.F (spouses have the right to hold community property as joint tenants); Wash. Rev. Code Ann. § 64.28.040(1) (presumption that joint tenancy interests held by spouses and domestic partners are community property).

[47] Jeremy T. Ware, *Section 1014(b)(6) and the Boundaries of Community Property*, 5 Nev. L.J. 704, 722 (2005).

subject to testamentary disposition or intestate succession by the decedent spouse. By contrast, a joint tenancy is based on the unity of title model: Both spouses (or co-owners) hold the same undivided whole interest, with ownership characterized by the unities of time, title, interest, possession, survivorship, and marriage. When one joint tenant dies, the survivor's title simply expands by operation of law.

There is a somewhat open question as to whether CP-WROS qualifies for the full basis adjustment under § 1014(b)(6).[48] Most commentators, including the authors, believe it should qualify. Most rely on Revenue Ruling 87-98 to support this proposition. There, the IRS treated property "held in a common law estate" (i.e., titled as JTWROS) as community property for purposes of § 1014(b)(6), because "if property held in a common law estate is community property under state law, it is community property for purposes of Section 1014(b)(6) of the Code, regardless of the form in which title was taken."[49]

However, critics note that the ruling never addressed whether the survivorship feature was actually operative, meaning it may not provide clear authority for CP-WROS. Also notable under Revenue Ruling 87-98 is that the spouses had also executed a joint will in which they declared the property to be a community asset, as further discussed later. One commentator, Arthur W. Andrews, argues that because CP-WROS passes by operation of law, the decedent technically holds no interest "at death," making it ineligible for inclusion in the gross estate under § 2033 and, by extension, ineligible for § 1014(b)(6).[50] He further reasons that § 2040, which expressly applies to tenancies by the entirety and joint tenancies with right of survivorship, does not include community property with right of survivorship within its plain language.[51]

Others counter that Andrews's reading is overly formalistic, and that the Service is unlikely to draw such a sharp distinction. I.R.C. § 2040(b)(2)(B) could easily be interpreted to include CP-WROS as a functional

---

[48] *Id.* at 704.

[49] Rev. Rul. 87-98.

[50] Arthur W. Andrews, *Community Property with Right of Survivorship: Uneasy Lies the Head that Wears a Crown of Surviving Spouse for Federal Income Tax Basis Purposes*, 17 Va. Tax Rev. 577 (1998).

[51] *Id.* at 588–89 (citing N.L.R.B. v. Amax Coal Co., 453 U.S. 322, 329 (1981)).

survivorship arrangement, satisfying the inclusion requirement and supporting a full step-up on the first death.[52]

Revenue Ruling 87-98 deserves further attention because the ruling more broadly stands for the proposition that property held in any state that is community property under state law is community property for purposes of § 1014(b)(6). In the ruling, a married couple purchased real property in a community property state using community funds but titled the property as JTWROS. The service noted that under the relevant state law, holding title in joint tenancy ordinarily gave rise to a presumption that the spouses intended to terminate the community character of the property and convert it into separate property interests. However, the spouses had subsequently executed joint wills explicitly stating that the property was intended to remain community property, and under the state's laws, such an expression of intent was sufficient to rebut the presumption of transmutation. Because the property remained community property under state law, the IRS held that both halves of the property received a basis adjustment to fair market value upon the first spouse's death, notwithstanding the joint tenancy title.

This ruling reflects the general principles that state law determines the character of property interests, and the federal tax consequences follow from that state law classification. Therefore, if property is treated as community property under the applicable state law, it is community property for purposes of § 1014(b)(6) even when held in a form of title traditionally associated with common law ownership.

[52] Ware, *supra* note 47, at 725. I.R.C. § 2040(b)(2)(B) provides: "For purposes of [§ 2040(b)(1)], the term 'qualified joint interest' means any interest in property held by the decedent and the decedent spouse as—(A) tenants by the entirety, or (B) joint tenants with right of survivorship, but only if the decedent and the spouse of the decedent are the only joint tenants."

Chapter 5

Creditor Rights and Community Property

Unlike noncommunity property states—where the debts and liabilities of one spouse are generally collectible from that spouse's separate property and, depending on the form of ownership, may or not be satisfied from jointly held assets—creditors in community property states often have substantially broader collection rights. In many community property jurisdictions, property characterized as "community property," whether held by one or both spouses, is generally subject to the claims of a creditor of either spouse.

By contrast, in noncommunity property states it is common for asset ownership to be structured with creditor exposure in mind. For example, the spouse who faces greater litigation or professional liability risk may hold no or nominal assets in his or her own name, while the other spouse acquires and holds assets during the marriage in a manner intended to reduce exposure to creditor claims.

Further, a number of the noncommunity property states recognize tenancy by the entirety as a form of marital ownership, which in many jurisdictions provides significant protection against the claims of a creditor of only one spouse. While exceptions exist, tenancy by the entirety remains an important creditor-protection tool in many noncommunity property states.[1]

[1] The bankruptcy code and state law under many noncommunity property tenancy by the entirety states further provide that a judgment creditor of an

As the result of these distinctions, married couples residing in community property states may, in appropriate circumstances and with advance planning, consider transmuting certain assets out of community property treatment before any creditor issues arise. Such planning must be undertaken carefully, as transmutation can have significant estate planning, estate tax, marital rights, and creditor protection planning implications for the family unit as a whole.

Moreover, even in community property states, certain categories of assets are often afforded statutory or constitutional protection from creditors, although the scope of these exemptions varies widely by jurisdiction. Common examples may include qualified retirement accounts, pension plans, the cash value of life insurance policies owned by an insured person, and annuity contracts, subject to state-specific limitations and exceptions.

The creditor rights and exposure associated with community property systems are therefore highly nuanced and fact dependent. A careful analysis of applicable state law in the U.S. Bankruptcy Code, combined with consultation with legal counsel specializing in creditor rights and marital property regimes, is often essential to effective planning.

The initial question as to creditor access to assets in a community property state depends on whether a particular debt is treated as a "community debt" (which can generally be satisfied from community property) or a "separate debt" (which can only be satisfied from the debtor-spouse's separate property or, in some states, from that spouse's share of the community). Because each state's statutory law and case law can differ dramatically, practitioners must be vigilant in understanding both the classification of the debt and the asset management rules in that particular jurisdiction.

Broadly speaking, two major approaches exist among the nine traditional community property states. One is the "community debt" system, which includes Arizona, New Mexico, and Washington, and the other is the "managerial system," which includes California, Nevada, Idaho, Louisiana, and (slightly differently than the rest) Texas.[2]

---

individual residing in a community property state cannot reach real estate owned as tenants by the entirety by such debtor-spouse and his or her nondebtor-spouse 11 U.S.C. § 522(b)(3)(B); *In re Cauley*, 374 B.R. 311, 316 (Bankr. M.D. Fla. 2007).

[2] The reader should note that only eight states were listed. The "missing" ninth state is Wisconsin. Wisconsin adopted a version of the Uniform Marital Property Act in 1986—rather than inheriting community property law from the civil law tradition. The primary division between community debt systems versus managerial

Although these general groupings are useful, each state has nuances that even further complicate creditor collection rights, tort liabilities, and spousal protections. On top of that, the federal government's treatment of tax liens can override state law classifications by attaching to "all property and rights to property" of the taxpayer spouse.[3] This section begins with an overview of how each system classifies debts and liabilities, followed by state-specific variations and special considerations for tort debts, federal tax liens, and conflicts of laws.

THE "COMMUNITY DEBT" SYSTEM

In Arizona, New Mexico, and Washington (often described as following a "community debt" framework), courts first determine whether a debt is community or separate. Debts incurred before the marriage are generally separate, while those incurred during marriage are presumed to be for the benefit of the community unless proven otherwise.

Arizona starts with a strong presumption that debts arising during marriage are community in nature, absent clear and convincing evidence to the contrary. In *Schlaefer v. Financial Management Service Inc.*, for example, the Arizona Court of Appeals held that medical debts incurred during marriage were presumptively collectible from the community. However, a spouse may overcome this presumption by showing that the debt benefited only that spouse's separate interest or was not connected with the marital partnership. This can happen, for example, if legal fees are incurred solely to protect a spouse's separate property interest.

Similarly, New Mexico broadly defines community debts, effectively making most obligations incurred during marriage collectible from community assets unless the debt is shown to be "unreasonable" or otherwise declared separate. Under the New Mexico Statutes, this definition means that creditors tend to have an easier time reaching community property.[4]

Washington employs a community debt system with unique rules for tort liabilities. Under Washington law, a tort committed by one spouse is treated as a community debt only if it is closely tied to managing or benefiting the community. If it is purely personal to the tortfeasor spouse, it is

systems usually concerns only those states whose community property law developed directly from the French or Spanish civil code.

[3] 26 U.S.C. §§ 6321, 6331(a).

[4] N.M. STAT. ANN. § 40-3-9(A).

deemed a separate obligation, but the creditor may still be able to reach the tortfeasor's one-half interest in the community property if that spouse's separate assets are insufficient.[5]

THE "MANAGERIAL" SYSTEM

A second major model for addressing creditor rights focuses on which spouse manages or controls the property. States like California, Nevada, Idaho, Louisiana, and Texas are usually grouped under this managerial approach.

California uses a statutory approach that ties liability to a spouse's power of management. Under the California Family Code, each spouse has broad authority to manage community property. California begins from the rule that the entire community estate is liable for a spouse's debts incurred before or during marriage, regardless of which spouse has management or control, subject only to specific statutory exceptions that largely track the management and control limitations in the Family Code.[6] This means a creditor may typically collect on a debt from whatever property the debtor-spouse can manage or control. In many cases, this includes most community property, unless a specific exemption applies. As a result, a spouse who takes on a debt (such as a personal loan to start a side business) may expose the entire community to liability if that spouse has authority over marital funds.

Nevada follows similar management rules, with the state's statutes allowing a spouse to control the community property under his or her dominion. Idaho similarly treats virtually all community assets as available to creditors, sometimes even for debts that could be characterized as separate.[7] In Louisiana, community property may be used to satisfy either spouse's debt obligations regardless of whether the debt is labeled separate or community.[8] In order to balance this, the nondebtor-spouse has a right of reimbursement

---

[5] deElche v. Jacobsen, 622 P.2d 835 (Wash. 1980) (permitting a tort creditor to collect from the tortfeasor spouse's share of the community assets once the debtor's separate estate had been depleted).

[6] Cal. Fam. Code Ann. § 910.

[7] Williams v. Paxton, 98 Idaho 155, 559 P.2d 1123 (1976); Gustin v. Byam, 41 Idaho 538, 240 P. 600 (1925).

[8] La. Civ. Code art. 2345.

if community assets are used to pay the other spouse's separate debt.[9] However, this reimbursement right may be difficult to enforce if the community assets have already been depleted. Finally, Texas follows its own variant of the managerial system. While Texas recognizes the category of separate versus community debt, many obligations during marriage end up collectible from at least some portion of the community. Certain community assets may or may not be reachable, depending on whether the debt arose from that spouse's actions. Even still, creditors must pay close attention to the intricate statutory scheme of when Texas courts will shield some community property from creditors who are owed separate debts.

CREDITOR RIGHTS IN ARIZONA

Statutory Framework

Arizona's modern creditor rights scheme is built on the community property definitions present in Arizona Revised Statutes §§ 25-211 and 25-213 and the management and liability rules in §§ 25-214 and 25-215, the purpose of which was to prevent avoidance. Section 25-211 presumes that all property acquired by either spouse during marriage is community property, except for assets acquired by gift, devise, or descent or as otherwise provided by law.[10] Section 25-213 correspondingly defines each spouse's separate property as assets owned before marriage and property acquired during marriage by gift, devise, or descent, together with rents and profits of that separate property.[11]

The statute carves out a limited set of transactions for which joinder is mandatory. Under § 25-214(C), both spouses must join in (1) any transaction for the acquisition, disposition, or encumbrance of an interest in real property (other than short-term leases of one year or less); (2) any transaction of guaranty, indemnity, or suretyship; and (3) transactions entered after service of a petition for dissolution of marriage, legal separation, or annulment if both spouses have actual notice of the proceeding.[12] These

---

[9] La. Civ. Code Ann. arts. 2345, 2364.

[10] Ariz. Rev. Stat. § 25-211.

[11] *Id.* § 25-213.

[12] *Id.* § 25-214(C).

joinder requirements define the situations in which a creditor must insist on both signatures to ensure access to the community estate.

Section 25-215 allocates which assets can be reached to satisfy different categories of debt. Subsection (A) provides the core protection for the nondebtor-spouse in that a spouse's separate property is not liable for the other spouse's separate debts or obligations unless the nondebtor-spouse expressly agrees to assume the liability.[13] Subsection (B) addresses premarital obligations. It provides that community property is available to satisfy a spouse's "premarital separate debts or other liabilities" incurred after September 1, 1973, but only up to the value of that spouse's contribution to the community that would have been separate property if the spouse were single.[14] Arizona courts have interpreted the phrase "other liabilities" in § 25-215(B) as referring to liabilities of similar nature to premarital debts, rather than creating a broader category of separate debts for which the community is liable.[15] Subsection (C) creates a quasi-community-debt rule. Community property is liable for debts a spouse incurs outside Arizona during marriage when those debts would have been community debts if incurred in Arizona.[16] This allows an out-of-state creditor to reach Arizona community property if the underlying obligation fits Arizona's concept of a community debt. Subsection (D) governs debts incurred "for the benefit of the community." It provides that, except as limited by § 25-214, either spouse may contract debts and otherwise act for the benefit of the community, and that in an action on such a debt, the spouses must be sued jointly; the judgment is satisfied first from community property and then from the separate property of the spouse who contracted the debt.[17] Arizona courts treat obligations incurred during marriage for the benefit of

[13] *Id.* § 25-215(A).

[14] *Id.* § 25-215(B).

[15] Schilling v. Embree, 575 P.2d 1262 (Ct. App. 1977). The *Schilling* case interpreted the term "other liabilities" under the doctrine of *ejusdem generis*, under which general words which follow the enumeration of particular classes of persons or things should be interpreted as applicable only to persons or things in the same general nature or class.

[16] ARIZ. REV. STAT. § 25-215(C); Arab Monetary Fund v. Hashim, 219 Ariz. 108, 193 P.3d 802 (Ct. App. 2008).

[17] ARIZ. REV. STAT. § 25-215(D).

the community as community debts, presumed to be chargeable to the community unless rebutted by clear and convincing evidence.[18] As a result, creditors typically look to community property to satisfy debts incurred during marriage for the benefit of the community and quasi-community debts under § 25-215(C); to community property (up to the debtor-spouse's contribution) for post-1973 premarital obligations under § 25-215(B); and to the debtor-spouse's separate property only for separate obligations that do not fall within those categories, absent an express agreement by the nondebtor-spouse.

Historical Background

Before 1973, Arizona law largely insulated community property from a spouse's premarital debts, and a creditor generally could not reach wages earned after marriage to satisfy obligations incurred while single.[19] Commentators and courts observed that this allowed a debtor to marry and then direct postmarital earnings into the community, effectively putting future income beyond the reach of existing creditors, a device sometimes described as the "two-dollar bankruptcy."[20] In 1973 the legislature repealed the prior community-property debt provisions and enacted the current §§ 25-214 and 25-215. The purpose of § 25-215(B) is to prevent this two-dollar bankruptcy, while preserving core protections for the nondebtor-spouse's separate estate.[21] The courts have read § 25-215(B) to be a narrow response to the premarital-debt problem rather than a general expansion of community liability for all separate debts.[22] For most modern planning and

[18] United Bank of Ariz. v. Allyn, 167 Ariz. 191, 805 P.2d 1012 (Ct. App. 1990); *Arab Monetary Fund*, 219 Ariz. at 111, ¶ 17, 193 P.3d at 805.

[19] *Schilling*, 118 Ariz. at 238–39.

[20] The phrase "two-dollar bankruptcy" refers to a pre-1973 feature of Arizona's community property regime under which a debtor could substantially shield postmarital earnings from existing creditors simply by marrying. Because a marriage license cost approximately two dollars at the time, commentators observed that a debtor could, in effect, obtain a form of bankruptcy protection for the price of the license.

[21] Hines v. Hines, 707 P.2d 969, 971 (Ariz. App. 1st Div. 1985).

[22] *Schilling*, 118 Ariz. at 238–39.

litigation, the pre-1973 regime matters primarily as context for understanding why premarital obligations receive special treatment under § 25-215(B).

Premarital Versus Marital Obligations

Arizona courts treat a debt as "incurred" at the time of the conduct that gives rise to the liability, not when a judgment is entered or the amount is later fixed.[23] For example, in *Flexmaster Aluminum Awning Co. v. Hirschberg*, the court held that a husband's purchase of goods before marriage created a premarital obligation even though judgment was entered during marriage.[24] This timing principle also governed *Arab Monetary Fund v. Hashim*, where the court classified an English costs judgment as a premarital debt because the debtor-spouse's wrongful receipt of funds occurred before marriage, thereby limiting the creditor's reach under § 25-215(B) to the debtor-spouse's contribution to the community.[25] The same statutory boundary has been reaffirmed in *Schilling v. Embree* and *Hines v. Hines*, both of which hold that § 25-215(B) applies only to premarital obligations and does not expose community property to separate debts incurred during marriage.[26]

Debts Incurred During Marriage: Community Versus Separate Obligations

Debts incurred during marriage are analyzed under § 25-215(D) and general community-property principles. Section 25-215(D) provides that, except as limited by § 25-214, either spouse may contract debts "for the benefit of the community," and such debts are satisfied first from community property and then from the contracting spouse's separate property.[27] Arizona decisions treat an obligation incurred during marriage as a community debt if it was undertaken for a community purpose or produced a community benefit. In *United Bank of Arizona v. Allyn* and subsequent cases, courts held that

---

[23] Arab Monetary Fund v. Hashim, 193 P.3d 802, 805 (Ariz. App. 1st Div. 2008).

[24] Flexmaster Aluminum Awning Co., Inc. v. Hirschberg, 839 P.2d 1128, 1130 (Ariz. App. 1st Div. 1992).

[25] *See generally Arab Monetary Fund*, 193 P.3d 802.

[26] Schilling v. Embree, 575 P.2d 1262 (Ariz. App. 2d Div. 1977); Hines v. Hines, 707 P.2d 969 (Ariz. App. 1st Div. 1985).

[27] Ariz. Rev. Stat. § 25-215(D).

a debt incurred during marriage for the benefit of the marital community is presumed to be a community obligation unless there is clear and convincing evidence to the contrary.[28] Tort liabilities are analyzed under the same "benefit of the community" framework, but the inquiry is necessarily fact specific. Arizona decisions and secondary authorities group Arizona with those jurisdictions that classify a tort as a community obligation when it arises from community activities or produces a community benefit (for example, business-related conduct or use of a community property motor vehicle for family purposes).[29] When the tort is purely personal and disconnected from the marital enterprise, courts tend to treat the resulting judgment as the tortfeasor's separate obligation, collectible from separate property only to the extent the statutory scheme otherwise permits access to community assets.[30] Because § 25-215(B) is limited to premarital obligations, a spouse's separate debts created during marriage that do not benefit the community generally fall on the debtor-spouse's separate estate, absent an express assumption of liability by the other spouse or another theory (such as fraudulent transfer or alter ego) that would justify reaching community property, but it therefore seems essential to offer married couples who live in Arizona the opportunity to cause their vehicles to be transmuted to separate property and to have each spouse drive only the vehicle that he or she separately owns.[31]

Procedural Protections and Joinder Requirements

Arizona couples enjoy significant procedural safeguards when creditors attempt to reach community assets. Section 25-215(D) requires that "[i]n an action on such a [community] debt or obligation the spouses shall be sued jointly," and courts treat this as a mandatory joinder requirement rather than a mere formality.[32] *Eng v. Stein* held that a creditor who obtained a judgment only against the husband could not garnish community wages

[28] United Bank of Arizona v. Allyn, 805 P.2d 1012, 1019 (Ariz. App. 1st Div. 1990).

[29] C.L. Williams, *Injured Victims and Robbed Spouses*, 61 ARIZ. L. REV. 403, 418–20 (2019).

[30] *Id.*

[31] *Schilling*, 118 Ariz. at 238–39.

[32] ARIZ. REV. STAT. § 25-215(D).

because the wife had not been joined or served, and the judgment therefore did not bind the community.[33] *Schilling v. Embree* likewise held that both spouses must be joined in an action seeking to reach community property, and that this joinder requirement applies to garnishment proceedings as well as foreclosure on community assets.[34] *Heinig v. Hudman* reaffirmed that a judgment against one spouse alone is not a community property judgment and cannot be transformed into one after the fact; if the creditor did not name and serve both spouses in the original action, the creditor may not use that judgment to execute against community property.[35] *Vikse v. Johnson* explained that the purpose of this joint-suit requirement is to ensure that each spouse receives notice of the proceeding and an opportunity to defend before community assets are exposed.[36]

Practical Implications for Planners and Creditors

For planners, the Arizona statutes and cases point toward careful segregation of separate and community assets. Keeping premarital assets in a clearly identified separate property vehicle and avoiding commingling with community funds limits the portion of community property that can be reached under § 25-215(B) for premarital obligations and clarifies which assets are exposed to creditors of community debts. Clients who operate businesses or incur substantial contractual obligations during marriage should understand that debts incurred for the benefit of the community will ordinarily be treated as community obligations, collectible from community assets and the contracting spouse's separate property. Creditors, correspondingly, are well advised to require both spouses' signatures in transactions involving significant credit risk, particularly where real property, guarantees, or other joinder-sensitive transactions under § 25-214(C) are involved.

Finally, litigators on both sides must pay close attention to joinder. A judgment obtained only against one spouse may be worthless against community property, even if the underlying obligation is substantively a community debt, if § 25-215(D)'s joint-suit requirement has not been satisfied.

[33] Eng v. Stein, 599 P.2d 796 (Ariz. 1979).

[34] Schilling v. Embree, 575 P.2d 1262 (Ariz. App. 2d Div. 1977).

[35] Heinig v. Hudman, 865 P.2d 110 (Ariz. App. 1st Div. 1993).

[36] Vikse v. Johnson, 672 P.2d 193, 195 (Ariz. App. 2d Div. 1983).

For that reason, Arizona creditor-rights practice in the community property context turns as much on procedure as on the substantive classification of the obligation.

CREDITOR RIGHTS IN NEW MEXICO

Statutory Structure: Separate Versus Community Debts

New Mexico allocates liability for marital obligations through a statutory priority scheme that distinguishes "separate" from "community" debts and then prescribes the order in which each category be satisfied to pay a debtor judgment instead of from marital property.[37] New Mexico's starting point is definitional. Section 40-3-9 classified a "separate debt" as one falling into specified categories (including certain premarital obligations and "separate torts" committed during marriage) and defines a "community debt" as any other obligation incurred by either or both spouses during marriage.[38] Because § 40-3-9(B) defines community debt by exclusion ("a debt contracted or incurred by either or both spouses during marriage that is not a separate debt"), New Mexico law presumes that debts incurred during marriage are community debts, with the burden on the party asserting separate characterization to establish that a separate debt category applies.[39]

Section 40-3-10 then establishes priorities for satisfying a "separate debt of a spouse."[40] Under § 40-3-10(A), a creditor holding a separate debt must look first to the debtor-spouse's separate property, excluding that spouse's interest in jointly held property.[41] If the debtor's separate property is insufficient, the creditor may next reach the debtor-spouse's one-half interest in community property and in property held in joint tenancy or as tenants in common, excluding the residence.[42] Only if those assets are insufficient may the creditor proceed against the debtor-spouse's interest in the marital residence, and even then this exposure is subject to the homestead

---

[37] N.M. Stat. Ann. §§ 40-3-9, 40-3-10, 40-3-11 (1978).

[38] *Id.* § 40-3-9.

[39] *Id.*

[40] *Id.* § 40-3-10.

[41] *Id.*

[42] *Id.*

protections in § 42-10-9, which exempt up to $150,000 of equity in an Arizona resident's primary residence from attachment, execution, foreclosure, and similar creditor process, subject to limited exceptions for secured creditors.[43] Section 40-3-10(B) further protects the nondebtor-spouse's interest in the residence by barring liens or foreclosure against that spouse's share unless that spouse joined in the encumbrance.[44] Section 40-3-10(C) ties these priorities to New Mexico's exemption regime by requiring a spouse who seeks the benefit of the statute to assert exempt status under § 42-10-13, which sets out the procedure for claiming exemptions in execution and garnishment proceedings.[45] Finally, § 40-3-10(D) limits the statute to debts contracted while both spouses are living, confirming that the separate-debt priority scheme does not govern obligations that arise after a spouse's death.[46]

Section 40-3-11 performs a parallel function for "community debts," prescribing a different order of satisfaction.[47] Under § 40-3-11(A), a community debt must first be satisfied from community property and from property in which the spouses hold an undivided equal interest as joint tenants or tenants in common.[48] If those sources are insufficient, the creditor may then proceed against the spouses' interests in the residence, again subject to the homestead protections provided in § 42-10-9.[49] Only after community assets and the residence have been exhausted may the creditor look to the separate property of the spouse or spouses who incurred the community debt.[50] As with separate debts, § 40-3-11(B) safeguards the nonjoining spouse's interest in the residence by prohibiting liens or foreclosure against that spouse's share when the spouse did not join in the obligation that created the debt.[51] Section 40-3-11(C) incorporates the same exemption-claim mechanism as § 40-3-10(C), requiring a party to file an exemption

43 *Id.*; *id.* § 42-10-9.

44 *Id.* § 40-3-10.

45 *Id.*

46 *Id.*

47 *Id.* § 40-3-11.

48 *Id.*

49 *Id.*; *id.* § 42-10-9.

50 *Id.* § 40-3-11.

51 *Id.*

claim under § 42-10-13 in order to invoke the statutory priorities.[52] Section 40-3-11(D) then mirrors § 40-3-10(D) by excluding from its reach debts incurred after the death of one or both spouses, thereby channeling those obligations into probate rather than community property administration.[53]

Read together, §§ 40-3-9, 40-3-10, and 40-3-11 create a two-step analysis: Practitioners must first characterize the obligation as separate or community and then apply the appropriate priority scheme to determine which assets are available to creditors and in what order.

Separate Debts

New Mexico Supreme Court decisions confirm that the text of § 40-3-10 is not merely aspirational; it sets real limits on how far a creditor can reach into the marital estate to satisfy a separate debt.[54] In *Central Adjustment Bureau, Inc. v. Thevenet,* the creditor held a judgment against the wife for her separate debt and sought to garnish the husband's earnings.[55] Because the trial court found that the wife's separate property was insufficient, the New Mexico Supreme Court held that § 40-3-10(A) permitted garnishment of only the wife's one-half community interest in the husband's wages, not his half.[56] The court awarded the creditor one-half of 25 percent of the husband's disposable income, explicitly recognizing the nondebtor-spouse's vested one-half community interest.[57] *Central Adjustment* confirms that even liquid community assets such as wages remain subject to the statutory one-half limitation: The debtor-spouse's half is available, while the nondebtor-spouse's half is not.

Delph v. Potomac Insurance Co. provides a related example in the insurance context.[58] There, the husband intentionally burned the parties' community residence, and the insurer attempted to deny recovery altogether by

[52] *Id.* § 40-3-11; *id.* § 42-10-13.

[53] *Id.* § 40-3-11.

[54] *Id.* § 40-3-10.

[55] Cent. Adjustment Bureau, Inc. v. Thevenet, 686 P.2d 954 (N.M. 1984).

[56] *Id.* at 958.

[57] *Id.*

[58] Delph v. Potomac Ins. Co., 620 P.2d 1282 (N.M. 1980).

imputing his arson to his wife.[59] The Supreme Court rejected that position and held that the innocent wife retained her vested interest in the community insurance proceeds and could recover her share, notwithstanding her spouse's wrongdoing.[60] The court classified the husband's arson as a separate tort because there was no evidence to suggest he was engaged in an act that could be to the benefit of the community.[61] The court explained that a tort is a community obligation only when the underlying conduct confers an actual or potential benefit on the marital community.[62] When it does not, the tort is a separate debt for which only the tortfeasor's separate or one-half of community assets may be reached.[63]

Federal bankruptcy decisions applying New Mexico law reinforce the same structure. In *In re Fingado*, the bankruptcy court held that New Mexico law permits a separate debt to be satisfied first from the debtor-spouse's separate property and then, if necessary, from that spouse's one-half interest in community property, but does not allow satisfaction from the nondebtor-spouse's one-half share.[64] The court emphasized that, even though all community property becomes property of the bankruptcy estate under 11 U.S.C. § 541(a)(2), state law continues to govern the allocation of that property between debtor and nondebtor interests, and § 40-3-10(A) forbids using the nondebtor-spouse's half of the community to pay the debtor's separate obligations.[65]

Appellate decisions addressing foreign judgments domesticated in New Mexico likewise apply § 40-3-10's separate-debt priorities. In *National Bank of Arizona v. Moore*, an Arizona judgment representing the husband's separate debt was domesticated in New Mexico so the creditor could garnish a New Mexico bank account the spouses held as community property.[66] Relying on *Huntington National Bank v. Sproul*, the Court of Appeals held that once the judgment was converted into a New Mexico judgment,

---

[59] *Id.*

[60] *Id.*

[61] *Id.* at 1285.

[62] *Id.*

[63] *Id.*

[64] *In re* Fingado, 113 B.R. 37 (Bankr. D.N.M. 1990), *subsequently aff'd*, 995 F.2d 175 (10th Cir. 1993).

[65] *Id.* at 41.

[66] Nat'l Bank of Arizona v. Moore, 122 P.3d 1265.

New Mexico's enforcement rules controlled, and § 40-3-10(A) permitted execution against the husband's one-half interest in the community funds, but not the wife's half.[67] *Moore* thus confirms that creditors cannot expand their reach beyond the debtor-spouse's half of community property simply by obtaining or domesticating a foreign judgment; the one-half limitation in § 40-3-10(A) remains a hard cap on recovery for separate debts.

Community Debts

New Mexico treats the characterization of an obligation as "community" or "separate" as a threshold question that controls both what property a creditor can reach and how liability is allocated between spouses.[68] Under § 40-3-9(B), any debt "contracted or incurred by either or both spouses during marriage which is not a separate debt" is a community debt, and the Supreme Court has repeatedly held that a debt incurred during marriage is presumptively a community obligation.[69]

In *First National Bank in Albuquerque v. Abraham*, the court stated the general rule that a debt contracted during marriage is presumptively a community debt and that the party asserting otherwise bears the burden of showing that the obligation falls within one of the separate-debt categories in § 40-3-9(A).[70] *Beneficial Finance Co. v. Alarcon* applied the same statute and held that, because § 40-3-9(B) defines community debt to include obligations incurred by "either or both spouses," one spouse alone may incur a community debt for which the entire community is liable.[71] The New Mexico Supreme Court in *Huntington National Bank v. Sproul* synthesized these principles, expressly presuming that a debt created during marriage is a community debt and confirming that the party who claims separate-debt status must prove that the obligation fits one of the enumerated separate-debt categories in § 40-3-9(A)(1)–(6).[72]

---

67 *Id.* at 1266.

68 N.M. Stat. § 40-3-9.

69 *Id.* § 40-3-9(B); Huntington Nat'l Bank v. Sproul, 861 P.2d 835, 939 (N.M. 1993); Beneficial Fin. Co. of New Mexico v. Alarcon, 816 P.2d 489, 491 (N.M. 1991); First Nat'l Bank in Albuquerque v. Abraham, 639 P.2d 575, 577–78 (1982).

70 *Sproul*, 861 P.2d at 939.

71 Beneficial Fin. Co. of New Mexico v. Alarcon, 816 P.2d 489, 491 (N.M. 1991).

72 *Sproul*, 861 P.2d at 939.

Naranjo v. Paull highlights the procedural side of tort classification.[73] In that case, the Court of Appeals rejected the notion that a personal judgment could automatically be entered against a non-tortfeasor spouse simply because the other spouse committed a tort, and emphasized that whether a particular tort obligation is a community debt may be determined either at trial or at the execution stage, depending on how the issues are framed.[74] Naranjo cautions creditors to align their pleadings, proof, and choice of defendants with § 40-3-9's separate-versus-community structure, rather than assuming that every tort during marriage is automatically a community obligation. *Jemko, Inc. v. Liaghat* underscores that even when a debt is properly characterized as community, enforcement must respect the distinct interests of debtor and nondebtor-spouses in community assets.[75] In *Jemko,* the creditor garnished payments on a promissory note payable to husband and wife, but the wife had not been a party to the underlying litigation.[76] The Court of Appeals held that a judgment creditor acting under a writ of garnishment may seize only the judgment debtor's interest in the garnished property, and remanded because the trial court had not distinguished between the debtor's and nondebtor-spouse's shares.[77]

Limits and Post-Death Obligations

Section 40-3-11(D) draws a critical line by providing that its community-debt priority rules "do not apply to the satisfaction of debts that are incurred after the death of either spouse," although guarantees or state liability statutes may expose assets as if a debt or other obligation was incurred by the surviving spouse.[78] *Karpien v. Karpien* demonstrates the practical effect of this limitation.[79] In *Karpien,* the wife died during pending divorce proceedings, and her parents advanced funds to pay post-death medical-related

---

[73] Naranjo v. Paull, 803 P.2d 254 (N.M. App. 1990).

[74] *Id.* at 267.

[75] Jemko, Inc. v. Liaghat, 738 P.2d 922 (N.M. App. 1987).

[76] *Id.*

[77] *Id.* at 296.

[78] N.M. Stat. § 40-3-11(D) (1978).

[79] Karpien v. Karpien, 207 P.3d 1165 (N.M. App. 2009).

costs,[80] funeral, and repatriation expenses incurred after her death.[81] The trial court treated those amounts as community debts and ordered the marital residence sold to satisfy them; the Court of Appeals reversed in part, holding that obligations incurred after the wife's death were not "community debts" within the meaning of § 40-3-11(D) and could not be charged against the community estate.[82] *Karpien* explains that while § 40-4-20 permits division of community property and preexisting community debts after a spouse's death in the context of a dissolution action, limits on post-death obligations are handled through the decedent's estate rather than through the community-debt scheme of §§ 40-3-10 and 40-3-11.[83] For practitioners, the timing of the underlying obligation relative to a spouse's death is therefore outcome determinative. Pre-death liabilities may fall within the community-debt framework, but post-death medical-related costs generally must be pursued in probate and cannot be satisfied from the surviving spouse's share of community property under § 40-3-11.[84]

Practical Considerations for Planners and Creditors

Three recurring themes emerge from New Mexico's community debt case law: the need to (1) plead and prove exemptions, (2) respect separate versus

---

[80] Post-death medical-related costs refers not to medical treatment rendered after death, but to obligations arising from a decedent's final illness and death that are incurred, billed, or paid after death. Such expenses may include unpaid hospital or physician charges associated with the decedent's last illness, hospice, or end of care billed after death; emergency transport or medical evacuation expenses; and related administrative charges, as well as funeral, burial, and cremation costs. Although these obligations may relate to events occurring during the marriage, they arise after the termination of the marital community by death and are therefore treated as separate obligations of the decedent, payable through the probate estate rather than as community debt.

[81] *Karpien*, 207 P.3d at 1166.

[82] *Id.* at 1170.

[83] *Id.*

[84] *Id.*

community classifications, and (3) pay close attention to cross-jurisdictional and temporal issues.[85]

First, the protections in §§ 40-3-10 and 40-3-11 are not self-executing. Both provisions expressly require the spouse or party claiming protection to file an exemption claim under § 42-10-13. In practice, if a debtor-spouse does not timely assert exemptions and the priority scheme in response to garnishment or execution, a creditor may succeed in reaching assets that would otherwise be partially shielded, such as the nondebtor-spouse's interest in a residence or other exempt community property.

Second, accurate classification of debts as separate or community is essential. Because debts that are incurred during marriage are presumed to be community, a spouse resisting collection from community assets (or from their own separate property) must produce evidence that the obligations fall within one of the separate debt categories in § 40-3-9(A), such as a separate tort that conferred no benefit on the community under the *Dell v. Heard* line of cases. Conversely, creditors who assume an obligation is community merely because it arose during marriage risk misstep if the transaction in fact served only one spouse's purposes or arises from a separate tort, in which case § 40-3-10 limits recovery to the debtor-spouse's separate estate and one-half of the community.

Third, cross-jurisdictional and timing questions require particular care. *Huntington National Bank v. Sproul* and *National Bank of Arizona v. Moore* teach that once an out-of-state judgment is domesticated in New Mexico, New Mexico's definition of separate and community debts and its enforcement rules, including the one-half limitation for separate debts and the full-community exposure for community debts, govern collection against New Mexico property, regardless of the originating state's law.

Karpien underscores that debts incurred after a spouse's death fall outside §§ 40-3-10 and 40-3-11 and must be addressed in probate, not by execution on the community estate. For planners, these rules counsel in favor of maintaining clear separations between separate and community assets, documenting the purpose of major obligations (particularly business and tort-exposed activities), and anticipating how a creditor will characterize and pursue a claim. For creditors, they highlight the importance of naming

---

[85] N.M. STAT. §§ 40-3-9 to 40-3-11, Huntington Nat'l Bank v. Sproul, 861 P.2d 835, 939 (N.M. 1993); Nat'l Bank of Arizona v. Moore, 122 P.3d 1265; Karpien v. Karpien, 207 P.3d 1165 (N.M. App. 2009).

both spouses when seeking to reach community assets, developing a factual record showing benefit to the community when asserting community-debt status, structuring garnishment and execution orders to respect the nondebtor-spouse's half interest, and conforming enforcement efforts to New Mexico's exemption procedures and statutory priority rules.

CREDITOR RIGHTS IN WASHINGTON

Statutory Framework: Classification, Management, and Liability

Washington's community property regime is codified primarily in Washington Revised Code chapter 26.16, which defines separate and community property and allocates management authority between spouses.[86] This classification framework is the starting point for any creditor-rights analysis, because liability generally follows the character of the property and the capacity in which a spouse acted when incurring an obligation.[87]

Washington Revised Code § 26.16.010 provides that property owned by a person before marriage or state-registered domestic partnership, and property acquired afterward by gift, bequest, devise, or descent, together with the rents, issues, and profits of that property, are that person's separate property.[88] The statute further authorizes the owner's spouse to manage, control, encumber, or dispose of separate property as if unmarried or not in a domestic partnership.[89] Washington Revised Code § 26.16.190 complements this rule by providing that for injuries committed by one spouse, there is no recourse against the other spouse's separate property except in situations where there would be joint responsibility even if the marriage or partnership did not exist.[90]

Washington Revised Code § 26.16.030 defines community property as all property acquired after marriage or domestic partnership by either or both spouses that is not separate under Washington Revised Code §§

---

[86] *See, e.g.*, WASH. REV. CODE ch. 26.16.

[87] *See id.*; *see also* WASH. REV. CODE chs. 4.56, 6.13, 6.15.

[88] WASH. REV. CODE § 26.16.010.

[89] *Id.*

[90] *Id.* § 26.16.190.

26.16.010 or 26.16.020.[91] As a default rule, either spouse may manage and control community personal property, and may bind the community to transactions, with "like power of disposition as [each] has over his or her separate property."[92] The statute, however, carves out several important exceptions requiring joinder; neither spouse may, without the other's consent, make a gift of community personal property, dispose by will of more than one-half of the community, convey or contract to convey community real property, purchase or contract to purchase community real property, grant a security interest in community household goods, or unilaterally manage a community business if both spouses participate in its management.[93] Washington Revised Code § 26.16.040 then confirms that community real property is subject to liens and execution for community debts, while preserving recorded homestead and other statutory exemptions.[94]

Washington Revised Code § 26.16.200 addresses premarital and separate obligations.[95] It provides that neither spouse is liable for the debts or liabilities of the other incurred before being married or entering into a state-registered domestic partnership,[96] nor is the rent or income of one spouse's separate property liable for the other's separate debts.[97] As an important qualification, however, the "earnings and accumulations" of a

[91] *Id.* § 26.16.030.

[92] *Id.*

[93] *Id.*

[94] *Id.* § 26.16.040.

[95] *Id.* § 26.16.200.

[96] Washington law expressly incorporates registered domestic partnerships into its community property regime and, for state law property and creditor purposes, generally treats registered domestic partners in the same manner as married spouses. Registered domestic partners are, therefore, subject to Washington's community property rules governing the classification, management, and division of property and liabilities. Notwithstanding this functional equivalence under Washington law, a registered domestic partnership is not a marriage per se, and the regime has become largely dormant following the legalization of same-sex marriage. For federal law purposes, registered domestic partners are not treated as spouses, and consequently may not file joint federal income tax returns, are not eligible for the federal estate and gift marital deduction, and do not receive spousal basis adjustments available to married couples in community property states.

[97] Wash. Rev. Code § 26.16.200.

spouse remain available to satisfy that spouse's premarital debts, and creditors may reach those earnings if the separate debt is reduced to judgment within three years after the marriage or partnership.[98] The statute also makes clear that one spouse is not deemed to have any ownership interest in the earnings of the other for purposes of this rule, thereby reinforcing the separation of liabilities for premarital obligations.[99] Finally, Washington Revised Code § 26.16.200 treats child support and maintenance differently: Those obligations may be collected from the obligor's separate property, earnings, and accumulations, and the obligor's share of community real and personal property, subject to an exemption for funds in a community bank account that can be identified as the nonobligated spouse's earnings.[100]

Outside chapter 26.16, lien and exemption statutes control creditor remedies against marital property. Under §§ 4.56.190 and 4.56.200, a judgment of a Washington court becomes a lien on the judgment debtor's nonexempt real estate in the county of docketing, and the lien generally runs for ten years.[101] The homestead statute, Washington Revised Code chapter 6.13, creates an automatic homestead in a debtor's principal residence and exempts a specified amount of equity from execution.[102] A homestead may consist of a dwelling, mobile home, or unimproved land intended as a residence, and the exemption amount is tied to the greater of a statutory minimum and the county median home price for the prior year.[103] Washington Revised Code § 6.15.010 and related provisions extend additional exemptions to personal property such as household goods, tools of the trade, certain vehicles, and various benefit payments.[104] Read together, § 26.16, § 4.56, and the exemption chapters create a two-step framework: Courts and practitioners must first characterize the relevant property and obligation as separate or community, and then apply the lien and exemption statutes to determine whether, and to what extent, a creditor may reach the debtor's interest.

---

[98] *Id.*

[99] *Id.*

[100] *Id.*

[101] *Id.* §§ 4.56.190, 4.56.200.

[102] *See generally id.* ch. 6.13.

[103] *Id.* § 6.13.010.

[104] *Id.* § 6.15.010.

Judicial Development of Community and Separate Liability

Because Washington Revised Code § 26.16 does not contain a comprehensive "liability" section, Washington courts have developed creditor-rights rules by combining the statutory classification and management scheme with common law principles.[105] The modern cases treat three questions as central:

1. When an obligation incurred during marriage is a community debt
2. How far a creditor may reach into community assets for a separate or premarital obligation
3. How tort judgments interact with community-property principles[106]

Washington adheres to the familiar presumption that property and obligations acquired or incurred during marriage are community in character.[107] In *Oil Heat Co. of Port Angeles, Inc. v. Sweeney*, the Court of Appeals explained that debts incurred during marriage are presumed to be community obligations unless evidence shows they were incurred after the marital community became defunct or otherwise fall within a separate-debt category.[108] Subsequent decisions reaffirm that a debt incurred by either spouse in the course of managing community affairs or for the benefit of the marital community is treated as a community obligation, even if only one spouse was a party to the transaction.[109]

Washington Revised Code § 26.16.200's treatment of premarital debts has been fleshed out in *Watters v. Doud.*[110] There, a creditor sought to collect on a note executed by the husband before marriage but renewed afterward, and argued that community property should be fully liable.[111] The Supreme Court rejected full community liability, holding that Washington

---

[105] *Id.* ch. 26.16; deElche v. Jacobsen, 622 P.2d 835 (1980).

[106] *See, e.g.*, Watters v. Doud, 631 P.2d 369 (1981); *deElche*, 622 P.2d 835; Clayton v. Wilson, 227 P.3d 278 (2010).

[107] WASH. REV. CODE § 26.16.030; Oil Heat Co. of Port Angeles, Inc. v. Sweeney, 613 P.2d 169, 171 (1980).

[108] *Oil Heat Co. of Port Angeles, Inc.*, 613 P.2d at 171.

[109] Keene v. Edie, 935 P.2d 588, 592 (1997).

[110] Watters v. Doud, 631 P.2d 369 (1981).

[111] *Id.*

Revised Code § 26.16.200 limits the creditor to the debtor-spouse's separate property and that spouse's postmarital "earnings and accumulations," even though those earnings may otherwise be community in character.[112] *Watters* thus confirms that, for premarital debts, the community is exposed only through the debtor's earnings and accumulations as defined in the statute, and the nondebtor-spouse's separate property remains insulated from those obligations.[113]

Washington also recognizes that the marital community can become "defunct" before formal dissolution of marriage, with consequences for creditor rights.[114] In *MacKenzie v. Sellner*, the court held that once spouses are permanently separated and no longer functioning as a marital unit, the community ceases to acquire new property interests, and later-incurred obligations are generally separate, even if the parties remain legally married.[115] *Oil Heat Co. of Port Angeles, Inc. v. Sweeney* applied this principle to a creditor-rights dispute, holding that where the evidence shows a defunct marital community, a creditor cannot rely on the ordinary presumption that a debt incurred during marriage is a community obligation.[116] These cases remind practitioners that characterization of both property and debt must account for the functional status of the marital community at the time the obligation arose.

Tort Liabilities

Tort obligations have generated some of Washington's most important creditor-rights decisions because they place the interests of tort victims in tension with those of innocent spouses.[117] Historically, Washington followed a strict rule under which a tort judgment could be satisfied only from the tortfeasor's separate property, leaving victims without recourse when the tortfeasor had only community assets.[118] In *deElche v. Jacobsen*, the Supreme Court modified that rule and adopted a middle ground: The tort victim

---

112 *Id.*

113 *Id.*

114 MacKenzie v. Sellner, 361 P.2d 165 (1961).

115 *Id.*

116 *Oil Heat Co. of Port Angeles*, 613 P.2d at 169.

117 622 P.2d 835 (1980).

118 Werker v. Knox, 85 P.2d 1041 (1938).

may satisfy the judgment from the tortfeasor-spouse's one-half interest in community property, but the non-tortfeasor spouse's one-half interest remains protected.[119] *DeElche* involved an intentional tort where the defendant husband had no separate property, but the couple owned community real estate.[120] The court held that the victim could reach the husband's half interest in the community real property to satisfy the judgment, but the wife's half interest could not be taken because she was not personally at fault.[121] The decision rests on two premises: first, that both spouses have present, vested one-half interests in community property and second, that a tort creditor should not be left entirely without recourse when the tortfeasor is solvent in terms of community assets.[122] *DeElche* therefore preserves the innocent spouse's interest while preventing the community form from becoming a liability shield for wrongful conduct.

Practical Considerations for Planners and Creditors

Washington's creditor-rights framework, built from Washington Revised Code § 26.16's classification and management rules, § 26.16.200's treatment of premarital debts, and the judicial doctrines developed over the years, produces several consistent themes for practitioners. These themes largely determine which assets remain exposed and which remain insulated in both transactional and litigation settings.

First, correct characterization of both property and obligations is essential. Washington applies a strong presumption that property and debts acquired or incurred during marriage are community in character, and the spouse resisting community liability bears the burden of rebutting that presumption. *Oil Heat Co. of Port Angeles, Inc. v. Sweeney* confirms that courts begin with community characterization unless the evidence shows a premarital obligation, a separate tort, or a defunct marital community at the time the obligation arose. A spouse resisting community liability must therefore be prepared to produce evidence establishing that the debt fits into a separate debt category recognized by statute or case law, such as a

---

[119] 622 P.2d 835 (1980).

[120] *Id.*

[121] *Id.*

[122] *Id.*

premarital obligation governed by Washington Revised Code § 26.16.200 or a tort obligation properly treated as separate under *deElche* and *Clayton*.

Second, timing often determines liability. Washington recognizes that a marital community may become "defunct" before dissolution of marriage, with the result that obligations incurred thereafter are treated as separate. Cases such as *MacKenzie v. Sellner* and *Oil Heat* show that when spouses are permanently separated and no longer acting as a marital unit, the presumption of community liability does not apply. Practitioners advising either creditors or spouses must therefore examine when the obligation arose, whether the marriage was functioning as a marital community at that time, and what property was acquired before or after the community ceased to function.

Third, tort judgments require special attention. Following *deElche v. Jacobsen*, a tort victim may collect from the tortfeasor-spouse's separate property and that spouse's one-half interest in community property, but not from the innocent spouse's vested half interest. *Clayton v. Wilson* reinforces this allocation even in the context of intentional misconduct. Thus, tort creditors must understand that the community form does not provide full insulation, but neither does it permit seizure of the entire community estate absent a true community obligation. Spouses, by contrast, should understand that Washington treats each spouse's one-half interest as a present, vested ownership interest that generally cannot be taken to satisfy the other's tort liability.

Fourth, premarital debts require careful application of Washington Revised Code § 26.16.200. Under *Watters v. Doud*, a creditor holding a premarital judgment against one spouse may reach the debtor-spouse's separate property and that spouse's "earnings and accumulations" during marriage, but not the nondebtor-spouse's separate property or vested one-half interest in community assets. Practitioners must therefore determine whether postmarital earnings qualify as "earnings and accumulations" under the statute, whether the debtor-spouse holds separate property, and whether wages or other income streams can be partially garnished without infringing on the protected share of the nondebtor-spouse.

CREDITOR RIGHTS IN CALIFORNIA

Statutory Framework: Classification and Liability of Marital Property

California organizes marital property and creditor liability through a combination of community-property classification rules and a separate set of liability provisions in the Family Code.[123] These rules create a managerial system in which the community estate is broadly liable for debts of either spouse, subject to targeted statutory exceptions and ordering rules.[124]

As a starting point, California presumes that "all property, real or personal, wherever situated, acquired by a married person during the marriage while domiciled in California is community property," except as otherwise provided by statute.[125] This presumption applies regardless of how title is held and gives each spouse a present, vested one-half interest in community assets.[126] By contrast, "separate property" consists of (1) all property owned by a person before marriage; (2) all property acquired after marriage by gift, bequest, devise, or descent; and (3) the rents, issues, and profits of that separate property.[127] Earnings and accumulations of a spouse while "living separate and apart" from the other spouse are also treated as that spouse's separate property.[128] These classification rules operate independently of creditor-liability rules but supply the baseline categories, community estate versus each spouse's separate estate, from which liability flows.[129]

For creditor-rights purposes, California defines "debt" broadly to include contract, tort, and other obligations, and specifies that a debt is "incurred" at the time of the act or omission giving rise to liability.[130] Under Family Code § 903, a contract debt is incurred at the time the contract is made, a tort debt is incurred at the time of the tortious act, and all other debts are incurred at the time the obligation arises.[131] These timing rules govern whether a debt is "premarital" or "during marriage" for purposes of the liability provisions that follow.[132]

Family Code § 910(a) supplies California's core conjugal-liability rule: "Except as otherwise expressly provided by statute, the community estate

---

[123] *Id.*

[124] *Id.*

[125] Cal. Fam. Code § 760.

[126] *In re* Marriage of Valli, 324 P.3d 274, 276 (Cal. 2014).

[127] Cal. Fam. Code § 770(a).

[128] *Id.* § 771(a).

[129] Lezine v. Sec. P. Fin., 925 P.2d 1002, 1007 (Cal. 1996).

[130] Cal. Fam. Code §§ 902, 903.

[131] *Id.* § 903(a)–(c).

[132] *Lezine*, 925 P.2d 1002.

is liable for a debt incurred by either spouse before or during marriage, regardless of which spouse has the management and control of the property and regardless of whether one or both spouses are parties to the debt or to a judgment for the debt."[133] The statute thus makes the entire community estate, not merely the debtor-spouse's one-half interest, available to satisfy debts of either spouse, subject only to specific statutory carve-outs.[134] Section 910 applies to all "debts," including obligations incurred solely for one spouse's personal benefit; the community-benefit concept is relevant to reimbursement between spouses, not to a third-party creditor's access to community assets.[135] In *Lezine v. Security Pacific Financial Services, Inc.*, the California Supreme Court emphasized that community property is liable for debts incurred by one spouse alone "exclusively for his or her own personal benefit," notwithstanding possible reimbursement rights between spouses.[136] Quasi-community property (property that would have been community had the couple been domiciled in California when it was acquired) is generally subject to the same liability rules as community property.[137] Family Code § 912(a) provides that quasi-community property is liable "to the same extent, and in the same manner, as community property" for debts of either spouse, including premarital debts brought into California.[138]

Family Code § 913(a) states the baseline rule for separate property: The separate property of a married person is liable for that person's own debts, whether incurred before or during marriage.[139] Section 913(b) then provides the mirror protection: Except as otherwise expressly provided by statute, the separate property of a married person is not liable for a debt incurred by the person's spouse before or during marriage, and the person is not personally liable for that debt.[140] These provisions insulate the nondebtor-spouse's separate estate from the other spouse's creditors,

---

[133] CAL. FAM. CODE § 910(a).

[134] *Id.*

[135] *Lezine*, 925 P.2d at 1006.

[136] *Id.*

[137] CAL. FAM. CODE §§ 63, 912.

[138] *Id.* § 912(a).

[139] *Id.* § 913(a).

[140] *Id.* § 913(b).

unless another statute (mainly § 914) creates personal liability.[141] Family Code § 911 creates a narrow but important carve-out in favor of the nondebtor-spouse's earnings. Under § 911(a), the "earnings of a married person during marriage" are not liable for a debt incurred by the person's spouse before marriage if: (1) the earnings are held in a deposit account in the name of the earning spouse; (2) the debtor-spouse has no right of withdrawal; and (3) the earnings are not commingled with other community property.[142] The statute does not recharacterize earnings as separate property; instead, it shields those earnings from levy for the other spouse's premarital debts, provided the segregation and no-access requirements are strictly observed.[143]

Section 914 operates as an express exception to § 913's separate-property shield.[144] It provides that, "[n]otwithstanding Section 913," a married person is personally liable for certain debts incurred by the person's spouse during marriage.[145] Subdivision (a)(1) provides that, before the date of separation, a married person is personally liable for debts incurred by the other spouse for the "necessaries of life."[146] Subdivision (a)(2) narrows this exposure after separation: Except as provided in Family Code § 4302, a married person is personally liable for debts incurred by the other spouse after separation only for the "common necessaries of life."[147] Personal liability under § 914 matters because it makes the nondebtor-spouse personally obligated to the creditor and thereby exposes that spouse's separate property to collection for the other spouse's qualifying debts.[148] In *Collection Bureau of San Jose v. Rumsey*, the California Supreme Court described § 914 as an "exception to the general rule that a married person's separate property is not liable for debts incurred by his or her spouse during marriage," and held that liability under § 914 attaches without regard to the character

---

141 *Id.*

142 *Id.* § 911.

143 *Id.*

144 *Id.* § 914.

145 *Id.*

146 *Id.*

147 *Id.*

148 *Id.*

of the nondebtor-spouse's property.[149] *Direct Capital Corp. v. Brooks* elaborates the distinction between "necessaries of life" and "common necessaries of life."[150] The court explained that "common necessaries" are those basic items all families need, such as food, clothing, and shelter, while "necessaires of life" depend on the particular marital standard of living and may include items or services appropriate to the couple's economic and social circumstances.[151] Courts therefore apply a broader, context-specific test for debts incurred before separation and a more restrictive baseline test for debts incurred afterward.[152]

After the community is divided in dissolution of marriage or legal separation, liability follows an assignment-based model. Family Code § 915(a)(1) provides that a spouse's separate property and the property received in the division remain liable for debts incurred by that spouse before or during marriage.[153] Section 915(a)(2) provides that the same property is not liable for debts incurred by the other spouse before or during marriage, and the spouse is not personally liable for those debts, unless the debt is expressly assigned to that spouse for payment in the division.[154] This scheme carries forward, in updated form, the principles discussed in *Lezine* concerning post-division liability and liens.[155] Section 916 complements § 915 by granting reimbursement rights when property of a spouse is applied to satisfy a debt assigned to the other spouse in the property division.[156]

Tort liability is governed by Family Code § 1000.[157] Subdivision (a) provides that, except as otherwise provided by statute, "the community estate is liable for a debt incurred by either spouse for a tort" committed during marriage.[158] Subdivision (b)(1) addresses torts committed while the spouse

---

[149] Collection Bureau of San Jose v. Rumsey, 6 P.3d 713, 718 (Cal. 2000).

[150] Direct Capital Corp. v. Brooks, 222 Cal. Rptr. 3d 601 (Cal. App. 3d Dist. 2017), *as modified* (Sep. 22, 2017).

[151] *Id.* at 605.

[152] *Id.*

[153] Cal. Fam. Code § 915(a).

[154] *Id.*

[155] *Lezine*, 925 P.2d at 1006.

[156] Cal. Fam. Code § 916.

[157] *Id.* § 1000.

[158] *Id.*

was performing an activity "for the benefit of the community," providing that the liability shall be satisfied first from the community estate and then, if necessary, from the tortfeasor's separate property.[159] Subdivision (b)(2) addresses torts not for the benefit of the community, providing that liability shall be satisfied first from the tortfeasor's separate property and then from community property that is subject to that spouse's management and control.[160] Thus, a tort creditor may generally reach both the tortfeasor's separate estate and the community estate, but the order in which those assets are applied depends on whether the tort occurred in the course of community-benefiting activity.[161] The non-tortfeasor spouse's separate property remains protected unless that spouse becomes personally liable under § 914 or some other statute.[162]

Practical Considerations for Planners and Creditors

California's statutory scheme is dense, but for community property planners and creditors a relatively simple road map emerges from the statutes and cases already discussed. Start with timing and characterization of the debt. Determine when the obligations was incurred under Family Code § 913 (before marriage, during marriage, or after separation) and whether it arises in contract, tort, or another source. This timing will control whether § 910, § 911, or § 914 is potentially implicated. Next, the property base must be mapped. The relevant assets should be classified as community property, quasi-community property, or separate property under §§ 760, 770, and 771, and, as a default, all property acquired during marriage should be assumed community unless a statutory separate property category clearly applies.

With the debt and property base identified, practitioners then apply the baseline liability rules. For debts incurred by either spouse before or during marriage, the working assumption is that the community estate is liable under § 910 unless a specific statutory exception (such as § 911 or § 916) applies. The debtor-spouse's separate property is liable for that spouse's debts under § 913(a), while the nondebtor-spouse's separate property is

---

[159] *Id.*

[160] *Id.*

[161] *Id.*

[162] *Id.* § 914.

protected by § 913(b) unless § 914 (or a similar statute) creates personal liability. *Lezine* reminds practitioners that the community estate's exposure is not limited to debts that "benefit" the community.

The next step is to test the statutory exceptions carefully. If the debt is a premarital obligation of the other spouse, counsel should evaluate whether the nondebtor-spouse's earnings can be sheltered under § 911 by strict segregation and denial of withdrawal rights. If the claim involves support, medical bills, or similar expenses, they must analyze whether the obligation falls within § 914's "necessaries" or "common necessaries of life" category and whether the spouses were separated at the relevant time. Practitioners must also account for tort ordering and post-dissolution assignments. For tort obligations, California Family Code § 1000 imposes ordering rules to provide that when the tort occurs in the course of community-benefiting activity, the creditor may look first to the community estate and then to the tortfeasor's separate property. If the tort is not committed for the benefit of the community, the order is reversed, and the liability is first satisfied from the tortfeasor's separate property and then (if that is insufficient) from the community estate. After dissolution of marriage, practitioners should assess how §§ 915 and 916, as interpreted in *Lezine* and subsequent cases, allocate liability and reimbursement rights between former spouses without disturbing the creditor's ability to enforce valid liens.

Finally, it is essential to document planning decisions. For clients entering marriage where one spouse has substantial premarital debt, planners should consider standalone earnings accounts structured to satisfy § 911, coupled with premarital agreements that clarify expectations about debt service and reimbursement. For operating businesses or professional practices, they should anticipate that community property will stand behind most trade obligations and that § 914 may expose the nondebtor-spouse's separate property for certain "necessaries of life" debts. Viewed as a whole, California's system can be summarized in one sentence: The community estate is broadly liable for debts of either spouse incurred before or during marriage, and the statute then carves out discrete pockets of protection for segregated earnings, nondebtor separate property, and assigned post-dissolution obligations. For practitioners, the task is less about finding an overarching "equitable" rule and more about working through the statutory sequence with precision, always asking which estate (community, quasi-community, or separate) answers for which debts, in what order, and subject to which limited exceptions.

CREDITOR RIGHTS IN TEXAS

Statutory Framework

Texas is a community property jurisdiction whose creditor rights rules are built on two pillars: (1) the constitutional and statutory classification of property as separate or community, and (2) a set of liability provisions that tie creditor reach to which spouse is personally liable and which "management" community estate the asset belongs to.[163]

The Texas Constitution provides that community property consists of property acquired by either spouse during marriage, while separate property includes property owned or claimed before marriage and property acquired during marriage by gift, devise, or descent.[164] The Family Code codifies this structure. Section 3.001 defines "separate property" as: (1) the property a spouse owned or claimed before marriage; (2) property acquired by gift, devise, or descent during marriage; and (3) recovery for personal injuries sustained during marriage, other than loss of earning capacity.[165] Section 3.002 defines "community property" as property, other than separate property, acquired by either spouse during marriage.[166] Section 3.003 adds a presumption: Property possessed by either spouse during or on dissolution of marriage is presumed to be community property, and the presumption may be rebutted only by clear and convincing evidence.[167]

Management and control overlay this characterization. Section 3.101 provides that each spouse has the sole management, control, and disposition of that spouse's separate property.[168] Section 3.102 allocates management of community property: Each spouse has sole management, control, and disposition of the community property that the spouse would have owned if single, including personal earnings, revenue from separate property, personal injury recoveries (other than loss of earning capacity), and community property held in that spouse's name alone, while other community property is subject to joint management, control, and disposition by

---

[163] Tex. Const. art. XVI, § 15; Tex. Fam. Code §§ 3.001–3.003.

[164] Tex. Const. art. XVI, § 15.

[165] Tex. Fam. Code § 3.001.

[166] *Id.* § 3.002.

[167] *Id.* § 3.003.

[168] *Id.* § 3.101.

both spouses.[169] Section 3.104 protects third parties by creating a presumption that property held in a spouse's name or in that spouse's possession is subject to that spouse's sole management, and it entitles third parties to rely on that apparent authority absent notice of a lack of authority or participation in fraud.[170] These management rules are central because the liability provisions of subchapter C look to whether community property is subject to a spouse's sole or joint management when determining what assets are exposed to that spouse's creditors.[171]

Personal liability and property-based liability are separated in subchapter C. Section 3.201 governs when one spouse is personally liable for the acts of the other.[172] Under § 3.201(a), a person is personally liable for the acts of the person's spouse only if: (1) the spouse acts as an agent for the person, or (2) the spouse incurs a debt for "necessaries" as provided by the duty-to-support provisions in chapter 2.[173] Section 3.201(c) underscores that a spouse does not act as an agent for the other spouse solely because of the marriage relationship.[174] Section 3.201(b) adds an important backdrop: "[E]xcept as provided by this subchapter, community property is not subject to a liability that arises from an act of a spouse," reinforcing that liability does not automatically follow marital status.[175]

Section 3.202 then sets out the "rules of marital property liability," distinguishing separate property, sole-management community property, joint-management community property, and tortious liabilities.[176] Subsection (a) states the baseline separate-property exemption: A spouse's separate property is not subject to the liabilities of the other spouse unless both spouses are liable under "other rules of law."[177] Subsection (b) provides that, unless both spouses are personally liable under subchapter C, community property subject to a spouse's sole management, control, and

[169] *Id.* § 3.102.

[170] *Id.* § 3.104.

[171] *Id.* §§ 3.201–3.203.

[172] *Id.* § 3.201.

[173] *Id.*

[174] *Id.*

[175] *Id.*

[176] *Id.* § 3.202.

[177] *Id.*

disposition is not subject to (1) liabilities the other spouse incurred before marriage or (2) nontortious liabilities the other spouse incurs during marriage.[178] Subsection (c) states the converse: Community property subject to a spouse's sole or joint management, control, and disposition is subject to the liabilities incurred by that spouse before or during marriage.[179] Finally, § 3.202(d) provides that all community property, regardless of management, is subject to tortious liability of either spouse incurred during marriage, reflecting a policy choice to make the entire community estate available for tort victims.[180]

Section 3.203 gives courts flexibility in enforcing judgments.[181] It authorizes a judge, "as deemed just and equitable," to determine the order in which particular separate or community assets (separate property, each spouse's sole-management community property, and joint-management community property) are subjected to execution and sale, instructing the court to consider the facts surrounding the transaction or occurrence on which the debt is based.[182] This ordering provision allows trial courts to tailor execution to the equities of the case while remaining within the liability categories set by §§ 3.201 and 3.202.

Read together, these provisions implement a hybrid system: Characterization statutes define separate versus community property and allocate management between the spouses, while subsection (c) determines when each spouse is personally liable and which marital estates (separate, sole-management community, joint-management community) answer for that spouse's debts.[183] Texas law does not recognize "community debt" as an entity-level obligation; a debt is always the obligation of the husband, the wife, or both, and the statutes then specify which assets may be reached to satisfy that obligation.[184]

---

[178] *Id.*

[179] *Id.*

[180] *Id.*

[181] *Id.* § 3.203.

[182] *Id.*

[183] *Id.* §§ 3.001–3.003, 3.101–3.104, 3.201–3.203.

[184] Tedder v. Gardner Aldrich, LLP, 421 S.W.3d 651 (Tex. 2013). The Texas Supreme Court's discussion in *Tedder* addresses the persistent misconception of "community debt." The court, quoting Professor Joseph McKnight, explained

Key Judicial Developments

The Texas Supreme Court's modern cases emphasize that creditor-rights analysis starts with personal liability, not with a free-floating notion of "community debt." In *Tedder v. Gardner Aldrich, LLP*, the court rejected arguments that turned on the label "community debt" and instead applied the statutory framework: The question is whether the spouse is personally liable and what the category of liability is under § 3.201, and, if so, which marital estates are exposed under § 3.202.[185] The court stressed that Texas law no longer recognizes community debt as a distinct category for liability purposes; rather, the community is not a separate entity that incurs debts, and the Family Code governs liability by reference to personal obligation and property classification.[186] Practitioners therefore must resist the temptation to treat "community debt" as a separate legal animal and instead walk through the statutory steps: Identify who is personally liable, and then identify which estates can be reached under § 3.202.[187]

Texas Family Code § 3.202(a) is explicit in its attempt to protect a nondebtor-spouse's separate property from the other spouse's creditors unless the nondebtor-spouse is personally liable under other rules of law, such as agency, partnership, or the necessaries doctrine.[188] Appellate decisions analyzing attempts to execute on the nondebtor-spouse's separate real estate or accounts generally begin by confirming that no personal liability

---

that the notion of a freestanding community obligation, equally binding on both spouses, is "an erroneous supposition" unsupported by the basic principles of Texas community-property law. Rather than treating debts as "community" or "separate" in the abstract, Texas law assigns every debt to a specific spouse (or to both spouses if jointly incurred) and then looks to the Family Code to determine which assets (separate, sole-managed community, or jointly managed community) may be reached to satisfy that spouse's obligation. Thus, a nondebtor-spouse is liable for the other spouse's debt only when a statute expressly imposes personal liability.

185 *Id.*

186 *Id.*

187 *Id.*

188 Tex. Fam. Code § 3.202(a).

exists under § 3.201 and then apply § 3.202(a) to bar execution.[189] By contrast, a debtor-spouse's sole-management community property is broadly available to that debtor-spouse's creditors.[190] Together with § 3.104's third-party reliance rule, creditors have substantial access to assets titled in or controlled by the debtor-spouse while they may be subject to significant protections for the nondebtor-spouse's separate estate and sole-management community property against the debtor's spouse's premarital and nontortious marital debts.[191]

Section 3.201(a)(2) incorporates the "necessaries" doctrine by making one spouse personally liable when the other incurs a debt for "necessaries" as defined in the duty-to-support provisions of subchapter F, chapter 2.[192] When the necessaries doctrine applies, both spouses may be jointly and severally liable, which in turn exposes all nonexempt marital estates, each spouse's separate property, and the various categories of community property to the creditor's claim, subject to statutory exemptions.[193] Other "rules of law" can also create personal liability for the otherwise nondebtor-spouse Agency, partnership, joint enterprise, and respondeat superior theories all can bring a spouse within § 3.201(a)(1), making that spouse personally liable for the acts of the other, and thereby opening that spouse's separate property and sole-management community property to execution under § 3.202(c).[194]

---

189 Martinek Grain & Bins, Inc. v. Bulldog Farms, Inc., 366 S.W.3d 800 (Tex. App.–Dallas 2012); Nelson v. Citizens Bank & Tr. Co. of Baytown, Tex., 881 S.W.2d 128 (Tex. App.–Hous. [1st Dist.] 1994).

190 Tex. Fam. Code § 3.202(b).

191 *Id.* § 3.104.

192 *Id.* § 3.201(a)(2); *id.* § 2.501; Daggett v. Neiman-Marcus Co., 348 S.W.2d 796 (Tex. Civ. App.–Houston 1961) (holding that whether items purchased by a wife constitute "necessaries" depends on the parties' station and condition in life and that, although the wife is ordinarily the judge of what items are necessary, the goods must nevertheless appear to the satisfaction of the court or jury to be reasonable and proper).

193 Tex. Fam. Code § 3.201(a)(2).

194 *Daggett*, 348 S.W.2d at 796.

Practical Considerations for Planners and Creditors

For Texas practitioners, the central insight is that creditor-rights questions are resolved by walking the statutory sequence rather than by appealing to an amorphous "community debt" concept. First, identify who is personally liable on the obligation. Section 3.201 makes clear that a spouse is personally liable for the other's acts only if an agency relationship or the necessaries doctrine applies; otherwise, the debt is purely the obligation of the contracting or tortfeasor spouse. Second, classify the relevant assets: Determine which property is separate, which is sole-management community for each spouse, and which is joint-management community, applying §§ 3.001–3.003 and 3.101–3.102. Third, apply the liability rules of § 3.202 to that map. The debtor-spouse's separate property and all community property subject to that spouse's sole or joint management are available to satisfy that spouse's liabilities before and during marriage, while the nondebtor-spouse's separate property is protected and that spouse's sole-management community property is insulated from the other spouse's premarital and nontortious marital debts unless both spouses are personally liable. All community property remains exposed to tort liabilities incurred by either spouse during marriage. Fourth, overlay exemptions under the Property Code to determine how much of the otherwise exposed property is actually available for levy or sale. Finally, use § 3.203's discretionary ordering power where appropriate to argue for, or against, execution on particular estates, based on the equities of the underlying transaction.

From a planning perspective, these rules suggest several recurring strategies. Spouses can reduce cross-exposure by maintaining clear separations between each spouse's business or professional activities and the other spouse's property, documenting the absence of agency or partnership relationships, and recognizing that the other spouse's sole-management community estate is generally insulated from premarital and nontortious marital debts. Where one spouse anticipates significant business risk, marital property agreements under chapter 4 and careful titling of assets may help concentrate risk in that spouse's separate and sole-management community estates, leaving the other spouse's property less exposed. For creditors, the statutes and cases counsel careful attention to (1) obtaining both spouses' signatures when joint liability is intended, (2) establishing agency or necessaries when relying on § 3.201(a), and (3) tracing which marital estates are reachable under § 3.202 before pursuing execution.

CREDITOR RIGHTS IN IDAHO

Statutory Framework: Classification, Management, and Liability

Idaho organizes marital property and creditor liability through a cluster of community-property provisions in Idaho Code §§ 32-901 through 32-929.[195] Idaho begins with the familiar distinction between separate and community property. Section 32-903 defines each spouse's separate property as (1) all property owned by that spouse before marriage; (2) all property acquired afterward by gift, bequest, devise, or descent; and (3) the rents, issues, and profits of that separate property.[196] Section 32-906 supplies the converse rule: Except as otherwise provided by statute or by an instrument making a gift expressly to one spouse, all other property acquired after marriage by either spouse, including the rents, issues, and profits of separate property, is community property.[197] These definitions create three estates relevant for creditor analysis: the first spouse's separate estate, the second spouse's separate estate, and the community's estate.

Management and control are governed by Idaho Code § 32-912.[198] After 1974 amendments, either spouse has equal "right to manage and control the community property," including the power to buy, sell, and encumber community personalty and to bind the community by contract.[199] Conveyances or encumbrances of community real property, however, require joinder; both spouses must execute the instrument in order to transfer or encumber community real estate.[200] The statute further provides that the separate property of a spouse who does not consent in writing to a "community obligation" is not liable for that obligation.[201] In combination, these provisions give each spouse broad authority to deal with community assets,

---

195 Idaho Code §§ 32-901–32-929.

196 *Id.* § 32-903.

197 *Id.* § 32-906.

198 *Id.* § 32-912.

199 *Id.*; Credit Bureau of E. Idaho, Inc. v. Lecheminant, 235 P.3d 1188 (Idaho 2010).

200 Idaho Code § 32-912.

201 *Id.*

while protecting the nonconsenting spouse's separate estate from community liabilities incurred by the other.[202]

Liability for separate and premarital debts is addressed primarily in §§ 32-910 and 32-911, read together with § 32-912. Section 32-910 provides that a spouse's separate property is liable for that spouse's debts contracted before marriage, while insulating the other spouse's separate estate from those antenuptial obligations.[203] Section 32-911 similarly protects a spouse's separate property from liability for the other spouse's postmarital debts, subject to specific statutory exceptions.[204] At the same time, Idaho courts have long held that separate debts of either spouse, whether incurred before or during marriage, may be satisfied from community property.[205] The current law thus reflects three basic propositions: (1) a debtor-spouse's own separate property is fully liable for that spouse's obligations; (2) community property is available to satisfy separate debts of either spouse; and (3) the nondebtor-spouse's separate property is not liable unless that spouse has personally obligated it, typically by written consent.[206]

Judicial Development of Community and Separate Liability

The Idaho Supreme Court has developed creditor-rights rules by combining the statutory classification and management scheme with common law principles. Modern cases focus on three recurring issues: (1) whether separate debts of a spouse may be satisfied from community property, (2) whether a debt must "benefit" the community to reach community assets, and (3) how far creditors may go against the nondebtor-spouse's separate property.[207] Idaho authority has long allowed creditors to satisfy a spouse's separate obligations from community assets.[208] In early cases such as *Holt v.*

---

[202] *Id.*

[203] *Id.* § 32-910.

[204] *Id.* § 32-911.

[205] *Lecheminant,* 235 P.3d 1188; Bliss v. Bliss, 898 P.2d 1081, 1085 (1995).

[206] IDAHO CODE §§ 32-910–32-912; *Lecheminant,* 235 P.3d at 1194.

[207] *Lecheminant,* 235 P.3d 1188; Action Collection Serv., Inc. v. Seele, 69 P.3d 173 (Idaho App. 2003).

[208] *Lecheminant,* 235 P.3d at 1194.

Empey and *Gustin v. Byam*, the supreme court held that community property could be reached to satisfy separate debts of a spouse, subject to the statutory protections for the other spouse's separate estate.[209] Later decisions reaffirmed that principle, describing it as settled law that separate debts of either spouse may be paid from community property.[210] The Idaho Supreme Court's more recent decision in *Credit Bureau of Eastern Idaho, Inc. v. Lecheminant* collects these authorities and confirms that there is no requirement that a separate debt benefit the community in order for community assets to be used in its satisfaction.[211]

Action Collection Service, Inc. v. Seele applies these principles in the garnishment context.[212] There, a creditor holding a judgment against one spouse for premarital debts sought to garnish the nondebtor-spouse's wages on the theory that earnings are community property.[213] The court of appeals held that a judgment creditor may garnish community property, including the nondebtor-spouse's earnings, to satisfy prenuptial debts of the other spouse, subject to any applicable exemptions.[214] *Lecheminant* later cited *Action Collection* as authority for the general proposition that prenuptial debts can be satisfied out of community property.[215] Together, these decisions make clear that, as between creditors and the community, the source and timing of the debt (premarital versus postmarital; separate versus community) do not limit access to community assets, absent a statute to the contrary.

Lecheminant also squarely rejects a "benefit of the community" requirement for creditor access to community property.[216] The Lecheminants argued that community assets could not be used to satisfy prenuptial debt that did not benefit the existing marital community.[217] The supreme court

---

209 Holt v. Empey, 178 P. 703 (Idaho 1919); Gustin v. Byam, 240 P. 600 (Idaho 1925).

210 Bliss v. Bliss, 898 P.2d 1081 (Idaho 1995).

211 *Lecheminant*, 235 P.3d 1188.

212 Action Collection Serv., Inc. v. Seele, 69 P.3d 173 (Idaho App. 2003).

213 *Id.*

214 *Id.*

215 *Lecheminant*, 235 P.3d at 1191.

216 *Id.* at 1192.

217 *Id.*

disagreed, holding that the debt does not need to be incurred for the benefit of the community in order for the community to be liable, again citing a line of authority allowing separate debts to be paid from community property.[218] While community benefit may be relevant for internal reimbursement between spouses, it is not a prerequisite to creditor recovery from community assets.[219] This places Idaho firmly in the managerial camp: Creditors look first to the statutory liability rules, not to equitable notions of benefit, when determining whether community property may be reached.

By contrast, Idaho law is protective of the nondebtor-spouse's separate estate.[220] Sections 32-910 and 32-911 prohibit creditors from executing on the separate property of a spouse for the other spouse's debts, whether incurred before or after marriage, unless a statute expressly provides otherwise.[221] Section 32-912 reinforces this protection by specifying that any community obligation incurred by either spouse without the other's written consent does not obligate the nonconsenting spouse's separate property.[222] Appellate decisions analyzing creditor efforts to reach the nondebtor-spouse's separate real estate or accounts generally begin by confirming that no personal liability exists under these provisions and bar execution against the nondebtor's separate assets.[223] As a result, Idaho creditors typically focus collection efforts on community property and the debtor-spouse's separate property, treating the other spouse's separate property as off limits absent a personal guaranty or similar written undertaking.

Practical Considerations for Planners and Creditors

For community property planners and creditors, Idaho's regime can be summarized in three working rules. First, creditors may reach community property (including earnings and other assets acquired after community) to satisfy separate debts of either spouse, whether incurred before

---

218 *Id.*

219 *Id.*

220 IDAHO CODE ANN. §§ 32-910–32-911.

221 *Id.*

222 *Id.* § 32-912.

223 Twin Falls Bank & Tr. Co. v. Holley, P.2d 893, 896–98 (Idaho 1986).

or during marriage, and need not show that the obligation benefited the community. Second, the debtor-spouse's separate property is fully liable for that spouse's obligations, but the nondebtor-spouse's separate estate is insulated absent personal liability created by statute or contract, and § 32-912 expressly bars extension of community obligations to the nonconsenting spouse's separate property. Third, equal management under § 32-912 means either spouse can, as a practical matter, expose the entire community estate to creditor claims, so the real planning leverage lies in how spouses structure and preserve their separate estates and to what extent creditors document personal guarantees and security interests. For planners representing spouses, these rules require carefully prepared documents evidencing separate-property status (particularly for premarital assets, inheritances, and gifts) and considering how much risk the marital community should bear for one spouse's existing or anticipated business debts. Where one spouse brings substantial premarital obligations into the marriage, practitioners should consider the limits of separate-property planning in Idaho: While separate property can be segregated and preserved, creditors will generally be able to satisfy prenuptial debts from the couple's community income and acquisitions. For creditors, Idaho's law makes community property a powerful collection resource (especially wages and other liquid community assets) while requiring attention to statutory protections for the nondebtor-spouse's separate estate.

CREDITOR RIGHTS IN LOUISIANA

Statutory Framework: Classification and Liability of Marital Property

Louisiana organizes marital property through the law of "matrimonial regimes," which govern the ownership and management of the spouses' property.[224] A matrimonial regime may be legal, contractual, or partly legal and partly contractual, but in the absence of a matrimonial agreement the

[224] La. Civ. Code art. 2325 (2024).

spouses are subject to the legal regime.[225] The legal regime is the community of acquets[226] and gains, which applies to spouses domiciled in Louisiana.[227]

Community property is broadly defined to include property acquired during the existence of the legal regime of marriage through the effort, skill, or industry of either spouse; property acquired with community things or with community and separate things when the community's contribution is not inconsequential in comparison; property donated to the spouses jointly; damages for loss or injury to community items; and all other property not classified by law as separate.[228] By contrast, separate property consists of property owned by a spouse before the establishment of the community property regime; property acquired by a spouse with separate things or with separate and community things when the community's contribution is inconsequential; property acquired by a spouse by inheritance or individual donation; damages awarded to a spouse in an action for personal injuries (with limited exceptions); and property declared separate by law or by judgment.[229]

Property in the possession of either spouse during the community property regime is presumed to be community, and a spouse who asserts separate status bears the burden of proving it.[230] The Code also addresses fruits and revenues of separate property: Fruits of separate property are community unless the owning spouse reserves them as separate by authentic act, and records the declaration when appropriate.[231] The combination of the presumption of community and the default rule for fruits (i.e., income, rents, profits, dividends, interest, and other returns produced by property)

---

[225] *Id.* art. 2326.

[226] In the civil law, "acquet" denotes self-acquired property. The term is derived from the French word "acquet" which means acquisition and Latin word "acquirere," which means to acquire. Acquets are property acquired by way of purchase or gift. Acquets include profits or gains of property between husband and wife. Acquets do not include property acquired by way of succession. Acquets is also termed as "acquest." Under Lousiana Civil Law acquets include profits from the labor of both husband and wife.

[227] LA. CIV. CODE art. 2334 (2024).

[228] *Id.* art. 2338.

[229] *Id.* art. 2341.

[230] *Id.* art. 2340.

[231] *Id.* art. 2339.

creates a large community estate that, as a matter of default, is available to satisfy most marital obligations.

Management of Community Property

Louisiana has adopted an equal-management model. Article 2346 provides that, except as otherwise provided by law, "each spouse acting alone may manage, control, or dispose of community property."[232] This general rule allows either spouse to bind the community property in ordinary transactions with third parties. Article 2347 then carves out important exceptions requiring the concurrence of both spouses.[233] In particular, the concurrence of both spouses is required for (1) the alienation, encumbrance, or lease of community immovables; (2) the alienation, encumbrance, or lease of furniture or furnishings located in the family home; (3) the donation of community property, unless authorized by law; and (4) certain other significant acts affecting the community patrimony.[234]

These management rules matter to creditors because they determine when a spouse acting alone can create obligations that may be satisfied from community assets.[235] Equal management and the broad authority to incur obligations for family expenses mean that a creditor dealing with one spouse will often acquire recourse against the community estate, even if the other spouse did not participate in the transaction.

Satisfaction of Obligations During and After the Community Regime

Article 2345 provides that "[a] separate or community obligation may be satisfied during the community property regime from community property and from the separate property of the spouse who incurred the obligation."[236] Article 2345 thus identifies two asset pools available to a creditor during the legal regime: (1) all community property, including the nondebtor-spouse's undivided interest, and (2) the debtor-spouse's

---

[232] *Id.* art. 2346.

[233] *Id.* art. 2347.

[234] *Id.*

[235] *Id.* art. 2345.

[236] *Id.*

separate property.[237] The separate property of the nondebtor-spouse is not available to satisfy the debtor-spouse's obligations absent an additional statutory basis.[238]

Article 2357 extends this scheme beyond termination of the community property regime.[239] It provides that an obligation incurred by a spouse before or during the community property regime "may be satisfied after termination of the regime from the property of the former community and from the separate property of the spouse who incurred the obligation."[240] If, however, a spouse disposes of property of the former community for a purpose other than the satisfaction of community obligations, that spouse becomes liable for all obligations incurred by the other spouse up to the value of the disposed property.[241] A spouse may also, by written act, assume responsibility for one-half of each community obligation incurred by the other spouse; in that event, the assuming spouse may dispose of former community property without incurring additional responsibility for those obligations.[242]

Read together, articles 2345 and 2357 establish a consistent creditor-oriented rule: Whether the regime is ongoing or dissolved, a creditor of either spouse may look to (1) community or former community assets and (2) the separate property of the spouse who incurred the obligation.[243] The nondebtor-spouse's separate property is insulated unless that spouse has disposed of former community assets for noncommunity purposes or has expressly assumed liability in writing.[244]

---

237 *Id.*

238 *Id.*

239 *Id.* art. 2357.

240 *Id.*

241 *Id.*

242 *Id.*

243 *Id.* arts. 2345, 2357.

244 *Id.*

Classification of Obligations: Community Versus Separate

The Civil Code separately classifies obligations as "community" or "separate." Article 2360 defines community obligations as those incurred during the existence of the community property regime "for the common interest of the spouses or for the interest of the other spouse," and those incurred during the regime for the ordinary and customary expenses of the marriage or of the family, or for the education of the children.[245] Article 2361 creates a presumption that obligations incurred by a spouse during the existence of the regime are community, and places the burden on the spouse claiming separate status to prove otherwise.[246] Article 2362 specifically classifies as community obligations the "alimentary obligations" of a spouse, which include obligations to support a spouse, former spouse, or children as imposed by law.[247] Article 2362.1 extends community-obligation treatment to certain obligations incurred in connection with actions for divorce, post-divorce relief, and related attorney's fees and costs, reflecting a policy that family-law litigation expenses frequently arise from the marital community's affairs.[248]

Article 2363 defines separate obligations. These include obligations incurred before the establishment of the community property regime; obligations incurred during the regime, "though not for the common interest of the spouses or for the interest of the other spouse"; obligations incurred during the regime for the separate property of a spouse to the extent they do not benefit the other spouse or the community; and obligations resulting from the intentional wrongs of a spouse not perpetrated for the benefit of the community.[249] Finally, articles 2364–2367 create reimbursement rights between spouses when one spouse's separate property is used to satisfy community obligations or when community property is used to satisfy a separate obligation.[250] From a third-party creditor's perspective, these reimbursement provisions do not limit the pools of property available under

[245] *Id.* art. 2360.

[246] *Id.* art. 2361.

[247] *Id.* art. 2362.

[248] *Id.* art. 2362.1.

[249] *Id.* art. 2363.

[250] *Id.* arts. 2364–2367.

articles 2345 and 2357 but instead affect the ultimate allocation of the economic burden between spouses.[251]

Taken together, articles 2345, 2357, and 2360–2363 create a two-level analysis. For third-party creditors, the key questions are: (1) which spouse incurred the obligation and (2) whether the community (or former community) still exists as a patrimony. For purposes of recourse against the community, classification of the obligation as community or separate is largely irrelevant; in either case, the creditor may satisfy the obligation from community property and the debtor-spouse's separate property. Classification matters primarily for internal allocation and reimbursement as between the spouses.

Practical Considerations for Planners and Creditors

For practitioners, Louisiana's system can be understood as creditor-friendly but conceptually straightforward. First, from the creditor's perspective, the main questions are: (1) is there (or was there) a community of acquets and gains, and (2) which spouse incurred the obligation? If the obligation was incurred by either spouse before or during the regime, all community property (and, after termination, all former community property) stands behind the debt, alongside the debtor-spouse's separate property. The nondebtor-spouse's separate property is generally out of reach unless that spouse has disposed of former community assets for noncommunity purposes or signed an explicit assumption of obligations.

Second, for spouses and planners, the classification of property as community or separate matters less for third-party exposure than for internal economics. Even a "separate" obligation can be paid out of community or former community assets. The payoff of careful classification, matrimonial agreements, and declarations of separate fruits is that they set up reimbursement rights and influence the economic outcome on partition or death, not that they automatically insulate the community from a spouse's creditors.

Third, termination of the community does not cut off preexisting creditors. Lawyers drafting divorce judgments and partition agreements need to assume that pre-termination creditors can still pursue former community property in either spouse's hands. The settlement should therefore address

---

[251] *Id.*

how those obligations will be handled, what reimbursement rights will exist between former spouses, and how to avoid exposing one spouse's separate estate by improper disposition of former community assets.

Finally, for debtors and their counsel, the key protective levers are: (1) structuring the matrimonial regime (through agreements) when appropriate, (2) preserving clear records of which obligations are separate and which are community, and (3) avoiding dispositions of former community property that could trigger personal liability under article 2357. For creditors, the converse is true: identify the debtor-spouse, locate community or former community assets, and be alert to any written assumptions of liability or problematic transfers that might expand the recovery base.

CREDITOR RIGHTS IN NEVADA

Statutory Framework: Classification, Management, and Liability

Nevada's community property regime is codified in chapter 123 of the Nevada Revised Statutes.[252] As in other community property states, Nevada distinguishes between each spouse's "separate" property and the spouses' "community" property. Separate property consists of all property owned by a spouse before marriage and all property acquired by that spouse afterward by gift, bequest, devise, or descent, together with the rents, issues, and profits of that separate property.[253] Community property is defined broadly as all property, other than separate property, acquired after marriage by either spouse or both spouses.[254] Property acquired by either spouse during marriage is presumed to be community property unless the party asserting separate status proves otherwise.[255] This presumption applies regardless of how title is held and reflects Nevada's policy of treating earnings and accumulations during marriage as belonging to the marital community.[256]

---

[252] NEV. REV. STAT. ch. 123 (2023).

[253] *Id.* § 123.130.

[254] *Id.* § 123.220.

[255] *Id.*

[256] *Id.* A conclusion that the presumption applies to all property acquired during marriage, regardless of how title is held, can be inferred from the statute's opening phrase, "All property."

Management of community property is governed primarily by Nevada Revised Statutes § 123.230.[257] Either spouse, acting alone, may control, manage, dispose of, or encumber community personal property, subject to specific statutory limitations.[258] For community real property, however, both spouses must generally join in any sale, conveyance, or encumbrance; a unilateral deed by one spouse alone is ineffective to transfer or encumber the community's real estate interest.[259] The joinder requirement for real property is designed to protect the nonacting spouse's undivided one-half community interest and to give third parties clear notice of the need to obtain both signatures.[260] Nevada law also restricts unilateral gifts of community property.[261] A spouse may not, without the other spouse's written consent, make a gift of community property that is not a usual or nominal gift, and an attempted gratuitous transfer in violation of this rule may be set aside as to the nonconsenting spouse's one-half interest.[262] These management rules form the backdrop for creditor-rights analysis and determine when one spouse, acting alone, has authority to bind the community in transactions with third parties.

Nevada's statutes do not use the term "community debt" as a defined category, but they do make clear which assets may be reached by a creditor of either spouse. The separate property of a spouse is always accessible for that spouse's own debts, whether incurred before or during marriage.[263] At the same time, Nevada treats the community property of the spouses as being liable for obligations incurred by either spouse during the marriage, unless a statute provides otherwise or the creditor has agreed to look only to separate assets.[264] The separate property of the nondebtor-spouse is not

---

257 Nev. Rev. Stat. Ann. § 123.230.

258 *Id.*

259 *Id.*

260 *Id.*

261 *Id.*

262 *Id.*

263 *Id.* § 123.050.

264 Randono v. Turk, 466 P.2d 218, 224 (1970). In *Randono*, the Nevada Supreme Court inferred spousal debt liability for community property from the statutory structure governing management and testamentary disposition. The court emphasized that Nevada Revised Statutes § 123.230 grants the husband entire

automatically liable for the other spouse's obligations.[265] In the absence of a personal guarantee or other direct undertaking, creditors of one spouse generally may not execute against the other spouse's separate estate.[266] Instead, Nevada's system exposes (1) the debtor-spouse's separate property and (2) community property to collection, while leaving the nondebtor-spouse's separate property insulated from the other spouse's creditors.[267] Read together, the classification, management, and exemption statutes create a two-step framework for creditor analysis. First, the practitioner must determine whether an asset is community or separate and whether it falls within an exemption. Second, they must identify which spouse incurred the obligation and then apply Nevada's general rule that the debtor-spouse's separate property and the community property are available to satisfy that obligation, absent an applicable statutory or contractual limitation.

Judicial Development of Community Liability

Because chapter 123 does not contain a single, comprehensive "liability" section, Nevada courts have developed creditor-rights principles by combining the statutory community property framework with general contract and judgment execution rules.

In *Randono v. Turk*, the Nevada Supreme Court affirmed a money judgment arising out of the husband's misuse of loan proceeds and upheld the district court's order amending that judgment so that it ran against the community property of the husband and his wife, even though the wife had not been named as a defendant.[268] The court concluded that "the entire community property" of the Randonos was subject to liability on the

management and control of the community property, with the absolute power of disposition. It then relied on § 123.260, which provides that upon the husband's death, the community property passing through his estate is subject to claims of his creditors. Reasoning from these statutes, the court concluded that if the husband may freely transfer community assets inter vivos and such assets are liable for his debts at death, it logically follows that community property must also be liable for his debts during his lifetime.

[265] Nev. Rev. Stat. Ann. § 123.050.

[266] *Id.*

[267] *Id.*; *Randono*, 466 P.2d at 224.

[268] 466 P.2d, 218.

judgments, irrespective of the wife's nonjoinder.[269] In reaching that conclusion, the court relied on Nevada Revised Statutes § 123.220's definition of community property as property acquired during the marriage through the toil or talent of either spouse, § 123.230's grant to the husband (under the then-existing statute) of "the entire management and control of the community property, with the like absolute power of disposition thereof, except as provided in this chapter, as of his own separate estate," and § 123.260's directive that community property passing from the husband's control at death is subject to his debts.[270] From these provisions the court reasoned that if community property can be given away by the husband during life and is subject to his debts at death, "we see no reason why it is not subject to his debts, whether arising out of tort or contract, during his lifetime."[271]

Nevada's community property system therefore tends to be described as a managerial regime: Assets characterized as community under § 123.220 are broadly exposed to liabilities incurred by either spouse under the management rules in § 123.230, while the principal protections for an innocent spouse lie in the insulation of separate property under statutes such as §§ 123.050 and 123.210 and in the statutory constraints on unilateral dispositions of community real property and jointly managed businesses.[272]

Practical Considerations for Planners and Creditors

From the creditor's perspective, the basic strategy is straightforward. If a debt was incurred by either spouse during the marriage, assume that both the debtor-spouse's separate property and the community estate are available to satisfy the obligation, subject to homestead and personal-property exemptions. Whether the nondebtor-spouse signed the contract often matters less than whether the debtor-spouse had authority to act under Nevada's equal-management rules. Unless the creditor affirmatively agreed to limit recourse to separate property, community assets are usually in play.

For spouses and their counsel, the most important planning moves involve front-end classification and documentation. Property brought into

---

269 *Id.*

270 *Id.*

271 *Id.*

272 Nev. Rev. Stat. Ann. §§ 123,050, 123,210, 123.220, 123.230.

the marriage, inheritances, and gifts should be kept separately titled if the goal is to preserve separate-property status. Commingling and using separate funds for community purposes will not necessarily destroy separate character, but clear records and separate accounts make it easier to prove separate ownership if a judgment creditor later appears. When one spouse has significant premarital or business liabilities, it is often worth considering a premarital or postmarital agreement that clarifies expectations about debt service and preserves room for equitable reimbursement between the spouses, even though such an agreement cannot, by itself, defeat the rights of existing creditors.

Because Nevada is an equal-management jurisdiction, a single spouse can, as a practical matter, expose the entire community estate to trade debt, tort judgments, or guarantee obligations. That reality should shape how practitioners counsel clients about signing personal guarantees, extending credit to closely held entities, and undertaking high-risk business activities. For the nondebtor-spouse, it means understanding that "I didn't sign" is not a complete defense where community assets are concerned; the more effective protections lie in monitoring major commitments, preserving separate property, and making thoughtful use of exemptions and homestead planning.

Chapter 6

Migratory Spouses and the Permutations of Marital Property

In Chapter 3, we explored how noncommunity property states constrain testamentary freedom through elective share statutes, the modern successors to dower and curtesy. As discussed, while the elective share reflects the common law states' solution for spousal protection at death, community property jurisdictions take a fundamentally different approach: They grant each spouse a present, vested one-half ownership interest in marital acquisitions during life.

This divergence matters most when a couple moves across jurisdictional boundaries. Community property rights are immediate and portable, so when a couple marries, works, and accumulates assets in a community property state but later relocates to a separate property jurisdiction, the question arises whether those vested community property rights survive the move. Conversely, if property is first acquired in a separate property state in the name of only one spouse and the couple later becomes domiciled in a community property jurisdiction, does the nontitled spouse immediately obtain an ownership interest, or does the original classification of the property as separate remain controlling? The resolution of these issues has significant implications for probate administration, estate planning, and family law.[1]

[1] Jeffrey Schoenblum, U.S. Conflict of Laws Involving International Estates and Marital Property: A critical Analysis of Estate of Charania v. Shulman.

At death, one of the central questions is identifying which assets properly form part of the decedent's estate for both state law and federal tax purposes. More specifically, the inquiry becomes: How much of the property titled in the decedent's name is, by virtue of community property rules, already owned by the surviving spouse?[2] To the extent that the surviving spouse is recognized as holding a community interest in the property, the value passing through the decedent's estate is generally cut in half, thereby reducing by 50 percent both (1) the share available to other heirs/devisees and (2) the amount subject to inclusion in the decedent's gross estate for federal estate tax purposes.[3]

GENERAL RULE: COMMUNITY PROPERTY RETAINS ITS CHARACTER AS SUCH AFTER MOVING TO A NONCOMMUNITY PROPERTY STATE

Community property retains its character as such after moving to a noncommunity property state.[4] While this general rule resolves most cases, how the spouses deal with the community property once they have established domicile in the noncommunity property state may change the character of the property, and there remains a significant minority in which courts diverge, particularly in the context of divorce or creditor claims.[5]

When spouses relocate from a community property state to a separate property state, all property acquired with community funds, or property traceable to those funds, should retain its community property character notwithstanding the change in domicile.[6] As to personal property, the Restatement explains, "Considerations of fairness and convenience require that the spouses' marital property interests in a chattel or right embodied

---

[2] *Id.*

[3] *Id.*

[4] *See* A.M. Swarthout, Annotation, *Change of Domicile as Affecting Character of Property Previously Acquired as Separate or Community Property*, 14 A.L.R.3d 404 § 2[a] (originally published in 1967). *See also* BRETT R. TURNER, EQUITABLE DISTRIBUTION OF PROPERTY § 3:13 (Choice of Law) (2019).

[5] Mbatha v. Cutting, 356 Ga. App. 743, 848 S.E.2d 920 (2020).

[6] RESTATEMENT (SECOND) OF CONFLICT OF L. § 259.

in a document should not be affected by mere removal of the chattel or document to another state. Likewise, these interests are not affected by a change of domicile to another state by one or both the parties."[7] "The Interest, however, may be affected by dealings with the chattel or document in the second state."[8]

An American Law Report, originally published in 1967, observes that "Whatever may be the underlying theoretical considerations that support it, the proposition that a change of domicil by a husband a wife from a state in which the community property system obtains to a state in which it does not, or vice versa, has no effect on the character, as separate or community property, of property acquired prior to the removal or property into which such property can be traced, is almost universally accepted."[9]

To support this proposition, the American Law Report cites 39 cases dating back as far as 1826. The ALR further observes that:

> It should be noted that the precise facts as to the nature or location of the property actually involved, whether personalty or real estate in which personalty has been invested, and whether left in the state of original domicil on removal to another state or brought with the parties to the new domicil, and the circumstance whether the removal was from a "common-law" state into a "community property" state, or vice versa, are different in many of the cases cited, although they all hold or recognize that no change in the character of the property resulted from the change of domicil.

"The question of which jurisdiction's marital property regime should prevail after spouses have changed their domicile is a recurring one in conflict of laws analysis."[10] This area of the law is best understood in the

---

[7] *Id.* § 259 cmt. b. *But see* § 258, providing that "the interest of a spouse in a movable acquired by the other spouse during the marriage is determined by the local law of the state which, with respect to the particular issue, has the most significant relationship to the spouses and the movable under the principles stated in § 6." As will be shown, this "most significant relationship" test is probably the closest thing to a general rule that practitioners can rely on in this area.

[8] *Id.* § 259.

[9] *See* Swarthout, *supra* note 4.

[10] Est. of Charania v. Shulman, 608 F.3d 67, 71 (1st Cir. 2010).

author's opinion as a dichotomy, with one set of rules applying to moveable properties, and another set of rules applying to immovable properties.[11]

Courts generally classify assets into two broad categories for conflict of laws purposes: movables and immovables. The terms come from the civil law tradition, and they roughly map onto the common law distinction between personal property and real property. Movables are assets that can be transported or transferred, such as cash, securities, and household goods, while immovables are fixed in place, such as land and buildings. Within the movable/personal property category courts further distinguish between tangible items, like jewelry or automobiles, and intangible interests, such as stocks, bonds, or digital assets. This classification matters because generally, and as further described later, marital rights in movables are typically governed by the law of the marital domicile at the time of the acquisition of the property, while rights in immovables are typically governed by the law of the situs of the property.

MOVABLE PROPERTIES: THE TRADITIONAL RULE—CHARACTER FOLLOWS THE MARITAL DOMICILE AT ACQUISITION (PARTIAL MUTABILITY)

There are generally two competing theories governing how the choice-of-law question should be answered as to *movable* property of the marital unit: (1) the doctrine of mutability (the marital property regime of the jurisdiction in which the spouses were domiciled when the property was acquired governs questions of ownership), or (2) the doctrine of immutability (the marital property regime of the jurisdiction in which the spouses were domiciled on the date of their marriage governs all personal property that they acquire thereafter, regardless of where they are living when the property is

[11] This is also an area where terminology can get confusing, because the vocabulary comes from different legal traditions. In the civil law, property is classified as either movables (i.e., property that can be physically moved from place to place such as furniture, jewelry, cars, cash, securities (even though intangible, treated as movable because they can be transferred easily)) or immovables (i.e., property that is fixed in place and cannot be moved without fundamentally altering it, such as land, buildings, and fixtures attached to land). This dichotomy is dominant in civil law systems and has been frequently used in conflict of laws and choice-of-laws analyses applied in U.S. courts.

acquired or whether their domicile changes).[12] In the United States, courts have tended to favor the doctrine of mutability.[13] "The primary rationale supporting this approach is that the jurisdiction in which a couple was domiciled at the time of the acquisition of property has the most significant interest in both the spouses and the property."[14] However, "[i]n continental European countries, the doctrine of immutability is favored."[15]

Within the United States, this issue is relatively straightforward, as states generally apply consistent choice-of-law principles. Matters become far more complex when foreign jurisdictions are implicated, since many apply fundamentally different conflict-of-law rules in determining marital property rights.[16]

Jeffrey Schoenblum observes that "For nearly 200 years, the prevailing doctrine in the United States has been 'partial mutability.'" Schoenblum describes the doctrine of partial mutability as follows:

> Under this conflict-of-laws rule, the right of a spouse in a movable asset acquired during marriage is determined by the law of the state in which the spouses had their marital domicile at the time of the acquisition of the asset. Thus, if the spouses change their marital domicile during the marriage, it is entirely possible that different movable assets will be governed by different laws. This

---

12 *Id.*, citing J.G. COLLIER, CONFLICT OF LAWS 282 (3d ed. 2001).

13 *Charania,* 608 F.3d, citing United States v. ITT Consumer Fin. Corp., 816 F.2d 487, 490 (9th Cir.1987); Saul v. His Creditors, 5 Mart. (n.s.) 569 (La. 1827).

14 *Charania,* 608 F.3d at 72, citing RESTATEMENT (SECOND) OF CONFLICT OF L. § 258.

15 *Id.*, citing DICEY, MORRIS & COLLINS, THE CONFLICT OF LAWS 1295 (14th ed. 2006); Friedrich K. Juenger, *Marital Property and the Conflict of Laws,* 81 COLUM. L. REV. 1061, 1061–62 (1981). And further noting that champions of the immutability doctrine tout its ease of administration and the desirability of applying a single marital property regime to the entire inventory of a couple's personal property. *See, e.g.*, Ernest G. Lorenzen, *The French Rules of the Conflict of Laws,* 38 YALE L.J. 165, 177 (1928); J. Thomas Oldham, *What If the Beckhams Move to L.A. and Divorce?,* 42 FAM. L.Q. 263, 264–65 (2008).

16 *See* JEFFREY SCHOENBLUM, U.S. CONFLICT OF LAWS INVOLVING INTERNATIONAL ESTATE AND MARITAL PROPERTY: A CRTICIAL ANALYSIS OF *ESTATE OF CHARANIA V. SCHULMAN.* Noting that the *Charania* opinion is deeply flawed in how it dealt with the international conflict-of-laws issues.

conflict-of-laws rule is widely known as "partial mutability" because the law of the original marital domicile does not remain the governing law as to assets acquired after a change in marital domicile has taken place. In other words, there is "mutability." However, it is only "partial" because with respect to rights acquired at a particular marital domicile, they are not mutable and are not lost simply by moving to a new marital domicile that does not recognize those spousal rights.[17]

IMMOVABLE PROPERTIES: THE TRADITIONAL RULE—"LEX SITUS," WITH TRACING BETWEEN THE SPOUSES

The partial mutability doctrine applies to *movable* properties (i.e., tangible property), but the doctrine does not apply to immovable property that is personally owned (i.e., real estate). For immovable property, the "lex situs" rule provides that real estate is governed by the law of the jurisdiction where the property is physically located. M. Read Moore observes that "The effect of the 'lex situs' rule followed by U.S. states is that the characterization of real property acquired in a community property jurisdiction during marriage will depend on the source of the funds used to purchase the property."[18]

CASE LAW

Courts in noncommunity property states have frequently recognized that personal property acquired while the spouses were domiciled in a community property state retains its community property character, or at minimum that the spouses retain the same ownership interests in the property after the couple relocates to the noncommunity property jurisdiction. 14 A.L.R.3d 404 (1967), cited earlier, is the most comprehensive source the authors have found with respect to the existing cases on point. Many of

---

[17] SCHOENBLUM, *supra* note 16.

[18] Coming Soon to Your State, ACTEC 2020 Fall meeting, citing Harding v. Harding, 36 Cal. Rptr. 2d 184 (Cal. Ct. App. 1963); *In re* Pugh's Est., 139 P.2d 698 (Wash. 1932); *In re* Gulstine's Est., 6 P.2d 628 (Wash. 1932).

these decisions arise in the context of divorce, but characterization questions can also surface at death.

There is divergence in the case law across the United States as to exactly how these rules are applied. With respect to property characterization issues at divorce, many jurisdictions have adopted the "most significant relationship" rule espoused by the Restatement (Second) of Conflict of Laws § 258, which requires an examination of specific factors to determine which state's law should govern as to the particular issue. Yet, courts frequently continue to apply traditional rules, such as the law of the spouses' domicile at the time of acquisition for movable property and the law of the situs for real property, rather than engaging in a full "most significant relationship" analysis under Restatement (Second) of Conflict of Laws § 258.[19]

For instance, in *In re Marriage of Whelchel*,[20] an Iowa court relied on Texas community property law to determine rights in a brokerage account funded while the parties lived in Texas for purposes of a divorce proceeding.

The court's opinion in *Whelchel* deserves further consideration, as it provides a solid outline of how an appellate court would seek to resolve the doctrinal issues at play, and concisely summarizes the applicable choice-of-law principles and how a court would apply them in a divorce proceeding. The holding of *Whelchel* generally supports the notion that personal property retains its character after the couple changes their domicile, but a review of the opinion illustrates that the rule is not all that general. How the court arrived at its holding must be understood by any practitioner seeking to truly understand the characterization issues for their migratory clients.

In *Whelchel*, the central dispute was whether a brokerage account, originally funded while the spouses resided in Texas, and continuing to be maintained in Texas, despite their move to Iowa, should be treated under Texas community property law or Iowa equitable distribution principles when the couple divorced in Iowa. This presented the classic choice-of-law problem of which state's law should govern the characterization of personal property acquired during marriage when the marital domicile later changes. The court began by acknowledging a long-standing challenge in family law conflicts: The First Restatement of Conflicts of Laws (1934) provided a rigid rule that property rights in movables were governed by the law of the

---

[19] Oldham, *supra* note 15, at 263.

[20] *In re* Marriage of Whelchel, 476 N.W.2d 104 (Iowa App. 1991).

spouses' domicile at the time of acquisition. This offered predictability but lacked sensitivity to competing state interests.[21] The Second Restatement (1971) introduced a more flexible, policy-oriented "most significant relationship" test.[22]

> The Restatement (Second) of Conflicts drops the territorial location of vested rights approach in favor of applying the laws of the state with the most significant relationship to the parties or property or issue. Although principles espoused by the first Restatement, such as choosing the law of the state of domicile, situs, or acquisition, are incorporated in the second Restatement's approach, they are relegated to the status of factors instead of rules used in choosing the correct law. The second Restatement is much more flexible in that it guides a court to the choice of the correct law by means of "Choice-of-Law Principles" instead of hard and fast rules of choice.[23]
>
> As applied to the interests of a spouse in movables acquired by the other spouse during marriage, this approach refers a court to the local law of the state with the most significant relationship to the spouses and the movable, with the greatest weight being given to the law of the state of the spouses' domicile at the time of acquisition.[24]

The *Whelchel* court, noting that it had not squarely addressed this issue in divorce cases,[25] expressly adopted the approach contained in the Restatement (Second) Conflict of Laws § 258: The interest of a spouse in a movable acquired during marriage is determined by the law of the state with the most significant relationship to the spouses and the property.

The *Whelchel* court then considered the factors outlined in § 6 of the second Restatement. Section 6 of the Restatement provides:

---

[21] *Id.* at 109.

[22] *Id.*

[23] *Id.*

[24] *Id.*

[25] But had addressed the issue in other areas such as contracts and torts, suggesting a natural extension into family law. *Id.*

[T]he factors relevant to the choice of the applicable rule of law include

a. the needs of the interstate and international systems,
b. the relevant policies of the forum,
c. the relevant policies of other interested states and the relative interests of those states in the determination of the particular issue,
d. the protection of justified expectations,
e. the basic policies underlying the particular field of law,
f. certainty, predictability and uniformity of result, and
g. ease in the determination and application of the law to be applied.

The court also observed that further guiding the court's analysis of which state has the most significant relationship to the spouses and the brokerage account was the following from the Restatement (Second) of Conflict of Laws § 258(2):

> In the absence of an effective choice of law by the spouses, greater weight will usually be given to the state where the spouses were domiciled at the time the movable was acquired than to any other contact in determining the state of the applicable law.[26]

"Guided by these principles, together with the fact that the parties acquired this account shortly after being married in Texas, we find that Texas has the most significant relationship to the issue of characterizing the corpus of the account."[27]

Ironically, whether Iowa or Texas law applied was of no substantive consequence to the outcome of the division of the brokerage account in the divorce proceeding in *Whelchel*, because, as the court explained, and as was explored in Chapter 3, the two states' laws provided substantially similar rules for dividing property at divorce.

---

[26] *Id.*

[27] *Id.*, citing generally "Wallack v. Wallack, 211 Ga. 745, 88 S.E.2d 154 (1955); Succession of Popp, 146 La. 464, 83 So. 765 (1920); Succession of Packwood, 9 Rob. (La.) 438, 41 Am. Dec. 341 (1845); *but see In re* Estate of Crichton, 20 N.Y.2d 124, 228 N.E.2d 799, 281 N.Y.S.2d 811 (1967)."

> However, once the property was characterized, the trial court should have applied Iowa law in dividing the property. Under the circumstances of this case, the two states' laws are not in apparent conflict on the issue of property division. Once the property has been characterized as marital or community property, both states' laws provide for equitable distribution of the property. Furthermore, the Texas property division statute, Texas Family Code Annotated section 3.63 (Vernon Supp. 1990), was not pleaded or proved. We, therefore, must treat the Texas law as though it were identical to Iowa law. See Berghammer v. Smith, 185 N.W.2d 226, 230 (Iowa 1971).

By contrast, in *Mbatha v. Cutting*,[28] the Georgia Court of Appeals expressly rejected the Restatement's "most significant relationship" methodology when it was faced with the question of whether South Africa's community property regime or Georgia's equitable division system should apply to the divorce proceeding.

In *Mbatha*, a South African husband (Mbatha) and a New Yorker wife (Cutting) married in New York, then lived together in South Africa under South Africa's community property regime. When the relationship broke down, the pregnant wife relocated to the state of Georgia in the United States to live with her parents and later gave birth there. The husband filed first in Georgia (initially for separate maintenance, then for divorce), and the wife argued that South African marital property law should govern the division of assets in the Georgia divorce.

The trial court treated the marriage as a "New York marital contract," and applied New York's "center of gravity" methodology to conclude that South African law should govern property division and alimony. On interlocutory appeal, the Georgia Court of Appeals vacated and remanded. The court held that the trial court used the wrong conflicts framework. It rejected the importation of New York's "center of gravity" approach and (consistent with prior Georgia precedent) declined to adopt the Restatement (Second)'s "most significant relationship" test. Instead, it directed the trial court to apply traditional choice-of-law rules to classify and divide marital property, with real property to be governed by the law of the jurisdiction where the property is sitused and personal (movable) property to be governed by the law of the owner's domicile at the time the property is acquired.

---

[28] Mbatha v. Cutting, 356 Ga. App. 743, 848 S.E.2d 920 (2020).

Brett Turner's well-respected and frequently cited treatise, *Equitable Distribution of Property*, categorizes *Mbatha* within the broader national landscape. Turner identifies three general approaches to marital property conflicts: (1) the traditional rule (i.e., situs for real property; domicile-at-acquisition for personal property), (2) the "modern rule in civil litigation" (i.e., the Restatement's "most significant relationship test"), and (3) "consistent practice in modern property division cases," which is to apply the law of the forum (lex fori).[29,30] Although the traditional rule continues to control legal title questions, Turner emphasizes that legal title is largely irrelevant in divorce, and only one equitable distribution state (Georgia) still applies the traditional rule to division at divorce.[31]

"The consistent practice in modern property division cases is to classify and divide all property under the law of [the] forum."[32] Turner emphasizes that divorce courts typically rely on their in personam authority over the parties to reach property situated beyond the forum. While a divorce decree may not directly transfer title to real property outside the state, courts regularly order a spouse to convey such property, and this order is enforceable through contempt or similar remedies. In practice, this jurisdictional device allows courts to apply forum law to assets wherever located.

Turner further notes that this reality explains the near-universal application of lex fori in equitable distribution cases. "The number of cases expressly adopting [lex fori] is even larger if one includes decisions applying the most significant relationship test but summarily determining that the forum state usually has the most significant relationship to the case."[33] Therefore, at least in the divorce context, the choice-of-law analysis, to the extent it appears, is often little more than a formal prelude to applying forum law. "Courts in the U.S. almost always apply the law of the forum to matters concerning divorce, even including the division of real and personal property (or at least to dividing the value of such assets) upon divorce."[34]

---

[29] This "consistent practice" of applying the law of the forum can be seen in *Whelchel*.

[30] TURNER, EQUITABLE DISTRIBUTION OF PROPERTY § 3:13.

[31] *Id.*

[32] *Id.*

[33] *Id.*

[34] JEREMY D. MORLEY, U.S. CHOICE OF LAW ISSUES, INTERNATIONAL FAMILY LAW PRACTICE § 4:93.

It may be said, then, that the legal title of spouses in personal property (movables) is governed by the law of the marital domicile at the time the property is acquired, and that the legal title of spouses in real property (immovables) is governed by the law of the state where the real property is physically located. Further, when issues beyond legal title arise, the court may apply the law of the jurisdiction with the most significant relationship to the case, but in practice this generally results in application of the forum state's laws.

In the New Mexico Supreme Court case of *In re Clarke's Will*,[35] the court determined that New Mexico law, and not Texas law, would apply to resolve the question of whether the income earned on real estate purchased in New Mexico by an individual domiciled in Texas with his separate property was community property.

Under Texas law, income from a married individual's separate property is generally treated as community property, but under New Mexico law such income is not community property and remains the separate property of the spouse who received the earnings. The New Mexico Supreme Court interpreted the lex situs principle to mean that earnings generated by rental property in New Mexico (purchased with source funds from separate property in Texas) must be evaluated according to New Mexico law. Because New Mexico does not treat income from separate property as community property, the court determined that the income belonged to the deceased individual as separate property. The court in *Clarke's Will* essentially interpreted the lex situs rule as applying to income from real property, which more accurately has no real situs or physical location.

The opinion by the Court of Appeals for the Fifth Circuit in *Commissioner v. Skaggs* sheds light on the application of the lex situs rule in this context, noting that the question of whether property is real or personal is to be solved by the law of the place where it is actually located.[36]

In *Skaggs*, in a 2–1 decision, the court held that the marital rights of spouses in property depends upon the law of the place where the property is located, and that the law of the situs governs the character of the income on real property. In *Skaggs*, a husband domiciled in Texas owned income-producing property in California that he had purchased with his separate

---

[35] 285 P.2d 795 (N.M. 1955).

[36] 122 F.2d 721 (5th Cir. 1941).

property. The central property characterization issue hinged on whether the income generated by the property should be governed by the laws of the property's location, as per the lex situs rule, or if the domicile of the property owners should influence the tax treatment on the income on the property. The wife argued that the income from the property would have been deemed community property under the laws of Texas. However, the court, in finding that California law applied to the characterization of the income on the property (thereby treating such income as separate property), emphasized that income taxation should adhere to the laws of the property's location, rendering the domicile of the property owners irrelevant in determining how the income should be taxed. The *Skaggs* court, in coming to its conclusion, enunciated the interplay of these rules effectively:

> Marriage is a very personal matter, and its incidents are in general regulated by the law of the matrimonial domicile. But the Spanish and French laws touching community property, and those of California and Texas and other States derived from them, are held to be, in the vocabulary of the civilians, statutes real and not statutes personal; that is to say, they apply to things within a country's jurisdiction rather than to persons wherever they may be or go. Hammonds v. Commissioner, 10 Cir., 106 F.2d 420. It should follow that things, whether movable or immovable, actually situate[d] in a State and effectively within its power, should be governed by the law of that State. It is universally held that real or immovable property is exclusively subject to the law of the country or State in which it is situated, and no interference with it by the law of any other sovereignty is permitted. 11 Am. Jur., Conflict of Laws, § 30. And the question whether property is real or personal is to be solved by the law of the place where it is actually located. Id., Sec. 29. These rules apply to questions of the marital rights of spouses in property. 11 Am. Jur., Conflict of Laws, Sects. 50, 85; Id., Community Property, Secs. 10, 11. The Board in this case recognized that the California land was subject to California law only, and that the rents from it prior to accrual were a part of the land, but thought that after accrual the rents were mere choses in action having no actual situs and would take a fictional situs at the domicile of Skaggs for tax purposes, and thus fall under the Texas law and become the property of himself and wife. We think the reasoning too artificial and

> tenuous. The receipt of the rents, issues or profits of land constitutes its enjoyment. A deed or devise of the income from property gives a corresponding right in the property itself. Commissioner f. Terry, 5 Cir., 69 F.2d 969; Irwin v. Gavit, 268 U.S. 161, 45 S.Ct. 475, 69 L.Ed. 897. If the Texas community law can transfer to Skaggs' wife a half interest in the rents and profits of his land in California, it in effect gives her a half interest in the land for the period of the marriage. An immature crop, like unaccrued rent, is a part of the land; and it becomes personalty when gathered—just as rent past due does—no longer passing with the land as part of it; but we think in neither case would the law of another State be effective to change the ownership of the crop on its gathering, or of the rent on its becoming due. In Robinson's Succession, 23 La. Ann. 174, the marital community of a Louisiana couple sought to have the husband's separate estate account for cotton raised on his separately owned farm in Mississippi. It was held the cotton was separate property. In the Hammonds case, supra, a wife whose earnings were her own at her domicile in Oklahoma, received her for services an interest in an oil lease in Texas, which she converted into money and an oil payment. The oil lease was realty in Texas, and what came out of it, cash and oil, was held governed for federal tax purposes by the Texas community law and not by the law of her domicile. The rent on this California land was certainly the property of Skaggs at the moment it became due. We do not think the Texas law, being a statute real, operates to change the ownership instantly afterwards.

As the *Skaggs* case indicates, generally the issue of determining the character of income from real property will be determined under the lex situs rule. It is worth noting that courts in noncommunity property states have recognized the community property nature of funds used to buy real property in the noncommunity property state, often finding that the spouses own the property as tenants in common.[37] Nevertheless, courts in community property states have held that real property in a noncommunity

---

[37] M. Read Moore, Coming Soon to Your State (citing Rozan v. Rozan, 129 N.W.2d 694, 694 (N.D. 1964); Stone v. Sample, 62 So. 2d 307, 307 (Miss. 1953); Rev. Rul. 72-433, 1972-2 C.B. 531, 1972 IRB LEXIS 172).

property state is community property where the source of the funds for the purchase of the real estate came from community funds, in defiance of the lex situs rule.[38]

As these cases suggest, it is not easy to predict whether a certain court will determine the property characterization issue to be one relating to personal property or real property, or even whether the court will apply American choice-of-law rules consistently and coherently.[39]

Similar choice-of-law issues have arisen in the context of property owned as tenancy by the entireties (TBE) that has been taken to a state that does not recognize TBE as a form of ownership. For example, two cases involving the same family, the Luries, and their impending bankruptcy claim, were decided by two different courts with conflicting outcomes. In *Lurie v. Blackwell*, the Supreme Court of Wyoming held that the law of the state of acquisition applied to determine the character of a sculpture.[40] The Luries had purchased the sculpture as husband and wife in Missouri, a TBE state, while both spouses resided there. The couple later moved to Montana, which does not recognize tenancy by the entireties. Years after moving to Montana, the couple sent the sculpture to Wyoming for a dealer to sell it. A Missouri bankruptcy proceeding was pending, and, in 1995, a judgment was rendered.[41] As a consequence, the sculpture was seized, but the wife claimed that it was held as TBE property and thus was not subject to creditors. The bankruptcy trustee, however, argued that Montana does not recognize tenancy by the entireties, and thus the sculpture should be subject to seizure.[42] The Wyoming Supreme Court held that the trustee could not seize the sculpture because the Luries were married at the time they acquired the sculpture in Missouri, they acquired the sculpture in a

---

[38] *See* Tomaier v. Tomaier, 146 P.2d 905, 905 (Cal. 1944) holding that the rights of California spouses are protected when community funds are invested in land in another state.

[39] J. Thomas Oldham, *Conflict of Laws and Marital Property Rights*, 39 BAYLOR L. REV. 1255 (1987).

[40] 51 P.3d 846, 846 (Wy. 2002).

[41] *Id.* at 847.

[42] *Id.*

state that recognized tenancy by the entireties, and creditors could thus not seize the sculpture.[43]

In contrast, the Montana Supreme Court in the related case of *Lurie v. Sheriff of Gallatin County* took the opposite approach and determined that the law of the forum controlled the characterization of tangible personal property.[44] Similar to *Lurie v. Blackwell*, at issue in *Lurie v. Sheriff of Gallatin County* was the sculpture purchased by the couple when they resided in Missouri (a TBE state) and moved to Montana (a state that does not recognize TBE) when the couple changed their marital domicile to Montana.[45] The court held that the sculpture was no longer held as tenancy by the entireties because Montana does not recognize that form of property ownership, and as such, the sculpture was subject to the bankruptcy judgment.[46]

The *Lurie* cases help demonstrate an important notion at the heart of this choice-of-law issue: The characterization of property may vary depending on the jurisdiction in which the issue is litigated and the interests that jurisdiction seeks to protect. Courts may be more inclined to preserve a marital property regime not recognized in the forum jurisdiction when doing so safeguards spousal rights—such as a noncommunity property state recognizing community property brought into the jurisdiction to prevent a spouse from being disinherited or otherwise having her rights in the property reduced[47]—than when the recognition would frustrate legitimate third-party creditor claims, such as a non-TBE state refusing to recognize the TBE character of tangible personal property purchased as TBE in a TBE state and brought to the non-TBE state.[48]

The Restatement (Second) of Conflict of Laws § 234 confirms this reading of the rules. It provides that the forum court will generally attempt to decide questions relating to land acquired during the marriage in the same manner that the courts of the situs themselves would. Importantly, those

---

[43] *Id.* at 851.

[44] Lurie v. Sheriff of Gallatin Cnty., 999 P.2d 342, 345 (Mont. 2000).

[45] *Id.* at 344.

[46] *Id.* at 345 (finding that the sculpture was owned as joint tenancy or as tenancy in common property in Montana and that the sculpture was subject to execution on a validly issued writ).

[47] Quintana v. Ordono, 195 So. 2d 577 (Fla. Dist. Ct. App. 1967).

[48] Lurie v. Sheriff of Gallatin Cnty., 999 P.2d 342 (Mont. 2000).

courts do not always apply their own substantive law in determining the effect of marriage on the property. Rather, they often "trace" the spouses' marital property interests from the funds used to acquire the land, so that, as between the spouses, the land takes on the same character that the purchase money funds had in the couple's state of domicile at the time they used such funds to purchase the property in the other state. Thus, if land in a common law state is purchased with community funds and acquired while the spouses were domiciled in a community property state, if the forum court is a noncommunity property state, it will usually hold that the wife regains her same one-half interest in the land, notwithstanding the forum state's lack of recognition of community property.

However, the Restatement (Second) of Conflict of Laws § 234 notes that this "tracing" principle tends to give way where the third-party rights are involved. In those situations, such as disputes with creditors or transferees, courts of the situs usually apply their own local law. This distinction highlights the underlying policy motivations at play: Courts are more likely to preserve marital property rights when doing so protects spousal interests, but more likely to apply local law rigidly when creditor rights or marketability of title are implicated.

The law governing migratory spouses is best understood as a patchwork of partial mutability for movables, lex situs for immovables, and lex fori in practical application at divorce. Courts often frame their analysis in doctrinal terms, but the real drivers are policy interests: spousal protection in disinheritance and divorce contexts, and creditor protection or title marketability in disputes with third parties. The challenge for estate planners is to anticipate these permutations, recognizing that a couple's rights in property may shift not only with time and domicile but also with the forum and context in which their claims are adjudicated.

THE SIMPLE(ST) SOLUTION: AN EFFECTIVE CHOICE-OF-LAW AGREEMENT

The best way to avoid the application of the aforementioned confusing principles from a marital law standpoint is to have the couple enter into an effective marital property agreement or premarital agreement that contains an effective choice-of-law provision. The courts will generally respect a married couple's choice of law to govern the property they acquire while married unless another state demonstrates a more compelling interest in seeing its laws applied.[49] For example, and as mentioned earlier, where cases deal with the rights of third parties, such as a creditor or someone who receives assets from one spouse, considerations of fairness may necessitate applying the law of the forum state.

Similarly, in cases involving movable property, greater weight will generally be given to the state where the spouses were domiciled at the time the movable was acquired than to any other contact in determining the applicable state law.[50]

Restatement (Second) of Conflict of Laws § 187 reinforces the aforementioned proposition. It states that, in a contract, a court will typically honor the choice of law made by a married couple unless the chosen jurisdiction has no connection to the parties or the transaction, or if applying the chosen law contradicts a fundamental policy of a state that has a significantly stronger interest than the chosen state. In such cases, the state with the greater interest in the matter, which absent the parties' choice of law would have been the governing law, takes precedence.[51]

On certain occasions, Florida courts have declined to uphold prenuptial agreements from foreign jurisdictions where public policy concerns have existed.[52] For instance, in 1961, before surviving spouses in Florida were given the right to an elective share (and the ability to waive such rights), a Florida court declined to enforce a prenuptial agreement from Quebec that waived dower rights. The court determined that enforcing

---

[49] *See* Restatement (Second) of Conflict of L. § 258, "Only in a rare case will the spouses have agreed to have their marital property interests in each other's movables determined by the local law of a particular state. When they have reached such an agreement, the local law of the selected state should be applied unless the value of protecting the justified expectations of the spouses is outweighed in the particular case by the intensity of the interest of another state, which would usually be the state of the spouses' domicile at the time of the acquisition of the particular movable, in having its own rule applied. In the normal situation, where the spouses have not reached an agreement on an applicable law, protection of their justified expectations will have relatively little role to play in the choice of the applicable law."

[50] *Id.* § 234.

[51] *Id.* § 187.

[52] Read Moore, *supra* note 37, at 24.

such an agreement would contradict a strong public policy of Florida to have its laws apply to real property situated in the state.[53]

However, in 1995, a Florida court upheld a choice-of-law provision designating Puerto Rico law regarding property other than real property in Florida, and remanded the case for further consideration of whether the choice-of-law clause was valid regarding the Florida real property.[54]

These cases underscore the importance of having a choice-of-law provision that designates both where the agreement will be litigated and what state law will apply.

---

53 *Id.*, citing Kyle v. Kyle, 128 So. 2d 427 (Fla. App. 1961).

54 *Id.* citing Estate of Santos & Franzen v. Franzen, 520 S.E.2d 74 (N.C. App. 1999); Brown v. Gillespie, 955 S.W.2d 940 (Mo. App. 1997); Estate of Santos, 648 So. 2d 277 (Fla. App. 1995).

Chapter 7

Transmutations of Property

Once the practitioner determines which jurisdiction's law governs the marital property of the spouses, the next question is how the character of that property may change over time, or has changed over time. As discussed in Chapter 4, property acquired while the couple was residing in a community property state will generally remain community property even after the spouses move to a noncommunity property state unless the spouses take affirmative steps to change the character.[1] Similarly, merely moving into a community property state does not convert previously acquired separate property into community property.[2]

Many community property states have a statutory concept known as "quasi-community property." The term generally describes all personal property owned that was acquired while the couple was residing outside of a community property state that would have been community property if it had been acquired while the spouses were residents of a community property state.[3] When spouses use community funds to acquire real property

---

[1] In states that have adopted the Uniform Disposition of Community Property Rights at Death Act, this proposition is nearly certain.

[2] Katherine D. Black et al., *Community Property for Non-Community Property States,* 24 Quinnipiac Prob. L.J. 260, 279 (2011).

[3] *See, e.g.*, N.M. Stat. Ann. § 40-3-8; Wash. Rev. Code Ann. § 26.16.220.

in a noncommunity property state, the spouses' equal one-half ownership interests are ordinarily preserved in the newly acquired asset.[4]

The law provides several avenues through which spouses may alter these default classifications. Through transmutation, the spouses may affirmatively change the character of their property—converting community property to separate property or separate property to community property.[5] This is typically accomplished by a clearly written agreement and a clear expression of intent. A transmutation agreement involving real property and converting community property to separate property, or vice versa, must be recorded in the county where the real property is located to be effective against third parties.[6] Because the formalities, requirements, and legal effects of transmutation vary considerably from state to state, practitioners should consult with counsel licensed in the particular community property state whose law governs the property before advising clients on or preparing any transmutation agreement.

California provides the most comprehensive statutory treatment of transmutations. Under California Family Code §§ 850–853, the spouses may,

---

[4] Rozan v. Rozan, 317 P.2d 11 (Cal. 1957). In *Rozan* the California Supreme Court held in an en banc opinion that real property purchased in North Dakota with community funds earned while the spouses were domiciled in California constituted community property. "A determination of the domicile is essential, for marital interests in movables acquired during coverture are governed by the law of the domicile at the time of their acquisition." Schecter v. Superior Court, 49 Cal.2d 3, 314 P.2d 10; In re Estate of Bruggemeyer, 115 Cal.App. 525, 538, 2 P.2d 534; Justis v. Atchison, Topeka and Santa Fe Ry. Co., 12 Cal.App. 639, 644, 108 P. 328; Civil Code, s 164; see Rest., Conflict of Laws s 290; Stumberg, Conflict of Laws (2d ed) p. 313; Goodrich, Conflict of Laws (3rd ed.) p. 385. Moreover, the interests of the spouses in movables do not change even though the movables are taken into another state or are used to purchase land in another state. Tomaier v. Tomaier, 23 Cal.2d 754, 759, 146 P.2d 905; Depas v. Mayo, 11 Mo. 314, 319; see also Beard's Ex'r v. Basye, 46 Ky. 133, 146; Avery v. Avery, 12 Tex. 54; Rest., Conflict of Laws ss 290, 291; Stumberg, Conflict of Laws (2d ed.) p. 314; Goodrich, Conflict of Laws (3rd ed.) p. 378. Rozan v. Rozan, 317 P.2d 11, 12–13 (Cal. 1957).

[5] 37 AM. JUR. PROOF OF FACTS 2d 379 (Originally published in 1984); 15B AM. JUR. 2D *Community Property* § 67; 120 A.L.R. 264 (Originally published in 1939).

[6] *See, e.g.*, CAL. FAM. CODE § 852(b) ("[A] transmutation of real property is not effective as to third parties without notice thereof unless recorded.").

by express written agreement or transfer, with or without consideration, transmute community property to separate property of either spouse, transmute separate property of either spouse to community property, or transmute separate property of one spouse to separate property of the other spouse.[7] To be valid in California, a transmutation must be in writing, made with the express intent to change the property's character, and be signed by both spouses.[8] This writing requirement was codified to curb litigation over oral and implied transmutations that had often produced conflicting claims after death or at divorce.[9]

Although California's statute serves as the model, all community property jurisdictions acknowledge the spouses' power to modify the character of property by mutual agreement or valid conveyance.[10] For example, in

---

[7] CAL. FAM. CODE § 850.

[8] *Id.* § 852(a). *Est. of MacDonald,* 794 P.2d 911 (Cal. 1990), *as modified* (Sep. 6, 1990). Cases prior to *MacDonald* permitted oral or conduct-based transmutations where intent could be inferred from use or title, but the modern California rule recognizes only those effected by clear, written declarations of intent.

[9] *See, e.g., In re* Raphael's Estate, 91 Cal. App. 2d 931, 206 P.2d 391 (1st Dist. 1949), where proof of an oral agreement to transmute the husband's inheritance into community property was found to exist, and was "corroborated by documentary evidence including income tax returns filed by or on behalf of Raymond Theodore Raphael, and his said wife, Bertha Rado Raphael." *Id.* at 938. Under Cal. Fam. Code § 852, a joint tax returned signed by both spouses lacks probative value; there must be a written express declaration of intent to transmute the character of the property. *See* William W. Bassett, *Transmuting the Classification of Separate Property, in* CALIFORNIA COMMUNITY PROPERTY LAW § 4:16 (2024–2025 ed.)

[10] Katherine D. Black et al., *Community Property for Non-Community Property States,* 24 QUINNIPIAC PROB. L.J. 260 (2011), noting that "[a]ll community property states permit couples to 'opt out' of the community property system either by antenuptial contract or by contract at any time during the marriage. Ariz. Rev. Stat. Ann. § 25-203 (2010); Cal. Fam. Code §§ 1620, 3580 (West 2004); Idaho Code Ann. §§ 32-906, 32-916 (2006); La. Civ. Code Ann. art. 2329 (2010); Nev. Rev. Stat. § 123.070 (2008); N.M. Stat. Ann. § 40-2-2 (LexisNexis 2010); Tex. Fam. Code Ann. §§ 4.102, 4.103 (West 2006); Wash. Rev. Code Ann. §§ 26.16.050, 26.16.120 (West 2005); Wis. Stat. Ann. §§ 766.58, 766.585, 766.587, 766.589 (West 2009). The courts and the IRS have generally respected contracts which partition community property for income tax purposes. See Clay v. United States, 161 F.2d 607, 611 (5th Cir. 1947); O'Bryan v. Comm'r, 148 F.2d 456, 458 (9th Cir. 1945); Helvering

Texas and Louisiana, spouses may alter their matrimonial regime by written contract, converting separate property into community property or vice versa.[11] Each system balances marital autonomy with evidentiary safeguards designed to prevent unintended or coerced changes in ownership.

While transmutations typically require an affirmative act reflecting intent, the commingling of assets often produces the same practical result through inattention. Commingling occurs when separate and community funds or assets are so intermixed that their origins cannot be reliably traced. In community property states, a separate property asset may be transformed into community property if it is commingled with other joint assets such that it cannot be reasonably identified as separate property. Similarly, in noncommunity property states, nonmarital assets may be transformed into marital assets if commingled into joint accounts to the extent that the nonmarital assets become untraceable.[12] If the commingling has only been for a short time and the separate property remains identifiable, the character of the separate property is not changed to community in the absence of other evidence that the commingled property was intended to be a gift to the community.[13]

In the following subsections, we walk through the transmutation laws in three of the community property states to provide a good overview for practitioners. For the practitioner in a noncommunity property state, it is important to be aware of transmutation, but a practitioner in a state whose community property regime applies to a particular asset should be consulted to address transmutation under the laws of that community property state.

---

v. Hickman, 70 F.2d 985, 986 (9th Cir. 1934); Rev. Rul. 73- 390, 1973-2 C.B. 12. A couple cannot, however, seek to assign community income already earned, but not received, as of the date of the contract. An attempt to do so returns to the question originally posed in Lucas v. Earl, 281 U.S. 111 (1930)."

[11] Tex. Fam. Code Ann. §§ 4.102, 4.103 (West 2006); La. Civ. Code Ann. art. 2329 (2010).

[12] Dravis v. Dravis, 170 So. 3d 849 (Fla. Dist. Ct. App. 2015). In *Dravis*, cash gifts that a wife's mother gave to the wife during marriage lost their nonmarital character when the gifts were commingled with marital money in a savings account. *Id.*

[13] 37 Am. Jur. Proof of Facts 2d 379 (Originally published in 1984), citing Myrland v. Myrland (1973) 19 Ariz. App. 498, 508 P.2d 757.

Although transmutation formalities vary across jurisdictions, practitioners advising clients in any community property state are well advised to follow California's statutory template: Use a written instrument signed by both spouses that contains an express declaration of intent to change the character of the property, avoid reliance on oral agreements or informal conduct, and record any instrument affecting real property. This belt-and-suspenders approach minimizes the risk of subsequent challenge and ensures that the transmutation will be respected by courts, creditors, and the IRS alike. Any such instrument should be prepared by or reviewed by a California community property practitioner.

ARIZONA

Arizona law generally determines whether property is community or separate property based on its status at the time of acquisition.[14] Any real or personal property acquired by a spouse during a marriage, except by gift or inheritance, is presumed to be community property while property acquired before marriage or after service of a petition for dissolution of marriage, as well as by gift or inheritance, is separate property.[15] Once the status of a property has been set, it does not change absent an agreement, gift, or commingling.[16] Arizona has also recognized that when community funds are used to increase the value of separate property, the improved

---

[14] Guthrie v. Guthrie, 242 P.2d 549, 426 (Ariz. 1952) (citing Lawson v. Ridgeway, 233 P.2d 459 (Ariz. 1951)); Bender v. Bender, 597 P.2d 993, 995 (Ariz. 1979); Schock v. Schock, 461 P.2d 697, 700 (Ariz. Ct. App. 1969) (citing Flynn v. Allender, 256 P.2d 560 (Ariz. 1953)).

[15] Ariz. Rev. Stat. Ann. § 25-211 (2025); Ariz. Rev. Sat. Ann. § 25-213 (also specifies property acquired before marriage and any "increase, rents, issues and profits of that property" is separate property); *In re* Marriage of Cupp, 730 P.2d 870, 873 (Ariz. Ct. App. 1986); *Bender,* 597 P.2d at 995–96; *In re* Sims' Est., 475 P.2d 505, 506 (Ariz. Ct. App. 1970).

[16] *Cupp,* 730 P.2d at 873 (citing Nation Wide Resources v. Massabni, 694 P.2d 290, 295 (Ariz. Ct. App. 1984) (citing Myrland v. Myrland, 508 P.2d 757 (Ariz. Ct. App. 1973))); *see, e.g., Guthrie,* 242 P.2d at 550 (discussing commingling); *Bender,* 597 P.2d at 996 (discussing gift by conveyance); *Sims,* 475 P.2d at (507) (discussing agreement by written conveyance); *Schock,* 461 P.2d at 700 (discussing oral agreement).

value that resulted from those funds is treated as community property, at least for purposes of reimbursement.[17]

Arizona Statutes

Arizona statutes do not specify how transmutation occurs, but do specify when property is or is not community property at the time of its acquisition.[18] Arizona does have a quasi-community property statute that provides that property purchased outside the state by an Arizona married couple will be treated as community property if, when it was acquired, it would have been considered community property if acquired within the state.[19] Courts, as opposed to statutes, have shaped the way Arizona treats transmutation.

Transmutation by Gift, Agreement, or Conveyance

Spouses in Arizona have the ability to transmute their property by agreement or conveyance, but are best advised to use a written instrument and have proof of intent to do so. Married couples in Arizona are free to decide what the status of their property is, and can convert such status of their property through the conveyance of their separate or community property to one another.[20] The transmutation of separate property into community property by conveyance requires a written instrument and contemporaneous conduct by the transferring spouse that demonstrates an intent to transfer the property interest to the receiving spouse.[21] However, when separate funds are used to buy a property that is subsequently titled as jointly owned by both spouses, the law presumes an intent to have gifted the property to

17 "[P]rofits, which result from a combination of separate property and community labor, must be apportioned accordingly." Honnas v. Honnas, 648 P.2d 1045, 1046 (Ariz. 1982) (quoting Cockrill v. Cockrill, 601 P.2d 1334, 1337 (Ariz. 1979); *Tester*, 597 P.2d at 196.

18 Ariz. Rev. Stat. Ann. §§ 25-211, 213, 318 (West 2025).

19 *Id.* § 318.

20 *Bender*, 597 P.2d at 996; *Sims*, 475 P.2d at 507.

21 *Bender*, 597 P.2d at 996; *Sims*, 475 P.2d at 507; *Schock*, 461 P.2d at 700.

the noncontributing spouse, and therefore transmute it into community property.[22]

This presumption can be overcome, however, if clear and convincing evidence demonstrates that a gift was not intended.[23] In *Cupp*, a wife was awarded a lump-sum payment for a worker compensation claim that she then used to purchase a car, furniture, and two parcels of real property titled in both spouses' names in order to avoid probate.[24] The court held that the property was the wife's sole and separate property.[25] The court reasoned that the wife's desire to avoid probate defeated the presumption that the jointly titled property was a gift.[26] Additionally, the lump sum covered lost wages extending past the end of the marriage and therefore the property was bought with separate funds.[27] In *Battiste*, a wife acquired a home in joint tenancy with her husband using her separate funds.[28] The costs of owning the home were all paid for by community funds; however the wife testified that she intended to keep the property as her separate property.[29] The court held that the husband's interest in the property was intended to have been a gift.[30] The court reasoned that the evidence presented did not overcome the presumption of intent to gift the property to the noncontributing spouse.[31]

If a spouse seeks to assert that transmutation occurred to real property by conveyance or agreement, they should do so with a written instrument

---

22 *Cupp*, 730 P.2d at 873; *Battiste*, 662 P.2d at 147 (citing Blaine v. Blaine, 159 P.2d 786 (Ariz. 1945)).

23 *Id.*

24 *Cupp*, 730 P.2d at 871.

25 *Id.* at 873.

26 *Id.* at 872.

27 *Id.*

28 *Battiste*, 662 P.2d at 147.

29 *Id.*

30 *Id.*, providing "[w]here separate funds of one spouse have been used to purchase real property and title has been taken in joint tenancy, a presumption arises that a gift to the noncontributing spouse was intended" (citing Sloane v. Sloane, 132 Ariz. 414, 646 P.2d 299 (App.1982)). Batesole v. Batesole, 24 Ariz. App. 83, 535 P.2d 1314 (1975).

31 *Id.*

and proof of corresponding intent to do so.[32] In *Schock*, a husband owned a ranch before his marriage to his wife and continued to own it throughout the marriage until his death, using community property to operate it and putting its earnings in a community bank account.[33] The court held that the ranch was not transmuted into community property, despite the wife's assertion that an oral agreement had been made to that effect.[34] The probate court relied on the fact that most other community property jurisdictions did not recognize an oral agreement being sufficient proof that transmutation occurred, while the ones that did tended to require a high burden of proof, and therefore found that this was insufficient to prove a transmutation.[35] The court reasoned that the use of commingled community funds to maintain the property, the fact that the property had been the family home for 19 years, and statements by the husband that he had provided for his wife in a will were insufficient proof that such an oral agreement had actually been made.[36]

In *Sims*, a widow in probate court argued that a property had been transmuted into community property when it was taken from the couple via a court judgment but then reacquired using community funds.[37] The court held that satisfying a judgment through a settlement that was paid for by community funds did not transmute the property.[38] The court reasoned that there was no evidence of either a conveyance by the husband or a corresponding intent to convert the character of the property.[39]

In *Holden*, a wife who solely owned property before her marriage executed a quitclaim deed to her husband after they married.[40] The court

32 *Schock*, 461 P.2d at 700; *Sims*, 475 P.2d at 507.

33 *Schock*, 461 P.2d at 698.

34 *Id.* at 701.

35 *Id.* (Neither commingling of community and separate funds and use thereof for taxes and improvements nor the fact that the dwelling had served as family home for 19 years accomplished change of status of such property from decedent's separate property to community property, and therefore, property could be set apart for use of widow for only a limited purpose.)

36 *Id.* at 701.

37 *Sims*, 475 P.2d at 506.

38 *Id.* at 507.

39 *Id.*

40 Ariz. Cen. Credit Union v. Holden, 432 P.2d 276, 279 (Ariz. Ct. App. 1967).

held that this was evidence that could support a claim of transmutation.[41] The court reasoned that because the property was acquired by the husband during the marriage, it became community property, and the quitclaim deed was evidence of an intent by the wife to transmute her separate property.[42]

Married couples residing in Arizona may be able to assert a transmutation to personal property without the need for a written conveyance.[43] In *Sellers*, a husband and wife married each owning their own vehicle prior to the marriage.[44] During a trial concerning insurance coverage of the husband's vehicle, the husband testified that he considered the vehicle as belonging to both him and his wife, and both spouses testified that community funds were used to repair it.[45] The court held that there was sufficient proof to conclude that the husband had intended that the vehicle be transmuted to community property.[46] The court's reasoning was based upon this testimony and the use of community funds toward the repairs.[47]

Spouses living in Arizona should typically be able to have community property ownership by transmuting their separate property into community property by gift, agreement, or conveyance. A gift to community property generally will be presumed when separate funds are used to purchase a jointly titled property, but with exceptions. Spouses should make sure their intent to gift the property is clearly documented, perhaps by other legal documents that could indicate a varied intention; otherwise their claim that property belongs to the community could be challenged.[48] Additionally, as the previously stated rules indicate, an intent to gift real property should also be accompanied by a written conveyance to ensure it is less likely to

---

[41] *Id.* at 279.

[42] *Id.*

[43] Sellers v. Allstate Ins. Co., 555 P.2d 1113, 1116 (Ariz. 1976) *disavowed on other grounds by* Darner Motor Sales, Inc. v. Universal Underwriters Ins. Co., 682 P.2d 388, 397 (Ariz. 1984).

[44] *Id.* at 1114.

[45] *Id.* at 1116.

[46] *Id.*

[47] *Id.*

[48] *See, e.g., Bender*, 597 P.2d at 996 (holding disclaimer deed stating wife had "no interest" in a property meant no transmutation of the separate property used to purchase the land had occurred).

face being challenged. Concerning property such as vehicles, a spouse may still be able to assert a transmutation to community property without a written title but should still have proof of intent to do so.

Transmutation by Commingling

Spouses seeking to transmute their separate property into community property in Arizona can do so by commingling it to the point that it is no longer identifiable. The touchstone of the commingling analysis in Arizona law is the ability to identify and distinguish the community property from separate property, or lack thereof.[49] Commingling occurs when separate and community property become mixed together in some way, either physically or, most commonly, in the case of funds in an account.[50] However, real property cannot be transmuted by commingling because of its "unique" nature.[51] The mere act of commingling, by itself, does not work a transmutation to separate property.[52] Neither does the mere fact that separate funds were used toward community interests[53] or that community funds were used to improve a separate real property.[54] In order for separate property to transmute into community property by commingling, it must be so intertwined that its identity is lost, and it can no longer be distinguished from the community property.[55]

For example, one spouse may enter into a marriage with separate funds. After getting married, both spouses open a joint bank account, and the separate funds are deposited in the joint bank account. Over time, frequent deposits and withdrawals of funds cause the overall balance of the account to fluctuate. Eventually, it becomes impossible for the spouse to determine how much of their original separate funds are left in the account and what amount of the funds in the account came from community property sources. This could come about from cash deposits or withdrawals

---

[49] *Guthrie*, 242 P.2d at 550–51; *Cupp*, 730 P.2d at 873.

[50] *See generally Guthrie*, 242 P.2d at 550 (concerning funds); *Cupp*, 730 P.2d at 873 (funds and real property).

[51] Potthoff v. Potthoff, 627 P.2d 708, 713 (Ariz. Ct. App. 1981).

[52] *Guthrie*, 242 P.2d at 551; *Cupp*, 730 P.2d at 873; *Potthoff*, 627 P.2d at 713.

[53] *Battiste*, 662 P.2d at 148.

[54] *Potthoff*, 627 P.2d at 715.

[55] *Guthrie*, 242 P.2d at 551; *Cupp*, 730 P.2d at 873; *Potthoff*, 627 P.2d at 713.

where the spouses did not document what the purpose of the withdrawals were or what the sources of the deposited funds were. At this point, a court would likely consider the original separate funds to have transmuted into community property through commingling because the funds can no longer be traced to their separate property origins.

If property that was separate can still be distinguished by a court from the community property, then it will not be considered to have undergone a transmutation.[56] In *Whitt,* a husband had a pre-marriage account he opened with his mother, which he kept after and during the marriage to his wife.[57] The husband continued to deposit earnings made during the marriage, which were community property, into the account and withdrew funds to use toward community interest while his mother also continued to deposit unspecified amounts.[58] The court held that funds deposited by the mother during the marriage belonged to her and could not be transmuted and that the pre-marriage account balance was not transmuted simply by commingling of the community funds deposited by the husband.[59] The court reasoned that the mother's property was never separate or community property because she was not a member of the marriage, and therefore she retained an interest in all of the money she contributed to the account.[60] As between the husband and wife, because some of the account balance was traceable at the time of marriage, it could be identified, and therefore it was not transmuted by subsequent commingling.[61] Again in *Cupp,* where the wife had a lump-sum award used to buy real property, the court held that because she had bought real property within a short time after being awarded the sum, it was easily identifiable as separate property.[62]

Arizona married couples can transmute their separate property into community property by commingling, but this process can be challenged if the separate property is still identifiable. First, couples should be aware that this concept will likely not apply to real property. When it comes to money,

---

[56] Whitt v. Meza, 545 P.3d 931, 936 (Ariz. Ct. App. 2024); *Cupp,* 730 P.2d at 873.

[57] *Whitt,* 545 P.3d at 935.

[58] *Id.*

[59] *Id.*

[60] *Id.*

[61] *Id.*

[62] *Cupp,* 730 P.2d at 873.

spouses should not rely on simply combining funds into a single account as a means to transmute premarital or other separate assets into community property. If the funds are considerable, it would likely take a long time for funds earned during the marriage to render the separate funds unidentifiable. Additionally, if one spouse is earning income that is considered separate under Arizona law, such as rent from separate property,[63] and it is traceable, depositing it in an account with community funds likely will not be enough to render it transmuted by commingling.

Transmutation by Community Effort

While Arizona does not recognize the transmutation of an entire separate property into community property as a result of contribution from community property, there could be a community property interest in the increased value resulting from that community effort. Profits from a separate property can be community property if they resulted from community contribution or from the individual efforts of the spouse.[64] Additionally, when community funds are advanced to improve separate property, there is a community property interest equal to the enhanced value of the property or its increased profits that resulted from the community fund contributions.[65] However, neither the contribution of community efforts nor community funds will transmute the underlying real property into community property.[66]

The language of the courts could be used to argue that there is community property in the value of otherwise separate property when community funds or individual efforts contribute to that value. However, no amount of contribution will likely transmute an entire property. Therefore, spouses should not rely on contribution as a means of asserting that property is transmuted. Other methods such as written agreement and conveyance should be relied on to ensure the property is treated as community property, but a spouse may have a community property interest in the increased value that stems from community effort.

---

[63] Ariz. Rev. Stat. Ann. § 25-213(A).

[64] *Honnas*, 648 P.2d at 1046; Cockrill v. Cockrill, 601 P.2d 1334, 1336 (Ariz. 1979); *Potthoff*, 627 P.2d at 715.

[65] *Honnas*, 648 P.2d at 1046; Kingsbery v. Kingsbery, 379 P.2d 893, 898 (Ariz. 1963).

[66] *Honnas*, 649 P.2d at 1048; *Cockrill*, 601 P.2d at 1338; *Potthoff*, 627 P.2d at 715.

CALIFORNIA

As noted earlier, California's community property scheme is statutorily driven. Property that a married person acquires while they are domiciled in California is community property, even if it is located outside the state.[67] When community property is placed in a trust, that trust is revocable as to that property, and it gives the spouses the power to modify the rights and interests in that property only with joinder or consent of both spouses, then it remains community property.[68] Property from before a marriage remains separate property during the marriage as does any property received by gift, bequest, or inheritance, and any rents and profits from that separate property.[69] California also recognizes transmutation by means of agreement or transfer.[70]

Guam adopted the California community property statutory scheme almost word for word in 1980, but does not have the benefit of the significant amount of California case law that has developed since then.[71]

Transmutation by Agreement

California statutes state that married persons may by agreement *or* transfer, with or without consideration, transmute community property to separate property of either spouse, transmute separate property of either spouse to community property, or transmute separate property of one spouse to separate property of the other spouse.[72] A transmutation of either "real or personal property is not valid unless made in writing by an express declaration that is made, joined in, consented to, or accepted by the spouse whose interest in the property is adversely affected."[73] This does not apply to gifts between the spouses such as "clothing, wearing apparel, jewelry, or other tangible articles of a personal nature . . . used solely . . . by the spouse

---

67 Cal. Fam. Code § 760 (West 2025); Rozan v. Rozan, 317 P.2d 11 (Cal. 1957).

68 Cal. Fam. Code § 761 (West 2025).

69 *Id.* § 770.

70 *Id.* § 850.

71 Sablan v. Sablan, Supreme Court of Guam, June 15, 2017 (Case No: CVA15-001).

72 Cal. Fam. Code § 850(a)–(c) (West 2025) (emphasis added).

73 *Id.* § 852(a).

to whom the gift is made and that is not substantial in value taking into account the circumstances of the marriage."[74]

"An 'express declaration' is an instrument that 'contains language which expressly states that the characterization or ownership of the property is being changed.'"[75] In *Brace*, a couple had used community funds to purchase real property that was titled as a joint tenancy.[76] The California Supreme Court held that the titling of a deed in joint tenancy did not transmute the community property into separate property.[77] This was because the deed did not "'contain[] language which expressly states that the characterization or ownership of the property is being changed' between the spouses."[78] The deed "expressly" saying that the title was in joint tenancy was insufficient to transmute the property.[79] The California Supreme Court distinguished this result from the conclusion of the California Court of Appeal in *Bibb*.[80]

In *Bibb*, a widow in probate court argued that a "grant deed"[81] conveying real property from her husband to himself and her as joint tenants transmuted the property into community property.[82] The court agreed that this was a valid transmutation.[83] The deed adequately demonstrated a "clear and unambiguous" intent to transfer the interest in the property because it contained on its face language, such as the word "grant," that was understood to mean transferring of an interest.[84] In the same case, the court held

---

[74] *Id.* § 852(c).

[75] *In re Brace*, 470 P.3d 15, 34 (Cal. 2020) (quoting *Estate of MacDonald*, 794 P.2d 911, 913 (Cal. 1990)). *Brace* held that the "form of title" presumption in California Evidence Code § 662 does not apply when it conflicts with the community property presumption in California Family Code § 760.

[76] *Id.* at 19.

[77] *Id.* at 35.

[78] *Id.* (alterations in original) (citing *MacDonald*, 794 P.2d at 911).

[79] *Id.*

[80] *Id.*

[81] A Grant Deed is a written instrument used to convey an interest in real property from a grantor to a grantee, carrying with it the implied covenants that the grantor has not previously conveyed the estate to another and that the estate is free from undisclosed encumbrances created by the grantor.

[82] *Estate of Bibb*, 104 Cal. Rptr. 2d 415 (Cal. Ct. App. 2001).

[83] *Id.* at 420.

[84] *Id.*

that DMV records that contained no signature and no language transferring an interest in a vehicle from the husband to the wife did not effectuate a proper transmutation of the vehicle.[85] The *Bibb* court also relied on *MacDonald* for guidance in its determination on whether a valid transmutation had occurred:

> Since the *MacDonald* court held that the consent paragraphs would have been adequate for a valid transmutation had they said, "I *give* to the account holder any interest I have . . .," and since "grant" is the historically operative word for transferring interests in real property, there is no doubt that [the husband's] use of the word "grant" to convey the real property into joint tenancy satisfied the express declaration requirement of section 852, subdivision (a).[86]

The court's decision was based around the wording of the document, which made clear to the party signing the document that there was to be a change in their interest over the community property.

In *MacDonald*, a consent agreement in an IRA beneficiary designation was held to be insufficient to effectuate a transmutation because it contained "no language . . . expressly stating that decedent was effecting a change in the character or ownership of her interest."[87] The court clarified, however, that a document does not need to contain the words "transmutation" or "community property" or terms of that nature to be a proper "express declaration," even though those terms could help.[88] Instead, it would have been sufficient for the consent agreement to have added the sentence referenced earlier in the *Bibb* case: "I give to the account holder any interest I have in the funds deposited in this account."[89] The *MacDonald* court's reasoning was guided by changes in the statutes and a corresponding commission report that asserted that transmutation by oral agreement was too easily achieved, encouraged litigation, and even incentivized perjury by the spouses.[90]

---

85 *Id.*

86 *Id.* (citing *MacDonald*, 794 P.2d 911) (italics in original).

87 *Estate of MacDonald*, 794 P.2d 911, 918–19 (Cal. 1990).

88 *Id.*

89 *Id.*

90 *Id.* at 268–69.

In *Lund*, an appeals court held that a transmutation agreement that stated that all of a husband's separate property was converted into community property was a valid transmutation agreement.[91] The court reasoned that the "motivations" behind the document were irrelevant; it only mattered that the document "contain[ed] the requisite express, unequivocal declarations of a present transmutation."[92] The instrument at issue in this case stated the following:

> All of the property, real and personal, held in the name of Husband having its origin in his separate property no matter how received and/or earned, is hereby converted to community property of Husband and Wife, and shall thereafter be the community property of the parties for estate planning hereto, each having a present, existing, and equal interest therein.[93]

Transmutation by Commingling

When separate and community property are blended and commingled in a manner that makes them indistinguishable from one another, and there is insufficient evidence that traces the separate property so that it can be identified, the entirety of the commingled property is community property.[94] When commingled funds, indistinguishable and therefore transmuted in the manner mentioned earlier, are used to purchase an asset, then the asset is also community property under the presumption that property acquired during the marriage is community property.[95] This presumption can only be overcome by adequate recordkeeping of the community and separate property that will allow for a direct tracing and identification of the funds used.[96]

---

[91] *In re* Marriage of Lund, 94 Cal. Rptr. 3d 84, 94 (Cal. Ct. App. 2009).

[92] *Id.* at 95.

[93] *Id.* at 94.

[94] *See, e.g., Estate of Murphy*, 544 P.2d 956, 964 (Cal. 1976); See v. See, 415 P.2d 776, 784 (Cal. 1966); Grolemund v. Cafferata, 111 P.2 641, 683 (Cal. 1941); Mason v. Mason, 186b Cal. App. 2d 209, 213 (Cal. App. 2d Dist. 1960); Pope v. Pope, 227 P.2d 867, 876 (Cal. App. 1st Dist. 1951).

[95] *See, e.g., Murphy*, 544 P.2d at 964; *See*, 415 P.2d at 784.

[96] *Murphy*, 544 P.2d at 964; *see* 415 P.2d at 784. While banks and brokerage firms probably keep records of deposits and values perpetually at present, previous

In *Murphy*, certain assets were acquired during a marriage at times when sufficient community funds existed to acquire such assets.[97] The husband did have separate property income earned during the marriage; however these earnings could not be directly traced to any of the assets in dispute.[98] The court held that the availability of separate funds was not sufficient to overcome the presumption of community property, and therefore affirmed a trial court ruling that the disputed property belonged to the community.[99] The court reasoned that either "direct tracing to a separate property source" or proof that all community property was exhausted at the time of purchase was required to prove the property was separate.[100] Additionally, the court held that the separate funds the husband earned, which were deposited into accounts with community funds, and for which there were no records that could distinguish the separate funds from the community funds, were commingled and properly treated as community property.

Walking Through a Tricky Example of Moving with Community Property

Assume spouses domiciled in California acquire Florida real estate during marriage using community funds and take title as "husband and wife," which under Florida law creates a presumption of tenancy by the entirety. From Florida's perspective, the property is treated as tenancy by the entirety (TBE) for purposes of creditor rights and survivorship. However, under California law, property acquired during marriage while domiciled in California is presumed to be community property regardless of title, and that presumption is not rebutted absent a valid written transmutation.

The Florida Uniform Disposition of Community Property Rights at Death Act introduces additional complexity to this example. Section 732.225 provides that when community property is reinvested in

---

technology has caused bank and financial facilities to not have any or at least to not have full information about previous account balances and values because this data was simply not maintained or in many cases was lost when software systems were changed.

97 *Murphy*, 544 P.2d at 963.

98 *Id.*

99 *Id.*

100 *Id.*

Florida real property held as tenants by the entirety, there is a conclusive presumption that the spouses agree to terminate the community property attribute of the reinvested property.[101] Although this provision appears to only apply in a death-time statutory scheme and has apparently not yet been interpreted by a published Florida or California court decision, its language suggests that, at least for probate and survivorship purposes, Florida courts would treat such property as tenancy by the entirety rather than retained community property. Whether this statutory presumption effects a binding inter vivos transmutation for all purposes appears to also remain unsettled.

So, when the married couple, domiciled in California, takes title to the Florida real estate "as husband and wife," is the property considered community property or TBE property? The best answer is: It depends on the forum and purpose of the characterization. A California court applying California marital property principles is likely to begin (and often end) with the presumption that the property is community property because it was acquired with community property funds during marriage while the spouses were domiciled in California, and the mere fact that Florida title is held as TBE would not, standing alone, appear to establish a valid transmutation under California law.[102] By contrast, a Florida probate court addressing death-time succession, creditor rights, or determining incidents of survivorship is more likely to treat the property as TBE, particularly in light of the conclusive

---

[101] It appears that § 732.225 is attempting to get rid of the problem that can arise when TBE, Florida homestead, and community property are coexisting. Florida's homestead laws are directly from the Florida constitution, and generally do not allow a principal residence to be left to someone other than a spouse (or minor children in certain cases). This is directly opposite of the general community property regime, which allows a decedent spouse to leave one-half of the community property at will. Section 732.225 likely deems that property that is considered homestead or TBE (jointly held property with rights of survivorship between spouses) cannot also be considered community property.

[102] If land in a common law state is purchased with community funds while spouses are domiciled in a community property state, a noncommunity property forum will usually restore the wife's one-half interest notwithstanding the forum's lack of community property law. *See, e.g.*, Tomaier v. Tomaier, 23 Cal. 2d 754 (1944); Rozan v. Rozan, 317 P.2d 11 (Cal. 1957). However, this rule is hard to fit within Florida's UDCPRDA, which conclusively presumes that community property reinvested into Florida TBE property severs the community property attributes of the property.

presumption in Florida Statutes § 732.225 when community property is reinvested in Florida real property held as TBE or homestead.

Ultimately, these authorities point to a meaningful and likely irreconcilable divergence between California and Florida courts when addressing real property acquired in the name of a married couple in Florida by spouses domiciled in California. A California court, applying its community property regime in a divorce or death proceeding, would likely focus on the marital domicile, the source of acquisition of funds, and the absence of a valid statutory transmutation and conclude that out-of-state real property purchased with community funds may retain its community character notwithstanding joint or entirety style title. A Florida probate court, by contrast, would likely reach the opposite result, relying on Florida Statute § 732.225 to conclude that the reinvestment of community property funds into Florida real estate titled as tenancy by the entirety effects a termination of the community property attribute and converts the asset into TBE property. In practice, this conflict is unlikely to create difficulty when the spouses have become Florida domiciliary, and the property qualifies for homestead treatment, as Florida law would govern both situs and succession. However, where characterization arises in a California forum, a California court is unlikely to accord significant weight to Florida's statutory severance rule and would instead apply its own community property principles, even if doing so leads to a result inconsistent with how the property would be viewed under Florida law.

LOUISIANA

As the only true civil law state in United States, Louisiana's community property jurisprudence is dictated by statute and will generally require a court order to transmute out of community property status.[103] Louisiana law recognizes three types of "matrimonial regimes," which are "system[s] of principals and rules governing the ownership and management of the property of married persons as between themselves and toward third

---

[103] La. Civ. Code art. 2329 "Spouses may enter into a matrimonial agreement that modifies or terminates a matrimonial regime during marriage only upon joint petition and a finding by the court that this serves their best interests and that they understand the governing principles and rules. They may, however, subject themselves to the legal regime by a matrimonial agreement at any time without court approval."

person."[104] These three regimes are (1) the legal regime, also known as the community of acquets and gains;[105] (2) the contractual regime, which arises from contractual agreements between spouses;[106] and (3) the partly legal and partly contractual regime.[107]

In other words, the default rule (i.e., the legal regime) is community property, but spouses can contract out of this via marital property agreement (i.e., a contractual regime), and such an agreement may contract the spouses out of the community property system as to certain property already owned by the spouses, but not as to future acquired property during the marriage (i.e., a partly legal and partly contractual regime).

As to transmutation, Louisiana law draws a distinction between converting the character of property already in possession of the spouses to separate property and attempting to classify all future property that may be acquired by the spouses as separate property. Spouses may voluntarily partition currently held community property, in whole or in part, without court approval, and this property will become the separate property of the spouses.[108] However, spouses can only enter into a matrimonial agreement that terminates or modifies the community property marital regime upon a joint petition and approval from a court finding it to be in their best interests.[109] When the interest of one spouse in community property is threatened by the other spouse's mismanagement or disordered affairs, the spouse may obtain a decree declaring the property separate.[110]

Transmutation by Transfer

Spouses may transfer their separate property to the other spouse, "with the stipulation that it shall be part of the community," in order to transform it

---

[104] *See id.* arts. 2325, 2326.

[105] *Id.* art. 2327; i.e., the regime that applies by default rule.

[106] *Id.* art. 2328.

[107] *Id.* art. 2326.

[108] *Id.* arts. 2336, 2341; Fargerson v. Fargerson, 593 So. 2d 454, 456 (La. Ct. App. 1992); Gachez v. Gachez, 451 So. 2d 608, 612 (La. Ct. App. 1984); Adams v. Adams, 2008 WL 607633, at 2 (La. Ct. App. 2008).

[109] La. Civ. Code art. 2329; Heyl v. Heyl, 445 So. 2d 88, 92 (La. Ct. App. 1984).

[110] La. Civ. Code. Ann. art. 2374 (West 2025); Pan American Import Co., Inc. v. Buck, 452 So. 2d 1167, 1168–69 (La. 1984).

into community property.[111] In *Faget*, a husband and wife entered into an agreement that transferred the separate assets of a family home and its furnishings into community property.[112] The assets had been made separate by a prior marriage contract, and the agreement at issue stated an intention by the parties that the residence and its furnishings be treated as a community asset again.[113] The court held that the agreement was enforceable as a valid transfer and partition of property, not a termination or modification of the matrimonial regime requiring court approval.[114] The court reasoned that the agreement only purported to transfer one single asset in a single transaction and did not govern assets acquired in the future.[115] Further, the court reasoned that the transfer conformed to article 2343.1 as a valid transfer, which was properly authenticated, and to article 2336, which allowed for spouses to partition property.[116]

The partitioning of property in Louisiana is similar to that of other community property states in that it is essentially a transmutation by agreement. The spouses may, at any time, voluntarily divide the community property into separate property under article 2336 or transfer their separate property, supported by a stipulation of the intent to do so, into community property under article 2343.1.

Is a Transmutation Ever "Voidable" or "Void"?

Third-party creditors do have standing to attack the validity of an interspousal transmutation that would adversely affect their rights of collection.[117] The California Supreme Court has held that the community property presumption applies to third-party disputes outside of the dissolution of marriage context.[118]

---

111 LA. CIV. CODE art. 2343.1; Faget v. Faget, 53 So. 3d 414, 419 (La. 2010).

112 *Id.* at 515.

113 *Id.*

114 *Id.* at 419.

115 *Id.*

116 *Id.* at 420.

117 J. Thomas Oldham, *Management of the Community Estate During an Intact Marriage*, 56 L. & CONTEMP. PROBS. 99 (Spring 1993).

118 *In re Brace*, 470 P.3d 15 (Cal. 2020).

If both spouses do not join in the transaction, it is "voidable" in most community property states, and "void" in others.[119] The distinction is significant here; if the transaction is "void" then a third party may seek to rescind or invalidate the agreement.[120] Voidable transactions, on the other hand, may only be challenged by the nonconsenting spouse.[121]

In California, a community property transaction lacking one spouse's signature is voidable, not void.[122] This means that the non-transferring spouse can later approve the transfer, and it will be considered to have occurred at the time it was transferred, as if the spouse had approved the transfer when or before it occurred. Therefore, it may only be challenged by the nonconsenting spouse, but not by third-party creditors, unless the transfer is also a voidable transfer under California's Uniform Voidable Transactions Act.[123]

Nevada's rule is substantially similar, but the case law is more convoluted. The Nevada Statute provides that neither spouse may devise or bequeath more than one-half of the community property,[124] and neither spouse may sell, convey, or encumber the community real property unless both join in the execution of the deed or other instrument by which the real property is sold, conveyed, or encumbered, and the deed or other instrument must be acknowledged by both.[125]

"The judicial interpretation of the statute in Nevada is that one spouse's conveyance of community property is merely voidable 'at the instance of the nonsigning spouse.'"[126]

---

[119] Case law in Idaho and New Mexico indicates that such transactions are void in those places. *See* Hannah v. Tennant, 589 P.2d 1035 (N.M. 1979) *cf.* Tew v. Man Waring, 480 P.2d 896 (Idaho 1971). (Failure of one spouse to sign may make the transaction void, but this rule is not followed when both spouses perform their part of the bargain.)

[120] Oldham, *supra* note 117.

[121] *Id.*

[122] *See* Trimble v. Trimble, 26 P.2d 477 (Cal. 1933).

[123] Thus, if a couple transmutes from community property to separate property with an actual intent to hinder, delay, or defraud creditors, the transmutation can be set aside.

[124] Nevada Stat. § 123.230(1).

[125] *Id.* § 123.230(3).

[126] *See* Richard W. Mollerup, *Improvements to Real Property During Marriage: It's Time for Idaho to Make a Decision*, 28 Idaho L. Rev. 1021 (1992), citing *In re* Lemons &

Although the Nevada Supreme Court has not directly commented on the issue, the *In re Lemons* court noted that: "While some community property states have decided that such statutes render noncomplying transactions absolutely void, this court believes, based on the decisions that have interpreted NRS 123.230(3), that the Nevada Supreme Court would follow those jurisdictions which hold that these noncomplying transactions are merely voidable, and then only at the instance of the non-signing spouse. The IRS and other tax authorities will therefore have to treat the transaction as if it was not voidable as long as the non-signing spouse does eventually approve it."

There may be some limited circumstances, particularly in the context of real property transactions, where the transaction is void, and not voidable, under both California and Nevada law. In *Dynan v. Gallinatti,* the court held that a husband's attempt to mortgage household furnishings, a joint management transaction in California, is void.[127] There, the husband borrowed money and gave the lender a chattel mortgage on the household furnishings; he forged the wife's signatures on the documents.

Similarly, the Nevada Supreme Court in *Neumann v. McMillan* upheld a trial court ruling that a nonsigning spouse could void a deed of trust affecting community realty where the deed of trust was signed only by the other spouse.[128] There, the Nevada Supreme Court determined that the real property in question, although nominally held by a married couple as joint tenants, was actually held as community property. Thus, the court found that because the note and deed of trust at issue had been executed by the husband without the wife's knowledge, the conveyance was void as against the wife.

The *Neumann* opinion itself is short and does not use the words "void ab initio" or "per se void." Instead, it describes the wife as having to bring an action to void the deed of trust. This suggests that the deed of trust signed by only one spouse was not treated as automatically void against the world, but rather as voidable at the election of the nonconsenting spouse.

Associates, 69 B.R. 360, 364 (Bankr. D. Nev. 1987); *see also In re* Crystal Palace Gambling Hall, 36 B.R. 947, 950 (Bankr. 9th Cir. 1984) (where the bankruptcy appellate panel based its holding on language in the Nevada Supreme Court decision of *Neumann v. McMillan,* 97 Nev. 340, 629 P.2d 1214 (1981), from which the court found an implicit duty on the non-signing spouse to "act without delay in asserting [his or her rights under NRS 123.230(3)]" 36 B.R. at 952).

[127] 197 P.2d 391 (Cal. Ct. App. 1948).

[128] 629 P.2d 1214 (Nev. 1981).

The *Crystal Palace* opinion confirms this reading of the *Neumann* decision. There, the United States Bankruptcy Appellate Panel of the Ninth Circuit of Appeal has confirmed this reading of the Neuman decision:

> [The Neumann decision] implicitly recognized a duty on the part of the wife to act without delay in asserting her rights when it noted as relevant the fact that the wife "seasonably filed the action to void the encumbrance."[129] Moreover, the doctrine of laches as a general rule is well established in Nevada. We thus conclude that the Nevada Supreme Court has already recognized that § 123.230(3) is subject to the nonsigning spouse's obligation seasonably to assert her rights. The court's finding that Nettie did not seasonably assert her rights in this case is fully supported by the record and will not be disturbed on appeal.

It is worth noting that the Nevada courts frequently cite to California law with respect to this issue.

Revenue Ruling 77-359: The Service Blesses a Transmutation of Separate Property into Community Property for Federal Tax Purposes

Revenue Ruling 77-359 squarely addresses the federal tax consequences of a Washington transmutation agreement that provided that all presently owned and subsequently acquired real and personal property would be community property of the spouses.

The taxpayers in the ruling were a Washington couple, each of whom owned separate property and expected to acquire additional separate property in the future. In 1975, the couple entered into the written transmutation agreement transmuting all then-owned or thereafter acquired property to be community property, in what was referred to as a "universal" transmutation "agreement." The Service framed the specific question as whether such an agreement "changes the status of presently owned separate property and subsequently acquired separate property of one spouse to community property under the laws of the State of Washington."[130]

---

[129] Citing *Neumann* 629 P.2d, at 1215.

[130] Rev. Rul. 77-359, 1977-2 C.B. 24.

To answer that question, the ruling first analyzes the Washington law and cites *Volz v. Zang,*[131] in which the Washington Supreme Court upheld a written agreement providing that "each parcel of land wherever situated, both presently owned or thereafter to be acquired, should be deemed community property," and held that such a contract operated to convert separate real property into community property.

The Service also noted that under Washington law, the status of real property could not be changed by mere oral agreement of the spouses, and that a written agreement was required, citing *Leroux v. Knoll.*[132]

The Service then held that:

> Accordingly, where a husband and wife residing in the State of Washington agree in writing that all presently owned property and all property to be acquired thereafter, both real and personal, will be community property, such agreement changes the status of presently owned separate property and subsequently acquired separate property to community property.
>
> Further, if such an agreement is entered into orally, it changes the status of presently owned separate personal property and subsequently acquired separate personal property to community property. However, the status of separate real property located in the State of Washington can be changed to community property only by a proper written agreement.[133]

Revenue Ruling 77-359 seems to follow the plain language of § 1014(b)(6). Washington considered property transmuted pursuant to an effective agreement to be community property, and thus it should be considered as such for purposes of § 1014(b)(6), which refers to property that is community property under the "community property law of any State."[134]

Revenue Ruling 77-359 concludes with a caveat:

> To the extent that the agreement affects the income from separate property and not the separate property itself, the Service will not permit the spouses to split that income for Federal income

---

[131] Volz v. Zang, 113 Wash. 378, 194. P. 409 (1920).

[132] Leroux v. Knoll, 28 Wash. 2d 964 (1974).

[133] Rev. Rul. 77-359, 1977-2 C.B. 24 (IRS RRU 1977).

[134] *See* Jeremy T. Ware, *Section 1014(b)(6) and the Boundaries of Community Property*, 5 Nev. L.J. 704, 711 (2005).

> tax purposes where they file separate income tax returns, citing *Harmon.*[135]

In other words, the ruling preserves the *Lucas v. Earl* style assignment of income limitation for "income-only" arrangements that do not alter ownership and where the spouses are not filing jointly. In the post-1948 world of the optional joint return, that caveat is largely a reminder of first principles: Spouses who file separately still may not split one spouse's earnings or separate property income by private agreement, but spouses who file jointly can in practice achieve the same rate effects through the joint return regardless of how state law attributes the income.

Jonathan Blattmachr has noted that the Service's view appears to be that *Harmon* applies only to income that becomes community property by agreement, whether in an opt-in or opt-out community system, where the property that generates the income remains the separate property of one of the spouses and where the spouses are not filing jointly.[136] In other words, the stated concern is confined to a relatively limited fact pattern. In most cases, the spouses will file jointly and make use of the community property characterization through the basis adjustments on the first death.

Finally, Revenue Ruling 77-359 addresses the gift tax consequences of a transmutation, which further underscores that the Service views them as a real shift in property rights. It states that:

> Whether the agreement affects only the income from separate property or the property itself, the Federal gift tax is applicable to the conversion of separate property into community property. Under section 2511 of the Internal Revenue Code of 1954, a single gift will take place with respect to the conversion of the separately owned properties and the value of the single gift will be the net difference between the value of the husband's (or the wife's) separate property before its conversion into community property and the

---

[135] Rev. Rul. 77-359, 1977-2 C.B. 24 (1977).

[136] Brandon J. Cintula, Jonathan G. Blattmachr & Abigail E. O'Connor, *Alaska Community Property: Gateway to a Powerful Estate Planning Tool, Peak Trust Company,* January 31, 2024. But this rule is even hard to wrestle with. Jeremy Ware notes that this part of the ruling appears to fly in the face of basic community property law. "For instance, Idaho Code § 32-906(1) states that income from separate property is community property (and thus could be split). The issue seems unresolved by the Service." *Ware, supra* note 134, at n. 55.

value of the husband's (or the wife's) interest in the community property resulting from the conversion. Compare Rev. Rul. 69-505, 1969-2 C.B. 179. Additional gifts will occur with respect to separate properties acquired in future years that will be converted into community property by reason of the 1975 agreement between the spouses. The value of the additional gifts will be determined in the manner indicated herein with respect to the presently-owned separate properties.

Sample Transmutation Agreement

***Important Notice:** The following sample transmutation agreement is provided solely as an illustrative example for educational purposes. It is not intended to serve as a template for use in any particular state or transaction. Community property laws vary significantly from state to state, and the requirements for a valid transmutation agreement differ among jurisdictions. Practitioners should consult with counsel licensed in and familiar with the specific community property state whose laws will govern the agreement before using this sample to create, review, or finalize any agreement regarding the character of marital property.*

With those caveats in mind, a sample transmutation agreement is provided here:

TRANSMUTATION AGREEMENT

THIS AGREEMENT is made effective as of [date of agreement], by and between [name of spouse 1] and [name of spouse 2], Husband and Wife.

RECITALS

WHEREAS, the parties to this agreement were married on [date of marriage], and since that time have been, and are now, Husband and Wife;

WHEREAS, since the date of their marriage, the parties to this agreement have acquired property, both real and personal, within [name of state(s)], all of which is now being held by the parties as community property under the laws of [name of state(s)].

WHEREAS, the parties to this agreement desire to separate and divide the property acquired by them since their marriage, to terminate its community property status, and to hold such property as tenants in common, each having an undivided one-half interest in such property.

NOW, THEREFORE, in consideration of the matters described above, and of the mutual benefits and obligations set forth in this agreement, the parties agree as follows:

1. Conveyance of Property. On or before [date of conveyance], they will convey all of their real and personal property held as community property to themselves as tenants in common, each to hold an undivided one-half interest in all such property.
2. Other Documents. The parties agree to execute and deliver any and all documents and instruments necessary to effectuate the described transmutation and to convey title to the parties as tenants in common, each holding an undivided one-half interest in such property.
3. Governing Law. This agreement shall be governed by, construed, and enforced in accordance with the laws of [name of state].

IN WITNESS WHEREOF, the parties have executed this Transmutation Agreement at [place of execution] the day and year first set forth above.

____

[name of spouse 1]

____

[name of spouse 2]

[acknowledgments]

Chapter 8

Federal Taxation of Community Property

Since the inception of the federal income tax and creation of the Internal Revenue Service in 1861 and 1862, respectively, Congress has been plagued with the issue of how to resolve the inherent inequities in the taxation of community property and noncommunity property. These issues became particularly apparent in the era following the passage of the Sixteenth Amendment, which rid the Constitution of the "apportionment" requirement.[1] Following the passage of the Sixteenth Amendment in 1913, Congress reintroduced the federal income tax in the Revenue Act of 1913, under which each spouse had to file a separate income tax return and could not redirect income as between them, causing many spouses to be in high tax brackets, while the person they were married to was in a very low tax bracket.[2]

The confusion was therefore centered around the issue of whether individuals, particularly spouses, should have the ability to "assign" or "split" income. The community property system simply did not comport with the assignment of income doctrine. *Lucas v. Earl* (1930) is one of the most

---

[1] The Sixteenth Amendment provides that "Congress shall have the power to lay and collect taxes on incomes . . . without regard to any census or enumeration."

[2] Congress has on many occasions addressed the issue of how to resolve the inherent inequities in the taxation of community property couples and noncommunity property couples, but they still exist.

famous U.S. Supreme Court tax cases, and provides that a taxpayer cannot avoid taxation on income by assigning it in advance of receipt.[3] The assignment of income doctrine provides that "fruit" (i.e., earnings) is attributable to the "tree" from which it grew. The assignment of income doctrine and a community property system that vests in each spouse one-half of the community income as it accrues could not theoretically coexist.[4]

In *Lucas v. Earl*, the U.S. Supreme Court confronted an early and influential effort to "split" earned income through a contract signed by a married couple. Nearly 20 years before the Revenue Act of 1948 and the invention of the optional joint return for married couples, Mr. Earl, a California attorney, attempted to share his earned income with his wife. The couple signed an agreement providing that any property that either of them currently owned or would thereafter acquire "in any way, either by earnings (including salaries, fees, etc.), or any rights by contract or otherwise, during the existing of our marriage, . . . and all the proceeds, issues, and profits of any and all such property"[5] would be owned by them as joint tenants with right of survivorship.

Mr. Earl argued that this agreement caused one-half of his salary and fees to vest in his wife the moment the income was earned. The Supreme Court rejected the argument, holding that the Revenue Act taxed compensation for personal services to the person who earned it and that taxpayers cannot avoid that result through "anticipatory arrangements and contracts," however skillfully drafted, that attribute the "fruits" to a different "tree."[6]

---

3 Lucas v. Earl, 281 U.S. 111, 111 (1930).

4 *See Harmon*, 323 U.S. at 46. "Under Lucas v. Earl an assignment of income to be earned or to accrue in the future, even though authorized by state law and irrevocable in character, is ineffective to render the income immune from taxation as that of the assignor. On the other hand, in those states which, by inheritance of Spanish law, have always had a legal community property system, which vests in each spouse one half of the community income as it accrues, each is entitled to return one half of the income as the basis of federal income tax." *Id.*

5 Lucas v. Earl, 281 U.S. 111, 113–14, 50 S. Ct. 241, 241, 74 L. Ed. 731 (1930).

6 "There is no doubt that the statute could tax salaries to those who earned them and provide that the tax could not be escaped by anticipatory arrangements and contracts however skillfully devised to prevent the salary when paid from vesting even for a second in the man who earned it. That seems to us the import of the statute before us, and we think that no distinction can be taken according to the

The Supreme Court held that the IRS could tax the attorney's entire salary despite the joint tenancy agreement.[7]

The astute practitioner would at this point ask, "But was one-half of the income not already the wife's by virtue of California's community property principles?" Important to understanding the outcome in *Lucas v. Earl* is the fact that the Supreme Court had recently held in the 1926 case of *U.S. v. Robbins*[8] that California's laws, "as construed by her own courts, gave the wife a mere expectancy and that the property rights of the husband during the life of the community were so complete that he was in fact the owner."[9]

However, just eight months after *Lucas v. Earl*, the U.S. Supreme Court held that while individuals could not change the incidence of initial taxation by contract, states could. In *Poe v. Seaborn*,[10] Seaborn and his wife were residents of the state of Washington, and it was undisputed that all of the property of the marital couple was community property and that neither owned any separate property or had any separate income. Mr. Seaborn earned a salary, interest on bank deposits and on bonds, dividends, and profits on sales of real property. He and his wife each reported one-half of the income and claimed one-half of the deductions in computing their respective net incomes. The IRS argued that all of the income should have been reported on the husband's return and assessed additional tax against him. In other words, the IRS argued that the spouses should not be able to "split" their income, even pursuant to Washington's community property laws. Mr. Seaborn paid under protest and sought a claim for refund. Upon rejection of the claim for refund, he brought suit.

The court held for Mr. Seaborn, and then distinguished *Poe* from *Earl* because in *Earl* the wife had only a mere expectancy because Mr. Earl's earned income was still his income under state law, and the private contract between the parties did not change that result. But in *Poe*, where the titling of the property was pursuant to a valid community property statute, it was

---

motives leading to the arrangement by which the fruits are attributed to a different tree from that on which they grew." Lucas v. Earl, 281 U.S. 111, 114–15 (1930).

7 *Id.* at 115.

8 269 U.S. 315, 46 S. Ct. 148, 70 L. Ed. 285.

9 Poe v. Seaborn, 282 U.S. 101, 116 (1930).

10 *Id.*

as if half of the husband's income was the wife's by law. The earnings were technically never the property of the husband, but that of the community.[11]

California thereafter amended its community property law to conform with the state of Washington's, as it was now blessed by the Supreme Court, and a flurry of other states, including Michigan, Nebraska, Oklahoma, Oregon, and Pennsylvania, adopted community property statutes between 1939 and 1947 in order to achieve community property status.[12]

> Before other states could similarly adopt community property statutes, Congress responded with the Revenue Act of 1948, which stated, in pertinent part, "[e]equalization is provided for the tax burden of married couples in common-law and community property states." . . . In less than a year after the adoption of the Revenue Act of 1948, Michigan, Nebraska, Oklahoma, and Oregon repealed their community property statutes. Pennsylvania may have, as well,

---

[11] "In the Earl Case a husband and wife contracted that any property they had or might thereafter acquire in any way, either by earnings (including salaries, fees, etc.), or any rights by contract or otherwise, 'shall be treated and considered, and hereby is declared to be received, held, taken, and owned by us as joint tenants. * * *' We held that assuming the validity of the contract under local law, it still remained true that the husband's professional fees, earned in years subsequent to the date of the contract, were his individual income, 'derived from salaries, wages, or compensation for personal service,' under section 210, 211, 212(a) and 213 of the Revenue Act of 1918 (40 Stat. 1062-1065). The very assignment in that case was bottomed on the fact that the earnings would be the husband's property, else there would have been nothing on which if could operate. That case presents quite a different question from this, because here, by law, the earnings are never the property of the husband, but that of the community." *Seaborn*, 282 U.S. at 117.

[12] *See* Jennifer E. Sturiale, *The Passage of Community Property Laws, 1939–1947: Was "More Than Money" Involved?*, 11 MICH. J. GENDER & L. 213 (2005) (observing that "[i]n response to the disparate treatment of taxpayers that resulted from *Earl* and *Seaborn*, a flurry of states adopted community property statutes between 1939 and 1947—Michigan, Nebraska, Oklahoma, Oregon, and Pennsylvania. Eight states—Arizona, California, Idaho, Louisiana, Nevada, New Mexico, Texas, and Washington—already had community property laws in place"). *Id.* at 215–16 (citations omitted).

had the Pennsylvania Supreme Court not already found its state's community property laws unconstitutional.[13]

A deeper dive into the legislative history behind the Revenue Act of 1948 provides clarity on why Congress believed the optional joint return was the best solution. The legislative history further sheds light on the pertinent questions before practitioners seeking to ultimately answer the question of whether a community property trust will be respected for purposes of obtaining the double step-up in basis under § 1014(b)(6).

CONGRESSIONAL HISTORY

By the late 1940s, lawmakers had a very specific diagnosis: The federal income tax treated otherwise identical married couples differently depending on whether they lived in a community property or a common law state.[14] Congress's 1948 reforms are best understood as a coordinated attempt to take the tax consequences of marriage out of the accident of state marital property law and place them on a nationally even footing.[15] The touchstone for the death time piece of the act is the 100 percent basis step-up for community property at the first spouse's death.[16] The operative text deems the survivor's one-half of community property to have been "acquired from" the decedent for § 1014(a) purposes, so long as at least half of the community is includible in the decedent's gross estate.[17] The Ninth Circuit later captured Congress's aim in crisp terms: § 1014(b)(6) was designed to equalize the incidence of taxation between community property and common law states, not to confer a bonus on the common law states.[18] That equalization method mattered due to the difference in circumstances at death in a common law versus a community property state. In the 1940s, regardless of which state a couple found themselves in, there was a high likelihood that

---

[13] *Id.*

[14] Jeremy T. Ware, *Section 1014(b)(6) and the Boundaries of Community Property*, 5 Nev. L.J. 704, 706 (2005).

[15] *Id.*

[16] I.R.C. § 1014(b)(6).

[17] *Id.*

[18] Ware, *supra* note 13, at 705 (2005) (discussing Willging v. United States).

most if not all of the marital assets were held solely by the husband.[19] The results, however, were far different depending on whether that couple was situated in a community property state or a separate property state. In the community property state, there was a step-up in basis on only that spouse's one-half interest in the community, meaning the surviving spouse would be left with an asset that was only partially stepped up.[20] However, in the separate property state, the husband would have had a 100 percent ownership stake in the property, meaning the entire piece of property would have been stepped up at his death.[21]

The mechanism Congress chose works because federal tax law lets state law be the divining rod on property interests. The Tax Court's formulation is straightforward: State law defines the parties' property interests, and then federal law applies the tax consequences to those interests.[22] Section 1014(b)(6) was drafted to fit that architecture; it asks only whether the asset is "community property under the community property laws of any State or any foreign country," and whether at least half of the community is includible.[23] Read this way, the 1948 solution is both minimalistic and powerful. It leaves ownership to the states but nationalizes the federal income tax treatment at death so that similarly situated couples do not face different basis outcomes simply because they married across state lines.

The equalization rationale underlying § 1014(b)(6) also illuminates how to resolve hard-edged cases. Because the provision looks to the property's character under applicable state law at the moment of death, rather than its characterization during life, the order of operations is (1) determine character under state law, and (2) if the property is community and at least half the community is includible, apply a full basis adjustment.[24] Ware's survey collects the leading applications of that sequence. For example, when title documents point one way but authoritative state law evidence establishes community character, the IRS has honored the state law characterization for § 1014(b)(6).[25] By the same token, if spouses trans-

---

19 *Id.*

20 *Id.*

21 *Id.*

22 *Id.* at 706.

23 *Id.*

24 *Id.*

25 *Id.* at 708 (discussing Rev. Rul. 87-98).

mute community assets into true common law form before death (tenancy in common), then the federal deeming rule has nothing to operate on, because the prerequisite "community property" element is gone.[26]

This state law approach explains why transmutation methods are outcome determinative. Courts and the Service have recognized that commingling can (under many state laws) convert separate property into community property, and those conversions have been respected for federal transfer tax purposes.[27] The same goes for universal community agreements. Where state law treats an agreement as effecting a valid transmutation, the IRS has indicated that the resulting assets are community property within the meaning of § 1014(b)(6), notwithstanding contrary inferences from title.[28] These are not loopholes granted after the 1948 structure; instead, they are predictable products of a federal design that intentionally piggybacks on the state property laws to accomplish national tax equality at death.

Finally, returning to the legislative purpose sharpens why § 1014(b)(6) belongs in any account of the 1948 Revenue Act's community property settlement. Without it, the move to nationwide income splitting during life would still have left a death time disparity. With it, Congress locked the death time treatment to the same equal treatment for married couples that would animate the broader 1948 reforms, converting what had been a geographic advantage to a national rule keyed to marital status, not state property laws.

Congress did not stumble into income splitting; it asked the Treasury for a neutral map of the problem and the options, and then argued obsessively about what "equal" should mean for families, singles, and the states. The Treasury's staff study opens by saying it makes no policy recommendations; its goal is to give facts and analyses to guide Congress on the treatment of family income.[29] It identifies three discrimination seams in the then-current law: by residence (community versus separate), by the nature of the income (earned versus investment), and among investors based on access to family

---

[26] Since § 1014(b)(6) does not create community property for federal tax purposes, it merely assigns a basis consequence to property that qualifies as community property under applicable state law at the decedent's death. Where that predicate classification is absent, the provision has no application.

[27] Ware, *supra* note 13, at 708–09.

[28] *Id.* at 709–12.

[29] Revenue Revisions, 1947–48: Hearings Before the H. Comm. on Ways and Means, 80th Cong., 1st Sess. pt. 2, at 844 (1947).

splitting devices like trusts and partnerships.[30] The numbers attached to those seams were not small; Treasury estimated 1.4 million couples were getting some savings annually from one or another splitting method, with the dollar advantage rising sharply at higher incomes.[31]

Treasury's Options

From there, the study lays out four options that Congress left unresolved for more than a quarter century.[32] These were (1) mandatory joint returns, (2) a management and control rule for community income, (3) a new dual rate schedule to strip the profit out of a separate filing, and, finally, (4) nationwide income splitting.[33] The first option would make division of income irrelevant by pooling everything on one return, which the study described as making equal income couples pay equal taxes.[34] But Treasury also flagged the fairness cost that had helped sink similar bids in 1934, 1941, and 1942: Beyond the first tax bracket, joint returns push a married couple's tax to no more than twice that of a single person with half the income, effectively creating an economic barrier to marriage for two-earner couples in the affected ranges.[35] That critique came not just from Treasury specialists; women's civic groups had repeatedly opposed a joint return mandate on the ground that it ignored actual ownership, penalized working wives, and set a premium on divorce, a political pressure the committee knew from earlier rounds.[36]

The "dual rate schedule" tried to solve that by keeping the option to file separately while erasing the tax payoff from doing so. Treasury's illustration literally halves the surtax brackets for single filers and for spouses filing separate returns, so that splitting income produces no tax advantage.[37] Treasury's distributional note is blunt: Under this scheme, spouses couldn't do any better than they would under mandatory joint returns, and single

---

[30] *Id.*

[31] *Id.* at 845.

[32] *Id.*

[33] *Id.*

[34] *Id.* at 854.

[35] *Id.* at 847.

[36] *Id.* at 914.

[37] *Id.* at 855.

filers would bear relatively heavier tax than under the present law, which is exactly how dual rate removes the separate filing arbitrage.[38] Treasury even priced it at about a $998 million revenue bump at 1947 income levels, drawn mainly from 7.2 million single persons and around 1.4 million married couples who, under the then-current law, would otherwise file separately.[39]

A third line of attack, the management and control plan, would tax earned income to the earner, and community investment income to the spouse who manages and controls it, on the premise that property rights are not different enough to justify the big interstate tax gaps created by automatic half and half splitting.[40] Treasury's estimate suggested this approach would initially raise the taxes of roughly 600,000 married couples in community property states, increasing receipts by about $82 million at 1947 income levels. This would price in the political reality that any fix aimed at equal treatment could not avoid creating regional winners and losers.[41]

The fourth option (and the one ultimately chosen) was nationwide income splitting. They allowed every married couple to pool income and deductions, compute the tax on one-half, and then multiply by two. Treasury sketches the computational steps explicitly and notes that this would extend the tax benefits of the community property system to married couples throughout the country, but without telling any state how to write its property law.[42] The political tailwind was visible: Eight states formally asked Congress to "place taxpayers in all States on a uniform income tax basis," and a number of bills were introduced that spring to implement the split income idea.[43] Treasury's score showed why the coalition was broad. About 4.9 million married couples would get relief, with an estimated $7.14 billion reduction in annual liabilities at 1947 income levels.[44]

---

38 *Id.* at 855–56.

39 *Id.* at 856.

40 *Id.*

41 *Id.*

42 *Id.* at 861.

43 *Id.* at 856.

44 *Id.* at 845.

If Treasury provided the map, the live hearings supplied the politics and the pictures.[45] Representative Albert L. Reeves came with tables (sourced from Stanley Surrey at Treasury) comparing identical incomes in community and common law states, showing the gap widening from $38 at $5,000 to $12,854 at $100,000 and $23,921 at $500,000.[46] The staff study drives the same point home by aggregating the ten-year savings (1937–1946): $320 at $5,000; $2,864 at $10,000; $20,633 at $25,000; $53,144 at $50,000—"more than an entire year's income before tax" at $50,000, an image designed to stick.[47]

Those tables sat beside another fact pattern the committee cared about, the states chasing the advantage. The study notes that Oregon had just enacted a "community property" law to qualify its residents for income splitting under federal law, evidence that the system itself was affecting state property choices, a uniformity problem Congress could only solve at the federal tax level.[48]

The estate and gift backdrop also entered the room. Witnesses reminded the committee that the 1942 estate tax amendments had, in effect, taxed the decedent on community assets on an economic attribution theory, an approach they argued singled out community property states, departed from the traditional "tax on the privilege of transmitting," and produced inequities when compared with common law states.[49] Split income would equalize income tax liability between community property and common

---

[45] *See generally* Revenue Revisions 1947–48: Hearings Before the H. Comm. on Ways and Means, 80th Cong., 1st Sess., pt. 2 (1947). The hearings are unusually rich in both technical detail and political rhetoric, offering a rare window into how Treasury officials and members of Congress framed the "community property problem" in terms of equality and fairness. They contain not only the Treasury staff study, complete with tables and revenue estimates, but also pointed exchanges with witnesses, state petitions, and testimony from civic groups. For researchers interested in the original intentions behind the 1948 Revenue Act, particularly its equalization provisions, a careful reading of these hearings is invaluable. The depth of argument and the contemporaneous context make them a uniquely revealing source compared to later committee reports or judicial gloss.

[46] *Id.* at 878–79.

[47] *Id.* at 850.

[48] *Id.*

[49] *Id.* at 780.

law state couples, paired with changes to the transfer tax system to unwind the earlier imbalance.

Treasury's study also catalogued the long legislative arc leading up to 1948. This was not the first time that many of these ideas had been presented and argued for and against.[50] A 1921 House bill to tax community income to the managing spouse died in conference; the 1933 and 1934 flirtations with mandatory joint returns likewise failed; and renewed pushes in 1937, 1941, and 1942 each ran aground because of drafting difficulties and fairness objections that joint returns might actually overtax two-earner marriages.[51]

Finally, the distribution tables in the staff study show that Congress was not using the term "equal" as a slogan; instead, they were budgeting it. Treasury prints both the revenue totals and the incidence (who pays more, who pays less) under each path, and highlights that income splitting relief would concentrate in noncommunity property states, while dual rate raised meaningful revenue mostly from single filers.[52] That is the hearing's main point: "Equal" meant making families with the same combined income face the same federal rate structure without forcing state law transplants, and "fair" meant doing it in a way that did not convert marriage itself into a surtax.

The Mandatory Joint Return Plan: The Path Ultimately Not Taken

Congress did not address the "mandatory joint return" in the abstract. By 1947–1948, members had a full, bruising history of trying (and failing) to make joint returns compulsory, and Treasury arrived at the 80th Congress with a fresh, deliberately nonprescriptive staff study that laid out the options without recommending one. The foreword to that study says it "makes no policy recommendations," and frames its purpose as providing "factual and analytic background" on four alternatives for taxing family income, including the mandatory joint returns.[53] Treasury's neutral map thus placed mandatory joint returns on the menu as a way to shut off tax

---

[50] *Id.* at 836.

[51] *Id.*

[52] *Id.* at 845–56.

[53] *Id.* at 846.

savings from spousal splitting, while also foreshadowing the political tradeoffs that had killed the idea in earlier rounds.

Treasury's summary of prior proposals opens with an observation that sets the tone for the hearing room: Community property spokesmen were intent on retaining the concepts underlying their property laws, and Congress had already built a substantial record analyzing the family income problem from multiple angles.[54] When Treasury turns to its first plan, the mechanics are straightforward: If joint filings were made compulsory, the division of income between spouses would no longer be a factor, and, as a result, equal income couples would pay equal taxes because liability would be determined on the combined income.[55] The study then states the incidence plainly: Mandatory joint returns increase taxes in general for couples who had been saving by filing separately, especially where the spouses' earnings are similar, and the combined income is large.[56]

Treasury did not leave that at the level of generalities. The study identifies who, exactly, would be hit: couples above the first surtax bracket living in community property states (these couples would automatically obtain an equal division of community income) and couples in noncommunity property states with separate income from wages, business, or property.[57] It attaches numbers to the change, estimating that roughly 1.4 million married couples could see tax increases, and that would raise around $542 million at 1947 income levels.[58]

The study also sets out the marriage penalty geometry that had sunk earlier efforts. So long as a couple's entire taxable income sits in the first bracket, a joint return simply yields twice the single person tax on half the income.[59] However, once the couple's taxable income exceeds the first bracket, the joint tax becomes more than twice the single person tax, with the wedge growing as the surtax graduation steepens.[60] Treasury goes fur-

---

[54] *Id.* at 854.

[55] *Id.*

[56] *Id.*

[57] *Id.*

[58] *Id.*

[59] *Id.*

[60] *Id.*

ther, acknowledging the economic barrier to marriage critique often leveled at this type of mandate.[61]

Those analytical cautions were not abstract for Ways and Means; they came layered over a two-decade chronology of failed attempts. The 1941 fight is memorialized in the record: On August 4, 1941, the House rejected a compulsory joint return plan. Weeks later, the Senate Finance Committee reported a different approach (taxing income "earned or controlled" in the eight community property states), which triggered Senator Connally's "ringing minority report" defending state law ownership and the wife's one-half interest.[62] Connally's objection is worth quoting because it captures the

---

[61] *Id.* Discussing the idea that two singles with separate earnings who marry would face higher tax if their combined income exceeds the first bracket; how much that matters would depend on how much weight people place on dollars and on the offsetting economies of shared living accommodations. A married couple could face less in actual dollar amounts; however, in reality the shared living accommodation may actually render an easier-to-live lifestyle. Although on its face, getting married would, in and of itself, create a heightened tax burden, referred to as the "marriage tax."

[62] *Id.* at 915–16. Senator Tom Connally of Texas filed a vigorous minority report in opposition to the Finance Committee's proposed amendment affecting community property states. Connally objected that, as "the only community-property State Senator on the Finance Committee," he was "vigorously dissent[ing] from an amendment" directed at the community property system of eight sovereign states that had been adopted without notice or hearing to those whose constitutions and laws governing property ownership were to be set aside or ignored. He emphasized that Texas, since entering the Union in 1845, had maintained a community property regime recognized in both its 1845 and 1876 constitutions, and that the state courts had long enforced the wife's ownership interest "as strongly as those rights in her separate property." Connally further noted that other community property jurisdictions (Louisiana, Arizona, New Mexico, Idaho, Nevada, Washington, and, later, California) shared systems of "equal historical and statutory dignity," and that the Treasury, the Attorney General of the United States, and the Supreme Court itself had consistently recognized that one-half of the community income is that of the wife. Condemning the proposed federal amendment as an intrusion on state authority, Connally argued that it "flies into the very face of the heretofore well-recognized principle that the States control the ownership of property and income." He contrasted this intrusion with the federal tolerance of income splitting through gratuitous transfers in common law states, which he described as "deliberate transfers of income producing property . . . made

federalism nerve the committee kept touching: It condemned treating the wife's community share as a "sham and a fraud for Federal income-tax purpose," and it insisted that federal tax should not ignore the "constitutional and statutory" recognition of the wife's ownership in community states.[63]

Outside the chamber, women's organizations were a constituent source of resistance to compulsory pooling, and their submissions were represented in the hearings. The General Federal of Women's Clubs' materials opposed "any law . . . requiring husbands and wives to file joint income tax returns," calling the plan an attempt to ignore the ownership of the wife's property by superimposing her income on the husband's and warning that it set a premium on divorce.[64] They also emphasized that the mandate had been advanced and defeated on five previous occasions (1921, 1924, 1934, 1941, and 1942), and argued the burden would fall not only on wealthy households but on two-earner couples in the middle brackets.[65] The National Woman's Party telegram to Chairman George similarly framed community property as an "attempt at economic equality for husband and wife" and opposed compulsion as a rollback of women's gains, linking the fight to equal rights language.[66]

Treasury's historical recap, used by members to explain why compulsion kept stalling, tracks the same pattern. Proposals in 1921 and 1924 faltered, in 1933 the Acting Secretary endorsed a joint return mandate, in 1934 Ways and Means tentatively approved universal mandatory joint returns but then dropped the idea for "drafting difficulties," 1937 brought renewed advocacy before the Joint Committee on Tax Evasion and Avoidance, and 1941–1942 saw the House and Senate sequence (summarized earlier), all culminating in rejection.[67] Treasury's chronology appears in the

---

expressly for tax purposes." Concluding, Connally urged that "instead of penalizing the community-property system . . . Congress should encourage its spread," observing that the system "recognizes the contribution of the wife to the marital partnership" and gives "legal and practical standing . . . to the concept of marital partnership which in common-law States remains spiritual only."

[63] *Id.*

[64] *Id.* at 914.

[65] *Id.* at 914–15.

[66] *Id.* at 917.

[67] *Id.* at 854.

study's proposals previously concerned section, and it is the institutional memory the Committee drew on when assessing this plan in 1948. Members also had on the table mitigation ideas from earlier rounds. (Randolph Paul's targeted credit concept aimed at cushioning two-earner households under a mandate, effectively a credit up to a cap keyed to the gap between joint and separate return liability.) That alternative appears in the hearings' citations to the 1942 revenue revision record and illustrates how seriously Congress had wrestled with the marriage penalty optics even before 1948.[68]

Fairness, in the Committee's vocabulary, was not reducible to the tidy statement that "equal income couples pay equal taxes." Treasury flags the comparative baseline problem head on: Under a mandate, single taxpayers' absolute liabilities would not change, but their relative burden would fall because some married couples would now pay more.[69] That is why the study prints, back-to-back, the observations about "more than twice" and the barrier to marriage discussion, to remind readers that any compelling story about equality across married households has to be squared with how the rule treats singles and incentives.[70]

The federalism thread, respecting state ownership while fixing a national tax distortion, also cut against compulsion. The Senate episode shows why: Attempting to tax income to the spouse who "earned or controlled" it (as a narrower substitute for a universal mandate) drew charges of overriding state constitutions and deeming wives' ownership unreal for federal purposes.[71] Connally's minority report, reprinted in the record, rests that critique on a simple proposition: States "control the ownership of property and income," and the Supreme Court, the Treasury, and the Attorney General had long recognized the wife's vested half in community income.[72] This is the same instinct that later makes the 1949 equalization scheme more attractive: Fix the computation federally and never relabel ownership.

The hearings preserve, finally, why the mandatory joint return plan struggled politically even when it looked tidy on paper. In the Committee's

---

[68] *Id.* at 858.

[69] *Id.* at 855.

[70] *Id.*

[71] *Id.* at 916.

[72] *Id.* at 915.

own words, mandatory joint returns would increase taxes for the very households most visible to constituents, two-earner couples in the middle and upper brackets, and would do so in a way that opponents would describe as a marriage tax.[73] The women's group submissions distilled that political message crisply, and the House's 242–160 vote in 1941 gave members an easy data point when they returned to the question in 1948.[74]

Put together, the Committee's 1947–1948 file on compulsory joint returns reads like a controlled experiment with clear observational results. Mechanically, a mandate would shut down spousal splitting and force equal-income couples into equal tax. Distributionally, it would raise revenue by increasing liabilities for about 1.4 million couples, concentrated where earnings are similar, and incomes higher. Normatively, it triggered sustained objections on marriage penalty grounds and on federalism/ownership grounds, especially in community states. And politically, it carried the baggage of five prior defeats and a prominent House floor repudiation. The hearings, therefore, set the stage for Congress to reach the same equalization without compulsion instinct that drives the 1948 package. If the goal is equal treatment across states, do it by computation (and later, at death by § 1014(b)(6)'s deeming rule), not by a federal rule that compels every marriage into one return regardless of state law ownership.[75]

Management and Control Approach

Treasury's staff study framed "management and control" as one of the four live ways to fix family income inequalities, alongside mandatory joint returns, a dual rate schedule for separate filers, and full income splitting. Mechanically, the plan was simple to say and hard to run: Wage and salary income would be taxed to the person who earned it.[76] Income from community-owned property would be taxed to whichever spouse had the legal right to manage and control that property under state law.[77] The appeal, on paper, was twofold: (1) It neutralized the "automatic" one-half split inside community property regimes by pinning tax to a single

[73] *Id.* at 854.

[74] *Id.* at 914.

[75] *Id.* at 914–17.

[76] *Id.* at 856.

[77] *Id.*

"manager," and (2) it promised formal parity with common law states, which already taxed earned income to the earner.[78] More practically, the plan's goal was to key federal liability to who actually controlled the investment base inside a marital community, while leaving wage income where it already sat, with the earner.[79] The study previews why this might narrow (although not erase) the residence-based gap: It removes the automatic 50/50 allocation of community income, which had made separate filing especially advantageous for high-income households.[80]

Treasury grounds the plan in a premise. The underlying property rights of spouses are not so different across regimes as to justify blanket tax differences.[81] If the law can identify who controls the investment assets that throw off income, it can assign that income consistently without rewriting state property systems. That is why the paper centers management rather than title formalities (especially because, in many community jurisdictions, the husband historically held broad managerial power over community personal property even while the wife owned an equal half).[82]

The hearings reminded members that this was not uncharted water. Congress had flirted with management and control ideas repeatedly: The House in 1921 actually passed a provision requiring community income to be included in the return of the spouse having management and control.[83] When the Senate in 1941 tried to cure the community advantage by taxing earnings to the earner while leaving other community income with the manager, a bloc led by Senator Connally blasted the approach as unworkable.[84] The 80th Congress thus came to 1947–1948 knowing both the logic and the political baggage of the management and control approach.[85]

---

[78] *Id.*

[79] *Id.*

[80] *Id.*

[81] *Id.*

[82] *Id.* at 867.

[83] *Id.* at 853. This was later dropped by the Senate, and in conference the House yielded in favor of the Senate action.

[84] *Id.* at 915. Senator Connally famously labeled this idea as a "sham and a fraud," and it was later withdrawn on the floor.

[85] *Id.* at 852–56.

Treasury included a side-by-side revenue table so that members could compare incidence across fixes. On those estimates, the management and control plan would raise a comparatively small $82 million.[86] The last figure mattered in the hearings: It signaled that "management and control" was a fine point calibration, it was tighter than the then status quo for community filers; however, it was not the kind of broad mechanical equalizer a dual rate schedule or joint return mandate would be.[87]

Running tax through the manager sounds tidy until the examiner must prove who managed which asset across a marriage. The record flags exactly that: In many community states, the husband retained "actual control and management" of community assets even as the wife held a vested half title, meaning the plan could collapse into defaulting investment income to the husband absent strong, state law–grounded proof to the contrary.[88] Louisiana illustrates the ambiguity from the other direction: If a court had shifted management to the wife for cause, she would be the "managing spouse"

---

[86] *Id.* at 847. In fact, of the four plans evaluated, the management and control plan was projected to raise the least revenue. The mandatory joint return proposal was estimated to generate approximately $542 million, the dual rate schedule was informally expected to yield nearly $1 billion, and the nationwide income-splitting plan—essentially the joint return system in place today—was projected to reduce revenue by roughly $744 million. Thus, among the three proposals expected to increase tax receipts, the management and control plan would have produced the smallest gain, surpassing only the income-splitting plan, which was ultimately adopted and lowered tax liabilities nationwide. This comparatively modest estimate provides at least some indication that the management and control proposal was narrowly targeted. Unlike the other plans, which would have affected taxpayers nationwide, this approach would have altered the treatment only of residents in community property jurisdictions—then numbering roughly 12 states. The limited projected revenue increase reflects that narrow reach: the plan's effect would have been confined to those community property states that lacked clear presumptions regarding which spouse exercised management and control over the income. In short, while not definitive proof, the revenue estimate supports the view that the management and control plan was primarily designed to eliminate the preferential tax treatment available in community property states by bringing their residents into parity with their common law counterparts.

[87] *Id.* at 845.

[88] *Id.* at 866.

for federal purposes, again requiring the Service to trace judgments and managerial changes at the moment the income was earned.[89]

Because it operated only inside community regimes, management and control could curb the existing advantage of curtailing 50/50 splitting on separate returns, but it did little to address the other two discrimination seams the Treasury documents, especially the earned versus investment tilt in common law states and the uneven access to private splitting devices.[90] The study shows how, outside the community states, families could and did use trusts, partnerships, and gifts to move investment income into lower brackets, a behavior management and control wouldn't touch on.[91]

The hearings repeatedly equate "equal treatment" with equal rules that don't penalize marriage or residency, not simply with closing a particular loophole.[92] On that metric, management and control was a half measure, it tried to normalize community filings toward the common law baseline by focusing on managerial power, but it would not, by itself, extend a symmetrical relief to common law couples with one primary earner.[93] Members also had fresh proof of how volatile the politics could be when tax design turns on intrafamily roles. Connally's 1941 broadside captured the fear that a manager control would be too formal to catch real sharing and too fact intensive to actually administer.[94]

Appendix A details that some states treat income from one spouse's separate property as community income, but others do not, a choice that would change the federal manager's tax exposure under this plan.[95] Even the remedy structure matters: In Louisiana, the wife can force partition or remove a mismanaging husband without divorcing. However, in many other states, that wife's only practical check is dissolution of the community.[96] This means the same federal plan would land differently across the

---

[89] *Id.* at 867.

[90] *Id.* at 850.

[91] *Id.*

[92] *Id.* at 851.

[93] *Id.*

[94] *Id.* at 915.

[95] *Id.* at 866.

[96] *Id.*

map, depending on the local rules, which is hardly a recipe for a single, national answer to a national equity problem.

Treasury put "management and control" on the menu because it is internally coherent: It links investment income to the spouse who directs the community capital and leaves wages with the earner. The plan promised only modest revenue impact relative to the other fixes and required the Service to adjudicate who managed what asset under a patchwork of state rules. As members weighed "equal" and "fair," the record shows this approach could shrink the community state advantage but not deliver the across-the-board symmetry they were pressing for by 1948. Two takeaways are durable. First, throughout the papers and the appendix, the federal analysis defers to state law to define ownership and management, an orientation that explains why later equalization at death keys on whether the property is community under state law at the moment of death. Second, the Committee's movement away from "management and control" and toward split income in 1948 rested on political judgment that national equal treatment meant national access to marital income splitting, rather than tighter policing of management within the eight community jurisdictions.

The Nationwide Income-Splitting Plan

Congress did not back into income splitting; it chose it after carefully reviewing its options and testing each path against what "equal" should mean across states and families. Treasury's staff paper is explicit that it makes no policy recommendations, and that, of the four options on the table, it presents the split-income plan in more detail because of its current widespread interest in this approach.[97]

In the Committee's own words, the idea was to "grant spouses in all States the option to divide equally their combined incomes, exemptions, and deductions for income tax purposes."[98] Treasury frames it as a response to formal requests; eight states petitioned Congress to place taxpayers in all states on a uniform income tax basis and noted that a number of bills to do exactly that had been introduced to the 80th Congress.[99] The same page explains the mechanics in four steps: (1) spouses filing a joint return

---

97 *Id.* at 846.

98 *Id.* at 856.

99 *Id.*

combine income; (2) subtract aggregate deductions and exemptions; (3) compute the tax on one-half of the aggregate taxable net income; and (4) multiply by two to find the combined liability.[100] The policy choice is clear, in that the community property system's benefits would be extended nationwide, but by a federal computational rule rather than by rewriting state property laws. Treasury then put numbers to the choice. It estimated that a spouses-only split-income plan would reduce individual income tax receipts by approximately $744 million at 1947 income levels, with relief concentrated among roughly 4.9 million married couples—predominantly in noncommunity states.[101] Treasury underscored that this policy left single taxpayers' absolute liabilities unchanged, though their relative burden would rise because they would not share in the married-couple relief.[102] The study also identified the structural winners within the married population: couples in noncommunity states where income was concentrated in one spouse's personal services or unincorporated business, and couples with significant property income who had been unable (or unwilling) to accomplish title splitting for tax purposes.[103]

Put against the full menu that Treasury laid before the Committee, the choice was candid. There were four paths: (1) make joint returns mandatory; (2) tax community investment income to the spouse with management and control while leaving earnings to the earner; (3) adopt a dual rate schedule that halves separate return brackets to remove the profit from filing separately; and (4) implement a nationwide split income by optional joint return.[104] Read in that light, three of the routes worked by narrowing or overriding the state law community split, while one route worked by extension—exporting the community property effect to every married couple through a federal computation rule that left ownership to the states. Treasury printed the budget stakes alongside the mechanics. On its estimates, the extension model would reduce receipts by roughly $744 million at 1947 income levels and benefit approximately 4.9 million married couples, largely in noncommunity states; singles absolute liabilities would not

100 *Id.*

101 *Id.* at 858.

102 *Id.*

103 *Id.*

104 *Id.* at 854–57.

change. By contrast, the curtailment paths were structured either to raise revenue or to shift liabilities by reassigning community income to a single filer, each premised on trimming the community property advantage rather than generalizing it.

Against that backdrop, the Committee's definition of equality is visible on the page. Any of the four could have been defended as "equal" in some sense, but Congress chose expansion, a nationalized computation that treats a Kansas couple like a California couple, even at a revenue cost, because it delivered a parity between the states while respecting the state law ownership principles.

Chapter 9

Community Property Trusts

Note: The elective community property trust statutes discussed in this chapter vary significantly from state to state in terms of their requirements, limitations, and tax implications. Practitioners considering the use of a community property trust should consult with counsel licensed in and familiar with the laws of the particular state whose community property trust statute they intend to use. The discussion that follows is intended as a general overview and does not substitute for jurisdiction-specific legal analysis.

THE EFFECTIVENESS OF A COMMUNITY PROPERTY TRUST FOR OBTAINING THE § 1014(B)(6) FULL STEP-UP

State of the Law and the Service's Position

Alaska's Community Property Act, enacted under the leadership of Jonathan Blattmachr,[1] provides that non-Alaskans can hold assets in Alaska community property trusts with the expectation that all community property

[1] "Mr. Blattmachr is a Principal in ILS Management, LLC and a retired member of Milbank Tweed Hadley & McCloy LLP in New York, NY and of the Alaska, California and New York Bars. He is recognized as one of the most creative trusts and estates lawyers in the country and is listed in The Best Lawyers in America. He has written and lectured extensively on estate and trust taxation and charitable giving."

assets in the trust will receive a step-up in income tax basis upon the death of the first dying spouse. Blattmachr has informed the authors that in drafting the Alaska Community Property Act, he closely followed the Uniform Marital Property Act as adopted by Wisconsin, which the IRS concluded in Revenue Ruling 87-13 caused Wisconsin residents to have community property for federal tax purposes.

Unlike Wisconsin's Act, however, Alaska residents must affirmatively elect into the community property regime.[2] Alaska was the first of its kind in this respect, providing an opt-in feature to community property treatment.[3] In addition, Alaska's Community Property Act, enacted in 1998, allows nonresidents to benefit from the elective community property regime by establishing a "community property trust" that has at least one trustee that is a resident individual or professional trust company or other certified trustee in the state.[4] More recently, in order to take advantage of the income tax planning advantages of community property, Tennessee, South Dakota, Kentucky, and Florida adopted elective community property systems in 2010, 2016, 2020, and 2021, respectively.

IRS Publication 555 (Rev. December 2024) entitled "Community Property" specifically provides that the publication "doesn't address the federal tax treatment of income or property subject to the 'community property' election under Alaska, Tennessee, and South Dakota state laws." This language has created doubt as to whether the IRS will respect a community property trust for purposes of affording a full step-up in basis to the assets of the trust on the death of the first dying spouse.

The uncertainty as to the effectiveness of an elective community property regime and community property trust planning is further amplified

---

InterActive Legal, https://interactivelegal.com/about-us/jonathan-blattmachr/ (accessed Dec. 7, 2025).

[2] ALASKA STAT. § 34,77.030(a) provides that "property of spouses is community property under this chapter only to the extent provided in a community property agreement or a community property trust." *See also* ALASKA STAT. § 34.77.030(f).

[3] *See* Jonathan G. Blattmachr, Howard M. Zaritsky & Mark L. Ascher, *Tax Planning with Consensual Community Property: Alaska's New Community Property Law*, 33 REAL PROP. PROB. & T.R. J. 615 (1998).

[4] ALASKA STAT. § 34.77.100(a).

by a 1944 Supreme Court decision, *Commissioner v. Harmon*,[5] where it was held that Oklahoma's version of an elective community property regime was ineffective for federal tax purposes. The *Harmon* Court held that Oklahoma's elective community property law violated the assignment of income doctrine as outlined in *Lucas v. Earl*.[6] The *Harmon* Court reasoned that because Oklahoma's community property system was optional rather than dictated by state policy as an incident of marriage that the system was ineffective to provide a married couple the tax benefits that would avail to receivers of community income.[7]

Moreover, Internal Revenue Manual 25.18.1.2.3 (updated May 3, 2023) specifically provides as follows with respect to the effectiveness of elective community property regimes:

> Alaska, South Dakota, and Tennessee have adopted a community property system, but it is optional. In Alaska, spouses may create community property by entering into a community property agreement or by creating a community property trust. See Alaska Stat. §§ 34.77.020–34.77.995. Similarly in South Dakota, property held in a special spousal trust becomes community property if the trust expressly declares that property transferred is South Dakota special spousal property. SD. ST. § 55-17. Tennessee also has adopted an optional community property system. TN. ST. § 35-17. The U.S. Supreme Court ruled that a similar statute allowing spouses to elect a community property system under Oklahoma law would **NOT** be recognized for federal income tax reporting purposes. *Commissioner v. Harmon*, 323 U.S. 44 (1944). The Harmon decision should also apply to all elective community property systems (such as those in Alaska, South Dakota, and Tennessee) for income reporting purposes.[8]

---

[5] Comm'r v. Harmon, 323 U.S. 44 (1944).

[6] Lucas v. Earl, 281 U.S. 111 (1930).

[7] Note that Oklahoma's community property legislation was not enacted to take advantage of § 1014(b)(6); instead, it was enacted prior to the creation of joint return filing in the tax code in 1948 in order to provide Oklahoma spouses with the same income tax treatment as spouses in community property states.

[8] The authors believe this language, or a similar version of this language, was first included in the IRM in 2017.

It seems more than reasonable to infer from Internal Revenue Manual quotation that the IRS will take the position that property subject to a community property election should not receive the full step-up in basis upon the first death, despite the clear meaning of the statute. At the same time, well-respected practitioners have concluded that "if a state incorporates characteristics of the community property statutes from the eight original community property jurisdictions in its community property trust legislation, it should be respected by the IRS (or at least the Tax Court if the IRS challenges a taxpayer's classification of property as community in nature)."[9]

The question, then, is whether the Tax Court would adopt the IRS's position. The theoretical basis for extending the *Harmon* decision to elective community property systems seems far from clear as opposed to secure. The IRS's position presumes that all elective regimes function as contractual assignments of income rather than as genuine property classifications under state law. Yet this assumption overlooks the substantive legal distinctions between Oklahoma's short-lived elective statute at issue in *Harmon* and the carefully drafted community property trust statutes enacted in the community property trust states. Once the election is made under these modern statutes, the spouses' ownership interests are fixed and defined by state law—mirroring the vested community property rights recognized in *Poe v. Seaborn*[10] and the eight traditional community property jurisdictions.

A Critical Analysis of *Harmon*

Harmon asked whether Oklahoma's 1939 elective community property statute required the federal income tax to honor spousal income splitting. The majority answered no, characterizing the Oklahoma régime as a consensual arrangement akin to *Lucas v. Earl*, rather than a state-defined property ("legal") system of the *Poe v. Seaborn* variety.

In a well-written dissent to the *Harmon* decision, Justice Douglas noted that the federal income tax law discriminated in favor of community property states and claimed that the Court's distinction between "consensual"

---

[9] Travis Hayes, *To Share and Share Alike: An Examination of the Treatment of Community Property in Florida and the New Florida Community Property Trust Act*, citing *Westerdahl v. Commissioner*, 82 T.C. 83 (1984) and *Angerhofer v. Commissioner*, 87 T.C. 814 (1986).

[10] Poe v. Seaborn, 282 U.S. 101 (1930).

and "legal" community property systems had no practical basis and could not be consistently maintained for federal tax purposes.[11] Justice Douglas went on to opine that:

> [t]he only apparent basis for such discrimination is that the community property systems in the eight states are traditional; that those eight states have a well settled policy; that Oklahoma merely gives its citizens a choice to get under or stay out of its community property system. Yet how can we say that the state which allows husband and wife to revoke or alter its community property system by contract has a more "settled" policy towards community property than a state which gives husband and wife the choice to invoke its community property system or to keep their marital property on a common law basis? The truth is that there is a wide range of choices in each. But the fact that there is a choice should not be deemed fatal when Oklahoma's case comes before the Court[.][12]

Douglas's dissent, joined by Justice Black, was not a mere protest over a one-off tax result; it was a sustained critique of a federal tax jurisprudence that allowed geography and legal pedigree to determine the outcomes for identically situated married couples. Read against the backdrop of the 1930s–1940s "copy-cat" experiments,[13] his reasoning amounts to an insistence that federal tax liability should track state-defined ownership wherever that ownership is substantively real, regardless of whether a legislature adopts it as a rule that applies to all married couples residing within the state. The dissent, therefore, meets the majority on its chosen ground (*Poe v. Seaborn*) and shows why *Poe*'s focus on state law ownership cannot coherently turn on whether the state's community regime is old and "inveterate" or new and elective. Crucially, Douglas also frames *Lucas v. Earl* and *Poe*

---

[11] *See Harmon,* 323 U.S. at 55–56. The *Harmon* Court distinguished between "Consensual community property," which arises out of contract, and "legal community property," which arises by "incident of marriage by the inveterate policy of the state." In this context, inveterate means long established and unlikely to change. *Id.*

[12] *Id.* at 55–56 (J. Douglas dissenting).

[13] Copy-cat experiments are studies or tests that replicate or closely imitate an original experiment to see whether the same results can be observed, often without introducing material new methods or insights.

as "competing theories of income tax liability,"[14] and he invites the Court to resolve the conflict forthrightly, rather than entrench a discriminatory carve-out for a handful of traditional community property jurisdictions. As the historical record shows, that discrimination was not an abstraction, since both taxpayers and states perceived and reacted to it in concrete ways, and those reactions illuminate why Douglas's uniformity principle was, and remains, the better rule.

To see why, one must begin with the context in which Oklahoma enacted its community property statute in 1939. Oklahoma officials were staring down a budgetary squeeze while neighboring Texas openly touted the federal tax advantages available to community property couples, prompting Oklahoma's bar and business community to explore statutory solutions that would keep affluent residents (and their tax base) at home. The governor's team understood that if Oklahoma could reduce the federal tax burden borne by its residents, it would soften the political blow of needed state tax measures and tamp down talk of flight to Texas. The community property bill was therefore pitched as a pragmatic "tax bill," with the purpose of saving state residents on their federal income tax and preventing a mass exodus of residents to Texas, and not as a sweeping social revolution in domestic relations law. This is not a conjecture floated after the fact; contemporary archival materials document the economic messaging and the comparative studies that preceded the statute's adoptions. That pragmatic posture matters because it explains why the legislature chose an elective design that would deliver the tax benefit to willing couples while minimizing perceived disruption elsewhere in the domestic relations code.

Just as important, the statute's elective design also explains its initial political success in a conservative era for women's rights in Oklahoma. Because couples had to opt in by filing a written election, households skeptical of community property's implications for management, creditors, and testamentary planning could remain safely within the common law system. Policymakers expected that only approximately 10 percent of taxpayers living in that state would benefit from electing, and the elective structure allowed the state to advertise a headline federal tax saving without imposing a one-size-fits-all property regime on the entire population. The point, for present purposes, is that this elective feature was a political compromise

[14] Comm'r v. Harmon, 323 U.S. 44, 49–57 (1944) (Douglas, J., dissenting).

and an implementation detail, not evidence that Oklahoma's law failed to create genuine co-ownership once elected. Treating that implementation choice as if it converted a property system into a mere private contract is the very formalism Douglas condemned. The article's unbiased careful reconstruction of Oklahoma's legislative motives and public messaging dispels any notion that the statute was a casual "assignment" device in the *Earl* sense; it was a deliberately engineered state law definition of ownership, activated by election for administrative and political reasons.

The litigation path to *Commissioner v. Harmon* underscores the point. After Oklahoma's enactment, the Tax Court upheld the electing couple's ability to split income, reasoning from *Seaborn*'s premise that state law had vested the wife with a present one-half interest in community income; the Tenth Circuit affirmed this. The Supreme Court then reversed, drawing a line between long-standing "legal" community property systems and Oklahoma's "consensual" version and aligning the latter with the anticipatory assignment condemned in *Lucas v. Earl*. Justices Douglas and Black resisted that line of reasoning, emphasizing that marriage itself and the decision to change domicile are themselves consensual acts, so the majority's distinction was a distinction without a difference. The dissent insisted that if federal law respects state-defined ownership in one jurisdiction, it cannot withhold the same respect when a neighboring state arrives at functionally equivalent ownership through an opt-in statute. That is not special pleading for Oklahoma; it is a claim about national uniformity and the Court's responsibility to avoid arbitrariness in federal tax administration.

The immediate fallout in Oklahoma shows how salient that uniformity concern was on the ground. The press misreported the Supreme Court's decision as having "overruled" the statute, but in reality the regime continued to operate for state law purposes, including limited state income tax splitting, even as federal income splitting was cut off. Business leaders warned that without the federal advantage, Oklahoma's affluent taxpayers would migrate, and political pressure mounted to enact a more effective community property framework that would satisfy federal standards. When rehearing was denied, state leaders publicly weighed the fiscal implications and the optics of remaining a holdout while Texas and other community property states retained their advantage. In short, the lived experience recapitulated Douglas's diagnosis. A federal rule that privileges identical family economics in one state over another solely because of legal pedigree invites precisely the interstate distortion and citizen resentment he decried.

The dissent's plea for either universal application of *Poe*'s logic or its forthright repudiation was not academic; it was responsive to conditions that the record lays bare.

Pennsylvania's brief embrace of community property in 1947 provides a counterpoint that further validates Douglas's concerns and reveals a different kind of institutional resistance: judicial hostility to importing a civil law regime into a common law state. The statute sailed through a legislature eager to tout an eye-popping projected $100 million in annual federal income tax savings for residents, and the governor's signing statement was candid that the law's "primary" purpose was the federal tax benefit. Yet within months the Supreme Court of Pennsylvania invalidated the regime in a friendly test case, *Willcox v. Pennsylvania Mutual Life Insurance Co.*,[15] characterizing the community property system as an "exotic" civil law transplant incompatible with the state's constitutional order. Tellingly, all sides in that litigation presented the statute as a vehicle for federal tax reduction rather than a comprehensive reform of Pennsylvania's domestic relations law, and the Attorney General's defense was tepid, couched as a last-ditch parity plea rather than a substantive defense of the property system adopted. The speed and tenor of the decision reflected a judiciary unwilling to accommodate a continental civil law import even where the legislature had spoken clearly, and the federal tax consequences were the point of the exercise. This episode, meticulously documented in the historical account, lends empirical weight to Douglas's observation that privileging "traditional" regimes bakes discrimination into federal tax, states that try to level the playing field by adopting substantively equivalent ownership rules will be thwarted by formalist objections, and their citizens will continue to labor under a federal disadvantage.

The Pennsylvania experiment also demonstrates why the majority's taxonomy is unworkable in practice. If the decisive criterion is "tradition," then even a mandatory community property statute enacted with unmistakable clarity can be dismissed as an inauthentic "civil law" graft and struck down before federal consequences can attach.[16] Conversely, if the criterion

---

[15] Willcox v. Penn. Mut. Life Ins. Co., 357 Pa. 581, 55 A.2d 521 (1947).

[16] The Service's recognition of Wisonsin marital property as community property for federal income tax purposes further illustrates that the decisive criterion cannot be "tradition." *See* Rev. Rul. 87-13.

is whether the state has, as a matter of positive law, vested each spouse with a present one-half interest in community acquisitions and income, then both Oklahoma's elective system and Pennsylvania's mandatory one pass muster on the attribute that matters. The Court cannot coherently demand that a state both adopt a settled policy and, simultaneously, avoid any signs of mere tax motivation; in a federal system where tax is one of many policy levers, legislative purpose will often include fiscal competition with neighbors. Douglas's dissent refuses to play that game; it measures state choices by their substance—do spouses own what the statute says they own, with the management, creditor, and death-time incidents that ownership implies? When the answer is yes, the federal tax law should treat the couple the same way it treats their counterparts across the border.

The broader national denouncement after *Harmon* proved the dissent's point by other means. Rather than continue to referee fine distinctions among state marital regimes, Congress brought parity to income splitting by adopting joint returns for married couples in 1948, blunting the interstate tax distortion that had motivated the many states to experiment. From that point forward, the federal question was less about who could split income under rate schedules and more about what state law said the spouses own for purposes of other parts of the Code. This is where Douglas's emphasis on state law ownership resonates most clearly with later federal doctrine. State property law continued to govern the definition of ownership for many federal tax questions, even as Congress altered rate structures to restore national uniformity. In other words, the federal system eventually migrated to the *Harmon* dissent's baseline: Respect state-defined ownership, but do not allow rate mechanics to create persistent geographic discrimination. The historical account makes this sequence explicit and provides the contemporaneous sources that show how legislative and administrative actors perceived the problem.

That historical sequence also explains why reading *Harmon* beyond its income-splitting holding is a mistake.[17] The *Harmon* case addressed whether an elective regime could force federal income attribution to follow a new state law during the pre-1948 rate environment; it did not answer how federal law should treat ownership at death, much less how it should

[17] *See Beyer*: "Accordingly, once could argue that *Lucas v. Earl* really has no relevance to the basis situation. When you take this step, *Harmon* cannot be seen as controlling the outcome."

treat basis rules enacted later with text that keys on property held "under the community property laws of any State."[18] Once joint returns leveled the rate playing field, the salient federal question became whether a given state statute genuinely creates community ownership, not whether the statute is old enough or sufficiently "mandatory" to satisfy a pedigree test. Douglas's insistence that either *Poe* applies uniformly or not at all delivers a clean doctrinal line for the post-1948 world in which federal law looks first to what property rights exist under state law and then applies federal consequences to those rights. The historical record confirms that this is how practitioners and administrators increasingly understood the system to work after parity returned to rate structures. The point is not to inflate the dissent into a basis rule; it is to recognize that the dissent's conceptual move, ownership over formalism, fits the statutory choices Congress later made.

There is, finally, a prudential strand running through the dissent that anticipates the post-war settlement. Douglas argues that if *Seaborn* is to persist, it should be available on equal terms to any state that substantively creates the ownership *Poe* respected; otherwise, the Court should abandon it and embrace a uniform *Earl*-based rule. Congress essentially made the first move unnecessary for rate purposes by adopting joint returns, but it left untouched the foundational principle that state law defines property rights for many federal tax consequences. In that environment, Douglas's rule is the natural one to apply to later questions: Respect ownership that exists "by law," whether that law is ancient or newly minted. The historical record collected in the article makes clear that when states drafted with care, whether by mandatory reform or by a carefully structured elective regime, they understood themselves to be creating real co-ownership with real incidents, not collusive assignments for tax purposes. That self-understanding, grounded in text and structure, is precisely what Douglas thought federal law should recognize.

In the end, the Douglas and Black dissent in *Harmon* offers a more coherent framework because it avoids tying federal tax consequences to the pedigree of a state's property system or to the particular mechanism by which co-ownership is established. Their approach would likely have reduced the period of experimentation that followed, during which similarly situated families faced different results based on formal labels rather than underlying ownership. It also fits more comfortably with the post-1948 landscape, in which state law defines property interests and federal law

---

[18] I.R.C. § 1014(b)(6).

attaches consequences to those interests. More broadly, the dissent's framework aligns with the Constitution's allocation of authority over property while promoting uniform federal treatment of like cases.

Additional Support for the Effectiveness of a Community Property Trust: *McCollum*, *Westerdahl*, and *Angerhofer*

The 1958 U.S. District Court decision of *McCollum v. United States* further supports the proposition that the § 1014(b)(6) step-up in basis will apply to community property created by spousal election.[19] In *McCollum*, a married couple elected under the then-applicable 1943 Oklahoma law to treat their assets as community property, and in 1945 Oklahoma changed its law to require that all of a married couple's assets had to be considered to be community property.[20] Mr. McCollum died after the community property status became mandatory, and Mrs. McCollum took a full step-up in basis for the full value of the community property that existed on Mr. McCollum's date of death.[21] The court allowed the full step-up in basis.[22]

The *McCollum* decision seems consistent with the notion that Internal Revenue Code § 1014(b)(6) applies to elective community property as well as mandatory community property. Although Oklahoma had a mandatory community property system by the time the decision was reached, because the property at issue was acquired before the change of law in 1945, the property would not have been community property under the 1945 Oklahoma community property law, except for the fact that the McCollums had previously designated it as community property under the elective system.[23]

Jonathan Blattmachr astutely observes that a mere labeling of assets as community property is not sufficient to make them community property for federal tax purposes.[24]

The state law property interest must actually provide a presently vested one-half interest in the community property, and the first dying spouse will only have the right to testamentarily dispose of one-half of the property.

---

[19] McCollum v. U.S., 2 A.F.T.R. 2d 6170 (N.D. Okla. 1958).

[20] *Id.*

[21] *Id.*

[22] *Id.*

[23] I.R.C. § 1014(b)(6).

[24] Blattmachr, Zaritsky & Ascher, *supra* note 3.

In that regard, *Angerhofer v. Commissioner* is instructive.[25] The married couple in *Angerhofer* were German citizens domiciled in Germany and took the position that they lived under a community property regime pursuant to German law, which actually provides that married couples who live there will be subject to one of three different marital property regimes.[26] Unless a German couple agrees otherwise, they basically live under a separate property regime, but they can opt in to one of the two other regimes.[27] The Tax Court found that one of those other regimes would be considered to be community property for federal income tax purposes, and the couple in *Angerhofer* ultimately conceded that they had never agreed to opt in to the German equivalent of community property status.[28] The Tax Court decision can be read as dicta to indicate that the couple could have opted in to the German community property regime and would have had their earnings treated as community property for U.S. federal income tax purposes. But the couple only opted in to the regime that did not grant each spouse full community property rights in the view of the Tax Court.[29] The missing key ingredient under the German marital regime the couple opted in to was that the first dying spouse would not have been able to bequeath his or her one-half of the marital assets however he or she wished to do so.

Similarly, in *Westerdahl v. Commissioner*, a majority of the Tax Court determined in a full Tax Court Opinion that Sweden should be treated as a community property jurisdiction for U.S. federal income tax purposes.[30] The taxpayers were Swedish citizens and domicilliaries temporarily working for IBM in New York; they and their wives filed separate nonresident alien returns, each reporting one-half of the husbands' U.S. wages. The IRS denied "community property benefits" on the ground that Swedish law did

---

[25] Angerhofer v. C.I.R, 87 T.C. 814 (1986). Before changes were made to the Internal Revenue Code in 1984, a nonworking spouse who filed separately was entitled to half of his or her spouse's income subject to U.S. taxation (because the spouse worked in the U.S. or for an American employer) but was not responsible for paying U.S. income tax on the nonworking spouse's half of such income.

[26] *Angerhofer*, 87 T.C. at 815.

[27] *Id.* at 820.

[28] *Id.* at 827.

[29] *Id.* at 829–30.

[30] Westerdahl v. C.I.R., 82 T.C. 83, 95 (1984).

not give a spouse a present vested interest in the other spouse's earnings. The Tax Court framed the sole issue as whether, under Sweden's 1920 Marriage Code, the wives held a present vested interest in one-half of their husbands' wages, an interest comparable to that recognized in *Poe v. Seaborn.*

The Tax Court's opinion in *Westerdahl* deserves a closer look, as it carefully walks through Sweden's marital property laws to answer the question of whether the system in place in Sweden was that of a "deferred community property system," with rights vesting only upon death or divorce, or a system that gave the spouses presently vested one-half interests.

The Service's basic contention was that Swedish law did not grant the wives a present vested interest in their husbands' wages. The court, however, undertook its own detailed comparison between Sweden's "giftorätt" regime and the eight original American community property states. The court observed that in *Seaborn,* to make the determination of whether Mrs. Seaborn clearly had a vested property interest in the community property, the Supreme Court looked at the spouse's legal obligations, responsibilities, and limitations with respect to one another and to the community property. The *Westerdahl* court observed that:

> [the *Seaborn* Court] regarded several factors as particularly important, but it did not label these factors as requisites for finding a present vested interest. The several factors, when combined and viewed as two broad attributes, include: Protection of the interest of each spouse in the community property (1) by legally assuring its testamentary disposition or its passage to the decedent's issue rather than to the surviving spouse, and (2) by limiting the managing spouse's powers of management and control so that detriment to the nonmanaging spouse from fraud or mismanagement will be minimized.[31]

Westerdahl then emphasized that even those two broad attributes are not the whole story. The court surveyed the statutes of the eight American community property states and identified a wider range of factors that bear on whether a spouse's interest is present and vested.

---

[31] *Id.*

> In reviewing the statutes of the eight American community property States, we are aware of the presence or lack of presence of rules that—
>
> 1. Make the community property liable for the managing spouse's separate torts;
> 2. Prevent the nonmanaging spouse from obligating by contract the community property;
> 3. Require, except in extraordinary circumstances, equal division of the community property upon its partition at divorce;
> 4. Allow the managing spouse to discharge his separate debts from community property; and
> 5. Require the managing spouse to make an accounting of all community property, including wages, when partitioned at the time of divorce.
>
> No one factor is determinative of the issue at hand.[32]

The Tax Court then showed that Sweden's Marriage Code lined up with the additional indicia of community property found in the American states.

> The Swedish Code addresses a number of these additional factors. For example, with the exception of debt incurred in connection with common household items and needs, in Sweden each spouse is responsible to repay his/her separate indebtedness; the spouse may make such repayments from his/her separate property or his/her interest in the marital property. Swedish Code, ch. 7, sec. I. *By comparison, the majority of the eight American community property States require similar treatment of the separate debts of spouses; some of the States that allow repayment of separate debts from community property require the spouse to reimburse the community for the expended funds.* Additionally, as above explained, the Swedish code requires that a married couple's marital property be divided equally upon separation or dissolution of the marriage by death or by divorce. After this initial equal division, the partition may be modified only where the nonmanaging spouse's interest has been unduly depleted through fraud or mismanagement of the managing spouse. *By comparison, the majority of the American community property States allow an ultimate*

---

32 *Id.*

> *unequal division of marital property only where the court deems it just and equitable.* The Swedish Code does not address specifically the question of whether the managing spouse must, at the time of partition, make an accounting of the acquisition and disposition of all marital property, including wages. However, the testimony reveals that, although an accounting would be necessary to divide the marital property in existence at the time of partition, a spouse may not be required to account for previously earned and expended wages. *Similarly, the laws of the eight American community property States are not clear in requiring an accounting of previously earned and expended wages* (emphasis added).

Westerdahl ultimately held that each spouse could report one-half of their U.S. earnings on each of their respective income tax returns, and concluded as follows:

> Although certain attributes of a spouse's giftoratt may appear to suggest a deferred interest or claim in marital property rather than a present vested interest,[33] all of these indicia are present in some of the recognized American community property States. We have weighed the presence and absence of the various attributes indicative of community property jurisdictions, and we are of the opinion that the laws of Sweden give a spouse a present vested interest in marital property which matures at the time the property is contributed to the marriage by the other spouse. Therefore, we conclude that petitioners' spouses had present vested interests in petitioners' U.S. earned income at the time the wages were earned. Accordingly, petitioners are entitled to report only one-half of their U.S. earnings on their respective Federal income tax returns for the years in issue.[34]

---

[33] Footnote 21 of *Westerdahl*: "Several attributes which suggest that a spouse's giftoratt is not a present vested interest are: (1) The giftoratt is not transferable during marriage; (2) a bank or other creditor likely will not value a spouse's giftoratt interest upon the spouse's application to obtain a loan and will not allow it to be used as collateral to secure a loan; and (3) a spouse may bind marital property contributed by the other spouse only for payment of children's educations and daily household needs."

[34] Westerdahl v. C.I.R., 82 T.C. 83, 95 (1984).

Westderahl is less about Sweden in particular and more about how federal tax law should evaluate any marital property regime that does not look exactly like the classic American community property model. The court's analysis notes that the eight American community property states themselves differ on questions of creditor rights, management powers, divorce allocations, and accounting rules, and yet all still qualify as "community property" for federal purposes. What unifies them, and ultimately brings Sweden into the fold, are the two "broad attributes" the court distills from *Seaborn*: First, each spouse's interest in the community is protected at death because the decedent may make testamentary disposition of only his or her half (with the other half preserved for the survivor or other heirs), and second, the managing spouse's powers are meaningfully constrained so that the nonmanaging spouse is protected against fraud, dissipation, and serious mismanagement.

Angerhofer and *Westerdahl* can be read to indicate that if a common law state includes these traditional attributes of community property from the laws of the original community property jurisdictions within its community property trust legislation, it should receive recognition in an elective from the IRS, or at the very least, from the Tax Court, in the event the IRS disputes a taxpayer's classification of property as community property.[35]

The Tax Court's analysis in *Westerdahl* establishes the functional requirements for federal recognition of community property, and those requirements do not depend on whether a regime is mandatory or elective. *Westerdahl* distilled the core inquiry into whether the foreign regime embodied two broad attributes derived from *Seaborn*:

(1) Protection of each spouse's interest at death by legally assuring that the decedent may dispose of only his or her one-half share, with the surviving spouse's half passing free of the decedent's control; and

(2) Meaningful limits on the managing spouse's power so that the nonmanaging spouse is shielded from detriment caused by fraud or mismanagement.

The court's willingness to find that Sweden's giftorätt regime satisfied these attributes—despite significant variations from "traditional" American community property states in areas such as accounting requirements,

---

[35] *See also* Joseph Percopo, *Understanding the New Florida Community Property Trust Part I*, 96(4) Fla. B. J., citing Travis Hayes, *To Share and Share Alike.*

debt allocation, and tort liability—confirms that federal tax law does not demand lockstep conformity with any particular "traditional" model.

Westerdahl's itemization of factors including tort liability rules, separate debt treatment, and division at divorce are corroborating indicia, not independent requirements. The court plainly stated that no one factor is determinative.

What matters for § 1014(b)(6) purposes is whether state law has created the ownership structure that justifies the full basis adjustment: a present vested interest in each spouse that arises at the moment property is contributed to the marriage, coupled with sufficient protections to ensure that each spouse's one-half share is preserved for testamentary disposition or partition upon divorce.

A common law state enacting elective community property legislation need not replicate every detail of California or Texas law, but it must vest each spouse with genuine co-ownership protected by the two core *Seaborn* attributes the *Westerdahl* court identified.

After an extensive review of the nation's brief but illuminating experiment with elective community property systems prior to the 1948 Act, along with *McCollum*, *Angerhofer*, and *Westerdahl*, the logical conclusion is that a properly drafted elective community property trust pursuant to a properly drafted elective community property act that provides a presently vested one-half interest in the property to each spouse should be fully effective to achieve the same federal tax results as "traditional" community property, specifically the full step-up in basis under I.R.C. § 1014(b)(6).[36]

The authors believe that the Service's position as outlined in Internal Revenue Manual 25.18.1.2.3 (updated as of May 3, 2023) is an incorrect reading of the applicability of the *Harmon* decision (pre-1948 Revenue Act) to the modern-day elective community property trust. The position is also hard to maintain considering post-1948 case law including *McCollum*, *Angerhofer*, and *Westerdahl*. Even in *Poe v. Seaborn*, the Commissioner conceded

---

[36] We note that, in *Commissioner v. Estate of Bosch*, 387 U.S. 456 (1967), the Supreme Court held that federal authorities are not conclusively bound by a state trial court's characterization of property interests for federal tax purposes. If the state's highest court has ruled on the issue, federal courts must follow that ruling. If it has not, federal authorities must apply what they find to be the state law after giving "proper regard" to relevant rulings of other courts of the State.

that the answer to the question "must be found in the provisions of the law of the state as to a wife's ownership of or interest in community property."[37]

> What, then, is the law of Washington as to the ownership of community property and of community income including the earnings of the husband's and wife's labor?
>
> The answer is found in the statutes of the state and the decisions interpreting them.
>
> These statutes provide that, save for property acquired by gift, bequest, devise or inheritance, all property however acquired after marriage, by either husband or wife, or by both, is community property. On the death of either spouse his or her interest is subject to testamentary disposition, and failing that, it passes to the issue of the decedent and not to the surviving spouse. While the husband has the management and control of community personal property and like power of disposition thereof as of his separate personal property, this power is subject to restrictions which are inconsistent with denial of the wife's interest as coowner. The wife may borrow for community purposes and bind the community property. . . . Since the husband may not discharge his separate obligation out of community property, she may, suing alone, enjoin collection of his separate debt out of community property. . . . She may prevent his making substantial gifts out of community property without her consent. . . . The community property is not liable for the husband's torts not committed in carrying on the business of the community.[38]

The IRS's reliance on *Harmon* to exclude elective regimes per se is thus indefensible on the authorities themselves. *Harmon* addressed income splitting in the pre-1948 era when the assignment of income doctrine was in tension with community property principles. Congress resolved that tension by extending income splitting nationwide and by enacting § 1014(b)(6) without any pedigree qualifier. To cite *Harmon* in 2025 for the proposition that elective community property regimes cannot qualify is to misapply

---

[37] Poe v. Seaborn, 282 U.S. 101, 110 (1930).

[38] *Id. See also Westerdahl,* footnote 15.

a pre-1948 decision to a statute enacted in deliberate rejection of *Harmon*'s distinctions.

Nothing in the Internal Revenue Code or its legislative history conditions the result on whether the state's regime is ancient, mandatory, or elective.[39] The "consensual" versus "legal" distinction in the *Harmon* majority opinion is best understood as the Supreme Court's attempt to coordinate the assignment of income doctrine with community property principles during an era in which the ability to split income was not available to those in common law states.

Section 1014(b)(6) refers simply to property held "under the community property laws of any State," and Congress's choice of that unqualified phrasing reflects its broader shift toward fully respecting state-defined property rights as the foundation for determining federal tax consequences.

ESTABLISHING A COMMUNITY PROPERTY TRUST

The next question for many practitioners will be: "So which state has the best community property trust legislation?" This chapter explores the answer to this question. At the outset, the authors note that Alaska's statute is the strongest, in part because Alaska law allows resident spouses of Alaskans to hold community property in non-trust form and allows the creditors of one spouse to receive community property titled in the name of the other spouse or jointly.[40] However, any state community property trust statute that effectively vests an undivided one-half interest in the community property trust in each spouse, and provides that one-half of the property in the community property trust will not be freely devisable by the first dying spouse, should be effective to obtain the § 1014(b)(6) step-up in basis with respect to such property, as long as at least one-half of the whole of the

[39] *Westerdahl* does make clear that the determination of whether property is "community" for federal tax purposes will include a review of factors such as whether laws are in place that limit the managing spouse's powers of management and control so that detriment to the nonmanaging spouse from fraud or mismanagement will be minimized, but that these factors are not prerequisites for finding a present vested interest.

[40] *See* Alaska Stat. § 34.77.090 ("community property agreement") and compare to § 34.77.100 ("community property trust").

community interest in the property is includible in determining the value of the decedent's gross estate.[41]

The rise of the elective community property trust over the past 25 years has produced five distinct legislative frameworks—those of Alaska, Tennessee, South Dakota, Kentucky, and Florida. Each state's Act enables spouses domiciled either within or outside the state to opt in to a community property regime by transferring assets to a properly structured trust (and also by a properly structured "community property trust agreement" in Alaska).[42]

Alaska

In 1998, Alaska became the first state to enact an elective community property trust regime pursuant to the Alaska Community Property Trust Act, codified in title 34, chapter 77 of the Alaska Statutes.[43] Under Alaska's framework, the property of a married couple is community property under Alaska law to the extent provided in a community property agreement or a community property trust.[44]

With respect to a CPT Trust Act, the Alaska Community Property Act provides that property held in a trust is community property if each of the following is satisfied:

1. One or both spouses transfer property to the trust.
2. The trust expressly provides that some or all of the transferred property is community property under Alaska law.
3. At least one trustee is an Alaskan "qualified person."[45]

---

[41] I.R.C. § 1014(b)(6).

[42] ALASKA STAT. § 34.77.090.

[43] *See* BLATTMACHR, ZARITSKY & ASCHER, TAX PLANNING WITH CONSENSUAL COMMUNITY PROPERTY: ALASKA'S NEW COMMUNITY PROPERTY LAW (1999).

[44] ALASKA STAT. § 34.77.030(a).

[45] Which is defined as any individual who resides in Alaska, whose true and permanent home is in Alaska, who does not have a present intention of moving away from Alaska, and who intends to return to Alaska when away or a trust company or bank that is organized under Alaska law or a banking association organized under federal banking law if the bank possesses trust powers and has its principal place of business in Alaska. ALASKA STAT. § 34.77.100(a).

4. The powers of the qualified trustee "include or are limited to maintaining records for the trust on an exclusive or a nonexclusive basis and preparing or arranging for the preparation of, on an exclusive or nonexclusive basis, any income tax returns that must be filed by the trust."
5. The trust is signed by both spouses.
6. The trust contains the following language in all capitalized letters at the beginning of the trust instrument:

> THE CONSEQUENCES OF THIS TRUST MAY BE VERY EXTENSIVE, INCLUDING, BUT NOT LIMITED TO, YOUR RIGHTS WITH RESPECT TO CREDITORS AND OTHER THIRD PARTIES, AND YOUR RIGHTS WITH YOUR SPOUSE BOTH DURING THE COURSE OF YOUR MARRIAGE AND AT THE TIME OF A DIVORCE. ACCORDINGLY, THIS AGREEMENT SHOULD ONLY BE SIGNED AFTER CAREFUL CONSIDERATION. IF YOU HAVE ANY QUESTIONS ABOUT THIS AGREEMENT, YOU SHOULD SEEK COMPETENT ADVICE.

An Alaska community property trust may also set forth the spouses' rights and obligations in the property transferred to the trust, regardless of when and where the property was acquired or located;[46] the management and control of the property transferred to the trust;[47] the disposition of the property transferred to the trust on dissolution of marriage, death, or the occurrence or nonoccurrence of another event;[48] the choice of law governing the interpretation of the trust;[49] and any other provision that affects the property transferred to the trust and does not violate public policy or a statute imposing a criminal penalty.[50]

Alaska's Act is comprehensive, and seeks to mirror many of the presumptions that are applied in historical community property states. For example, the Act includes a statute that provides that mixing community property with property of another character will reclassify the property as

---

46 ALASKA STAT. § 34.77.100(d)(1).

47 *Id.* § 34.77.100(d)(2).

48 *Id.* § 34.77.100(d)(3).

49 *Id.* § 34.77.100(d)(4).

50 *Id.* § 34.77.100(d)(5).

community property unless the noncommunity property that was commingled into the community property fund can be traced.[51]

In Alaska, an obligation incurred by only one spouse before or during marriage may be satisfied only from the property of that spouse that is not community property and from that spouse's one-half interest in the community property.[52]

Tennessee

Tennessee's Community Property Trust Act was passed in 2010, and is codified in Tennessee Code §§ 35-17-101 to 37-15-108. Unlike Alaska, in Tennessee, the only way to hold property as community property is in trust.

Under Tennessee law, a trust arrangement qualifies as a community property trust if one or both spouses transfer property to a trust that: (1) expressly declares that the trust is a Tennessee community property trust, (2) has at least one trustee who is a "qualified trustee,"[53] (3) is signed by both spouses, and (4) contains the following language in capital letters at the beginning of the trust:

> THE CONSEQUENCES OF THIS TRUST MAY BE VERY EXTENSIVE, INCLUDING, BUT NOT LIMITED TO, YOUR RIGHTS WITH YOUR SPOUSE BOTH DURING THE COURSE OF YOUR MARRIAGE AND AT THE TIME OF A DIVORCE. ACCORDINGLY, THIS AGREEMENT SHOULD ONLY BE SIGNED AFTER CAREFUL CONSIDERATION. IF YOU HAVE ANY QUESTIONS ABOUT THIS AGREEMENT, YOU SHOULD SEEK COMPETENT ADVICE.

A Tennessee community property trust may also set forth the spouses' respective rights and obligations in the property contributed to the trust, regardless of when the property was acquired or where it is located.[54] The instrument may further address the management and control of trust

---

[51] *Id.* § 34.77.130.

[52] *Id.* § 34.77.070(j).

[53] A qualified trustee is defined as a natural person who is a resident of Tennessee or a company authorized to act as a fiduciarty in Tennessee pursuant to TN Code § 45-2-1001. *See* TN CODE § 35-17-102(6).

[54] TENN. CODE § 35-17-104(a)(1).

assets[55] and the disposition of property upon dissolution of marriage, death, or other specified events[56] and may designate the governing law applicable to its interpretation.[57] The trust may also include any other provisions affecting the property as long as such provisions are not contrary to public policy or a law imposing a criminal penalty.[58]

In Tennessee, an obligation incurred by only one spouse before or during marriage may be satisfied from that spouse's one-half share of a community property trust.[59]

Either spouse may amend the trust as to the disposition of his or her one-half share of the community property upon death.[60] Otherwise, a Tennessee community property trust may not be amended or revoked unless the agreement itself provides for amendment or revocation.[61]

Tennessee Code § 35-17-105(e) specifically provides that once property is distributed from a community property trust, it shall no longer constitute community property. Upon dissolution of the marriage of the settlor spouses, the community property trust terminates, and the trustee has a statutory duty to distribute one-half of the trust assets to each spouse, "with each spouse receiving one-half of each asset, unless otherwise agreed to in writing by both spouses."[62]

---

[55] *Id.* § 35-17-104(a)(2).

[56] *Id.* § 35-17-104(a)(3).

[57] *Id.* § 35-17-104(a)(4).

[58] *Id.* § 35-17-104(a)(5).

[59] *Id.* § 35-17-106(a).

[60] *Id.* § 35-17-104(b)(1).

[61] *Id.* § 35-17-104(b)(2). The authors note that it is odd for the Tennessee Act to presume irrevocability for a community property trust. By contrast, Florida's Act states that a community property trust is amendable or revocable by the spouses unless the trust agreement specifically provides that the trust is irrevocable. FLA. STAT. § 736.1504(3). Importantly, an irrevocable community property trust's assets would not receive a § 1014(b)(6) full step-up on the first death, unless the trust contained other features that caused it to be an incomplete gift trust, since a requirement of § 1014(b)(6) is that at least one-half of the whole of the community property is includible in determining the value of the decedent's gross estate.

[62] TENN. CODE § 35-17-108.

Kentucky

In 2020, the Commonwealth of Kentucky enacted the Kentucky Community Property Trust Act, codified at Kentucky Revised Statutes §§ 386.620–386.624 (effective July 15, 2020), creating an elective community property trust regime. Under this framework, married spouses may elect to treat some or all of their property as community property by transferring it to a trust that meets the statutory requirements of a community property trust.[63] To qualify, one or both spouses must transfer property into an express trust that: expressly declares itself a Kentucky community property trust, has at least one "qualified trustee" whose powers include maintaining records and preparing or arranging preparation of any trust income tax returns, is signed by both spouses, and contains the required warning language in all caps at the beginning of the document.[64] The warning states:

> THE CONSEQUENCES OF THIS TRUST MAY BE VERY EXTENSIVE, INCLUDING BUT NOT LIMITED TO YOUR RIGHTS WITH YOUR SPOUSE BOTH DURING THE COURSE OF YOUR MARRIAGE AND AT THE TIME OF A DIVORCE. ACCORDINGLY, THIS AGREEMENT SHOULD ONLY BE SIGNED AFTER CAREFUL CONSIDERATION. IF YOU HAVE ANY QUESTIONS ABOUT THIS AGREEMENT, YOU SHOULD SEEK COMPETENT ADVICE.[65]

The statute further provides that whether or not one or both spouses are domiciled in Kentucky, the trust may classify property as community property,[66] and that the trust is enforceable without consideration.[67] Once property is held in a properly constituted community property trust, all property owned by the trust is considered community property during the marriage, and when distributed from the trust it ceases to be community

---

[63] Ky. Rev. Stat. § 386.622(1)(a)–(d).

[64] *Id.* A qualified trustee is defined in the Kentucky Act as a natural person who is a resident of the state or a bank or trust company authorized to act as a trustee within the state. Ky. Rev. Stat. § 386.620(6).

[65] *Id.* § 386.622(1)(d).

[66] *Id.* § 386.622(5).

[67] *Id.* § 386.622(6).

property.[68] For obligations incurred by only one spouse before or during the marriage, only that spouse's one-half share of trust property may be used to satisfy the obligation, whereas obligations incurred by both spouses may be satisfied from the trust.[69] Upon the death of a spouse, one-half of the aggregate value of the trust property reflects the survivor's share, one-half reflects the decedent's share, and unless otherwise agreed, the trustee may distribute assets pro rata or non–pro rata.[70] Upon dissolution of the marriage, the trust terminates, and the trustee is required to distribute one-half of the assets to each spouse (unless the spouses agree otherwise in writing).[71]

Interestingly, the Kentucky community property trust, like Tennessee's, is presumed irrevocable unless the trust instrument expressly provides otherwise.[72] The statute allows a community property trust to be made revocable if the agreement itself includes provisions permitting amendment or revocation by one or both spouses.[73] From a planning perspective, this distinction is significant and can serve as a trap for the unwary. For purposes of the double step-up in basis, practitioners should ensure that any Kentucky community property trust contains language making it revocable. If the trust is irrevocable, property held within it would generally be excluded from the decedent's gross estate, thereby failing to meet the requirements for obtaining the double step-up in basis.[74]

---

68 *Id.* § 386.622(7)–(8).

69 *Id.* § 386.624(1)–(2).

70 *Id.* § 386.624(3).

71 *Id.* § 386.624(4).

72 *Id.* § 386.622(4).

73 *Id.*

74 I.R.C. § 1014(a); § 1014(b)(6). Gross estate inclusion appears to be a prerequisite to the step-up in basis under I.R.C. § 1014, in order to satisfy § 1014(a)'s requirement that the property be acquired from a decedent. Even the Regulations specifically provide that, in addition to the property described in 1.1014-2(a), "in the case of a decedent dying after December 31, 1953, property shall also be considered to have been acquired from the decedent to the extent that both of the following conditions are met: (i) the property was acquired from the decedent by reason of death, form of ownership, or other conditions (including property acquired through the exercise or non-exercise of a power of appointment), *and* (ii) the property is includible in the decedent's gross estate under the provisions

South Dakota

South Dakota's "special spousal trust" regime is anchored in S.D. Codified Laws § 55-17-5, which expressly ties these trusts to the federal community property basis rules in I.R.C. § 1014(b)(6).[75] For purposes of applying § 1014(b)(6), the statute provides that a South Dakota special spousal trust is treated as a trust established under the state's community property laws, and that "special spousal property" is community property for that limited federal income tax purpose.[76] Community property classified as such under another jurisdiction's law retains its community property character when transferred into a South Dakota special spousal trust and, upon revocation and distribution, continues to be treated as community property to the extent South Dakota law otherwise permits.[77] These provisions allow married couples, including couples migrating from community property states, to seek a full step-up in basis on both halves of the special spousal property at the first spouse's death.[78]

An arrangement qualifies as a South Dakota special spousal trust if one or both spouses transfer property to a trust that expressly declares some or all of the transferred property to be South Dakota special spousal property and has at least one trustee who is a "qualified person" within the meaning of §§ 55-3-39 and 55-3-41.[79] A "qualified person" includes a South Dakota resident individual, a South Dakota-chartered trust company, or a bank or savings association with trust powers and its principal place of business in South Dakota, provided the state's jurisdictional requirements for trusts are satisfied.[80] The special spousal trust is enforceable without consideration, may be revocable or irrevocable, and may have one or both spouses serving

---

of the Internal Revenue Code of 1954, or the Internal Revenue Code of 1939, because of such acquisition" (emphasis added). Treas. Reg. § 1.1014-2(b)(1). This is the Service's position as well. Rev. Rul. 2023-2.

[75] S.D. Codified Laws § 55-17-5 (2024); I.R.C. § 1014(b)(6).

[76] S.D. Codified Laws § 55-17-5 (2024).

[77] *Id.*

[78] *Id.* Note that the Internal Revenue Service has not yet issued specific guidance on South Dakota special spousal trusts or similar elective community property techniques.

[79] *Id.* § 55-17-1; *id.* §§ 55-3-39, 55-3-41.

[80] *Id.* § 55-3-41.

as trustee, but it must be signed by both spouses.[81] These requirements enable married couples nationwide to avail themselves of South Dakota's elective community-property-by-designation regime without changing their domicile, so long as the statutory trustee and drafting conditions are met.[82]

Every special spousal trust must include, at the beginning of the document, an all-caps warning stating that the trust may have significant consequences for the rights of each spouse, including how those rights may be affected during the marriage, in the event of divorce, and at death, as well as potential implications for creditors and third parties.[83] The warning must also advise the spouses to seek independent legal advice.[84] From a drafting standpoint, practitioners should reproduce the statutory warning language verbatim and place it conspicuously at the front of the document to avoid any argument that the trust fails to satisfy this mandatory condition. Because the warning expressly references creditor and marital-rights consequences, it also provides later evidentiary support that the spouses were put on notice of the legal implications of electing special spousal property treatment.

Spouses may classify all or any portion of their property as special spousal property by transferring it to a South Dakota special spousal trust and expressly declaring in the trust that the property is community property for purposes of the statute.[85] Absent a contrary provision in the governing instrument, each spouse is deemed to own a 50 percent interest in the special spousal property held in the trust.[86] A special spousal trust may not be amended or revoked unless the trust agreement itself authorizes

---

81 *Id.* § 55-17-1.

82 *Id.* §§ 55-17-1, 55-3-39.

83 *Id.* § 55-17-2.

84 *Id.* "THE CONSEQUENCES OF THIS TRUST MAY BE VERY EXTENSIVE, INCLUDING YOUR RIGHTS WITH RESPECT TO CREDITORS AND OTHER THIRD PARTIES, AND YOUR RIGHTS WITH YOUR SPOUSE BOTH DURING THE COURSE OF YOUR MARRIAGE, AT THE TIME OF A DIVORCE, AND AT THE DEATH OF YOU OR YOUR SPOUSE. ACCORDINGLY, THIS TRUST AGREEMENT SHOULD ONLY BE SIGNED AFTER CAREFUL CONSIDERATION. IF YOU HAVE ANY QUESTIONS ABOUT THIS TRUST AGREEMENT, YOU SHOULD SEEK INDEPENDENT LEGAL ADVICE."

85 *Id.* § 55-17-3.

86 *Id.*

amendment or revocation, or the trust is amended or revoked by a later South Dakota special spousal trust, and any such amendment or revocation is enforceable without consideration.[87] After the first spouse's death, and unless the instrument provides otherwise, the surviving spouse may unilaterally amend the trust with respect to the "surviving spouse's property," defined to include the survivor's non–special spousal property and the survivor's share of the special spousal property as of the first spouse's date of death.[88]

A transfer to a South Dakota special spousal trust may also constitute a "qualified disposition in trust" if the transfer satisfies the requirements of the state's domestic asset-protection trust statute in chapter 55-16, permitting the couple to combine elective community property treatment with South Dakota's asset-protection regime.[89] As a practical matter, some practitioners may prefer to segregate designated community property into a standalone South Dakota special spousal trust and hold noncommunity property in a separate trust or trusts in order to reduce the risk that the trust fails to achieve its intended federal income tax or asset protection objective. In addition to direct conveyances, property is treated as transferred to a special spousal trust when assets such as life insurance, retirement accounts, or similar arrangements designate the trust as beneficiary, in which case the property received at the first spouse's death is treated as the surviving spouse's non–special spousal property unless the trust expressly classifies it as special spousal property.[90] The trustee is obligated to maintain records identifying which trust assets are South Dakota special spousal property and which are not, a practical requirement if the trust will hold both designated community property and separate-type assets.[91]

Within a South Dakota special spousal trust, the spouses may agree on the rights and obligations in the transferred property, its management and control, its disposition on dissolution of marriage or death (subject to default South Dakota law if the instrument is silent on dissolution), the choice of governing law for trust interpretation, and any other matter

87 *Id.* § 55-17-4.

88 *Id.*

89 *Id.* § 55-17-6; *id.* ch. 55-16.

90 *Id.* § 55-17-7.

91 *Id.* § 55-17-8.

affecting the transferred property that does not violate public policy or a criminal statute.[92] Those contractual freedoms are limited, however, by explicit protections for children and creditors. A special spousal trust may not adversely affect a child's right to support, and creditor rights are preserved in revocable trusts for creditors without actual knowledge, and in irrevocable trusts to the extent provided under the qualified-disposition rules in South Dakota statute chapter 55-16.[93] The statute also imposes a non-waivable duty of good faith between spouses in matters involving South Dakota special spousal property, reinforcing the marital fiduciary overlay on these arrangements.[94]

Transactions with bona fide purchasers are protected notwithstanding the existence of a special spousal trust or the parties' marital status, thereby preserving the alienability of special spousal property and protecting third parties who transact in reliance on record title or management authority. Notice of the trust or the marriage does not defeat bona fide purchaser status, and a purchaser from a spouse who has the right to manage and control special spousal property takes free of any claim of the other spouse.[95] A "bona fide purchaser" is defined as a good-faith purchaser for value who is not a party to fraud or illegality, has no notice of an adverse spousal claim, and acquires property for value in a voluntary transaction, with value broadly defined to include consideration such as new credit, satisfaction of preexisting claims, or other contract-sufficient consideration.[96] Finally, a South Dakota special spousal trust executed during marriage is unenforceable if (1) it was unconscionable when made, or (2) the spouse against whom enforcement is sought did not execute the agreement voluntarily or with fair and reasonable disclosure (or a valid waiver) of the other spouse's property and financial obligations, with unconscionability determined as a matter of law.[97] From a planning perspective, South Dakota's special spousal trust regime allows married couples, including those relocating from community property jurisdictions, to designate community property

---

[92] *Id.* § 55-17-9.

[93] *Id.* §§ 55-17-10, 55-17-11; *id.* ch. 55-16.

[94] *Id.* § 55-17-11.

[95] *Id.* § 55-17-12.

[96] *Id.* § 55-17-13.

[97] *Id.* § 55-17-14.

treatment for selected assets in order to pursue a double step-up in basis under § 1014(b)(6), but careful drafting is essential to ensure that the trust both satisfies the statutory formalities and achieves the desired estate-tax inclusion and creditor-rights outcomes.

Florida

Florida's Community Property Trust Act was passed in 2021 and is codified in Florida Statutes §§ 736.1501–736.1512.

The Act provides that "'Community Property' means the property and the appreciation of and income from the property owned by a qualified trustee of a community property trust during the marriage of the settlor spouses."[98]

A community property trust is a "trust that complies with s. 736.1503 and is created on or after July 1, 2021."[99] Therefore, it appears that a preexisting trust cannot be converted into a community property trust, but trust assets existing on or before July 1, 2021, can be "decanted" or transferred into a new community property trust.

A trust arrangement qualifies as a Florida community property trust if one or both spouses transfer property to a trust that: (1) expressly declares that the trust is a community property trust within the meaning of § 736.1503; (2) has at least one trustee who is a qualified trustee, provided that both spouses or either spouse also may be a trustee; (3) is signed by both spouses consistent with the formalities required for the execution of a trust under the Florida Trust Code; and (4) contains language substantially similar to the following at the beginning of the community property trust agreement:

> THE CONSEQUENCES OF THIS COMMUNITY PROPERTY TRUST MAY BE VERY EXTENSIVE, INCLUDING, BUT NOT LIMITED TO, YOUR RIGHTS WITH RESPECT TO CREDITORS AND OTHER THIRD PARTIES, AND YOUR RIGHTS WITH YOUR SPOUSE DURING THE COURSE OF YOUR MARRIAGE, AT THE TIME OF A DIVORCE, AND UPON THE DEATH OF YOU OR YOUR SPOUSE. ACCORDINGLY, THIS TRUST AGREEMENT

---

[98] Fla. Stat. § 736.1501(2).

[99] *Id.* § 736.1502(2).

SHOULD BE SIGNED ONLY AFTER CAREFUL CONSIDERATION. IF YOU HAVE ANY QUESTIONS ABOUT THIS TRUST AGREEMENT, YOU SHOULD SEEK COMPETENT AND INDEPENDENT LEGAL ADVICE. ALTHOUGH NOT A REQUIREMENT, IT IS STRONGLY ADVISABLE THAT EACH SPOUSE OBTAIN THEIR OWN SEPARATE LEGAL COUNSEL PRIOR TO THE EXECUTION OF THIS TRUST.[100]

In the agreement establishing the Florida community property trust, the settlor spouses may also agree upon the rights and obligations in the property transferred to the trust, notwithstanding when and where the property is acquired or located;[101] the management and control of the property transferred into the trust;[102] and the disposition of the property transferred to the trust on dissolution of marriage, death, or the occurrence or nonoccurrence of another event, subject to two important limitations.[103]

Limitation 1. Under Florida Statute § 736.1507, upon "the death of a spouse, one-half of the aggregate value of the property held in a community property trust . . . is not subject to testamentary disposition by the decedent spouse or distribution under the laws of succession. . . . The other one-half . . . reflects the share of the decedent spouse and is subject to testamentary disposition or distribution under the laws of succession of the state."

Limitation 2. Florida Statute § 736.1508 states that, upon dissolution of the marriage of the couple, the community property trust will terminate, and the trustee will distribute one-half of the trust assets to each spouse.

The spouses may further provide for provision of any other matter that affects the property transferred to the trust and does not violate public policy or general law imposing a criminal penalty, or result in the property not being treated as community property under the laws of a relevant jurisdiction.[104]

The spouses can agree whether the trust is revocable or irrevocable,[105] and the presumption is that the trust is revocable unless the agreement

---

[100] *Id.* § 736.1503.

[101] *Id.* § 736.1504(1)(a).

[102] *Id.* § 736.1504(1)(b).

[103] *Id.* § 736.1504(1)(c).

[104] *Id.* § 736.1504(1)(e).

[105] *Id.* § 736.1504(1)(d).

itself specifically provides that it is irrevocable.[106] Regardless of whether agreement provides that the community property trust is irrevocable, in the event of the death of one of the settlor spouses, the surviving spouse may amend a community property trust regarding the disposition of his or her one-half share of the community property.

An obligation incurred by only one spouse before or during marriage may be satisfied from that spouse's one-half share of a community property trust, unless a greater amount is otherwise provided in the community property trust agreement.[107]

Upon the death of a spouse, one-half of the aggregate value of the property held in a Florida community property trust reflects the share of the surviving spouse and is not subject to testamentary disposition by the decedent spouse or distribution under the laws of succession of the state. The other one-half of the value of that property reflects the share of the decedent spouse and is subject to testamentary disposition or distribution under the laws of succession of the state.[108] Unless provided otherwise in the trust agreement, the trustee has the power to distribute assets of the trust in divided or undivided interests and to adjust resulting differences in valuation.[109] A distribution in kind may be made on the basis of a non–pro rata division of the aggregate value of the trust assets, on the basis of a pro rata division of each individual asset, or by using both methods.[110] The decedent's spouse's one-half share is not included in the elective estate.[111]

An advantage of the Florida community property trust is that it provides that the settlor spouses shall be deemed to be the only qualified beneficiaries of the trust, regardless of whether the trust is revocable or irrevocable, notwithstanding any other provision of the Florida Trust Code.[112] Because Florida Statute § 736.1504 dictates that settlor spouses will be considered the only qualified beneficiaries of the trust until the death of one of the spouses, the trustee of a Florida community property trust owes no duty to

---

[106] *Id.* § 736.1504(3).

[107] *Id.* § 736.1506(1).

[108] *Id.* § 736.1507.

[109] *Id.*

[110] *Id.*

[111] *Id.*

[112] FLA. STAT. § 736.1504(4).

the settlor spouses' descendants or other would-be qualified beneficiaries (while both settlor spouses are alive) to keep them reasonably informed of the trust and its administration. As a result, this statutory quirk can offer a real privacy advantage by eliminating a duty to keep a first-line remainder beneficiary informed while both spouses are alive.[113]

Upon the dissolution of marriage of the settlor spouses, the community property trust shall terminate, and the trustee shall distribute one-half of the trust assets to each spouse in accordance with § 736.1508(3).[114] For purposes of Florida's Act, Florida's statute on equitable distribution does not apply to the disposition of the assets and liabilities held in a community property trust.[115]

The initiation of an action to dissolve the settlor spouses' marriage does not automatically terminate the community property trust unless otherwise agreed to by the settlor spouses in writing or otherwise ordered by the court having jurisdiction over the dissolution of marriage proceedings between the settlor spouses.[116]

However, if an action to dissolve the settlor spouses' marriage remains pending for 180 days, the trust automatically terminates, and the trustee must distribute one-half of the trust assets to each spouse in accordance with § 736.1508(3), unless: (1) one spouse objects to the termination within 180 days following the filing of the dissolution action, at which time either party may request that the court having jurisdiction over the dissolution of marriage determine if good cause exists to terminate the community property trust during the pendency of the dissolution of marriage action; (2) the court overseeing the dissolution of marriage action enters an order directing otherwise; (3) the spouses otherwise agree, in writing, while the dissolution of marriage action is pending; or (4) the community property trust agreement provides otherwise.

With respect to distributing property at divorce, Florida Statute § 736.1508(3) provides that, unless otherwise provided in the Florida

[113] *See* Gassman, Blattmachr & Exline, *Using the Florida Irrevocable Community Property Trust to Protect an Elderly Couple from Abuse, Leimberg Information Services Newsletter* – Archive Message #2914, Oct. 14, 2021.

[114] Fla. Stat. § 736.1508(1).

[115] *Id.*

[116] *Id.* § 736.1508(2).

community property trust agreement, the trustee has the power to distribute assets of the trust in divided or undivided interests and to adjust resulting differences in valuation. A distribution in kind may be made on the basis of a non–pro rata division of the aggregate value of the trust assets, on the basis of a pro rata division of each individual asset, or by using both methods.[117] A trustee may not distribute real property or business interests in a manner that would leave the settlor spouses as co-owners of such assets after divorce or termination of the community property trust, unless otherwise agreed to by the settlor spouses in a separate written agreement executed during the dissolution of marriage action.[118] Finally, § 736.1508(3) provides that "notwithstanding any other provision of this section, the community property trust cannot be terminated, and the assets cannot be distributed, in a manner that could cause the trust assets to not be treated as community property."

The last sentence of § 736.1508(3) contemplates the distribution of assets upon termination of a Florida community property trust due to divorce; however, the subsection appears to conflict with § 736.1505(5), which provides that "when property is distributed from a community property trust, the property shall no longer constitute community property within the meaning of this part[.]" Thus, if § 736.1508(3) were read literally, the clause would make the trust practically irrevocable.[119]

Upon divorce or death, the community ceases to exist. Just as nonspouses cannot hold property as tenants by the entireties, they likewise cannot hold property as community property. Certainly, the provision was added to Florida's Act with the intent of a belt-and-suspenders measure to reinforce eligibility for the benefits of § 1014(b)(6). However, when

---

117 *Id.* § 736.1508(3).

118 *Id.*

119 If the property is no longer community property once the trust is terminated, how can a Florida community property trust be terminated in a manner that satisfies § 736.1508(3) and that would allow the trust assets to continue to be treated as community property? The inconsistency in the drafting more importantly reminds us that the ability to hold community property outside of trust form (such as by simple community property agreement that provides that all property now owned or hereafter acquired by either spouse is community property) is what makes Alaska's statutory scheme so much closer to that of a traditional community property state.

read literally, it would prevent the spouses from ever terminating the trust during their lifetimes.

In states such as Florida that only recognize and allow for community property treatment in trust form, when assets are distributed out of the trust, the assets do not retain their character as community,[120] at least insofar as the assets were not community property before they were transferred to the trust. Florida Statute § 736.1511 provides that "[c]ommunity property, as classified by a jurisdiction other than this state, which is transferred to a community property trust retains its character as community property while in the trust. If the trust is revoked and property is transferred on revocation of the trust, the community property as classified by a jurisdiction other than the state retains its character as community property to the extent otherwise provided by [the FUDCPRDA]."

Thus, married couples moving from California to Florida could establish a Florida community property trust to hold their community property, and later revoke the trust, and the assets would continue to be treated as community property. However, couples may instead fund a standard joint revocable trust with community property prior to moving from a community property state with terms that reflect and preserve the community character of the trust assets.

For practitioners focused on ensuring eligibility for the full step-up in basis under § 1014(b)(6), previously acquired community property generally should not be used to fund an elective community property trust. Instead, assets that are already community property should be placed into a standard joint revocable trust that reflects and preserves their existing community character. Only assets that are not already community property should be contributed to the elective community property trust, thereby converting *those* assets to community property under Florida's elective regime. This structure preserves the original community property character of assets acquired in the former community property state, while clearly segregating and documenting the elective community property treatment applied to assets acquired after moving to Florida.

---

[120] Florida's, Kentucky's, and Tennessee's Community Property Trust Acts all specifically provide that the assets are no longer community property once distributed from the trust.

Chapter 10

Life Insurance, IRAs, Preparing the Form 706, and Other Issues with Community Property

PREPARING FORM 706

Community property presents a unique reporting classification on Form 706 because, as a matter of state law, each spouse owns a present, vested one-half interest in every community asset. At death, only the decedent's one-half interest is includible in the gross estate under § 2033, but the federal return requires that the full property itself be identified and described wherever it would normally appear—on Schedule A if it is real property, Schedule B if it is stock, Schedule F if it is tangible personal property, and so on.

Although community property may be jointly owned by spouses, it is not reported on Schedule E because Schedule E is limited to property held as joint tenants with right of survivorship or tenants by the entirety. Those forms of ownership include a survivorship feature that causes the decedent's interest to be extinguished at death and therefore require special inclusion rules under § 2040. Community property, by contrast, is not a survivorship estate. Each spouse owns a present, vested, undivided one-half interest during life, and that interest does not pass to the surviving spouse by operation of law at death. Instead, the decedent's half of the community must be administered as part of the probate or trust estate, and the survivor retains only his or her existing half.

Because community property lacks the survivorship element that defines Schedule E property, it is not reported on Schedule E but instead is listed on the schedule corresponding to the type of asset involved.

Once reported on the appropriate asset schedule, the preparer must show only the decedent's one-half community interest in the value column. There are two accepted ways to accomplish this:

(1) Under the gross method, the full fair market value of the asset is entered in the value column of the relevant schedule, and the spouse's one-half community interest is then subtracted as the final line item on that schedule. This method reflects the full value on the face of the return and may be useful when reconciling totals across schedules, but it requires the additional subtraction entry to arrive at the includible amount.

(2) Under the net method, the full value of the asset is still disclosed in the description section, often with an explicit notation that only one-half is includible as community property, but the value column carries only the decedent's one-half community interest (or the discounted value of that half, if valuation adjustments apply). This avoids the need for a separate subtraction line and typically produces a cleaner interface with preparation software and Form 8971.[1]

The net method does seem to be preferred over the gross method.[2]

---

[1] Portfolio 822-3rd: Estate, Gift, and Generation-Skipping Transfer Tax Returns and Audits, V. Community Property and Form 706, B. Differences in the Community Property Form 706.

[2] "Community property assets are commonly reported on the estate tax returns by showing the full value of the property and then a separate line item backing out the one-half portion attributable to the surviving spouse. Consider instead reporting these assets as a one-half community property interest in the property, which will require less adjustments in the software when preparing Form 8971 [ ]. When this is done, it is recommended that the full value of the property be reported in the asset description but place only one-half the value in the value columns (or the discounted value if so determined). Years later, when heirs are referring to the Form 706 for basis information, it is administratively simpler to have the full value of the property listed rather than starting with one-half of the value." *Id.*

Determining What Is Community Property: A State Law Inquiry

Before turning to any particular schedule on the Form 706, the preparer must confirm which assets are truly community and which are separate. This characterization drives both inclusion and deduction, because only the decedent's one-half community interest is included in the gross estate, and only the portion of debts and expenses properly chargeable to the decedent's half of the community are deductible.

The Form 706 instructions and federal case law make clear that § 2033 includes only the property interests that the decedent actually owned under state law. In a community property state, this inquiry begins with the presumption that property acquired during marriage is community property unless proved otherwise. That presumption may be strengthened or weakened, but in all cases it is the estate's burden to demonstrate the property's character as community property, and the IRS may be more likely to question that classification when the spouses have lived particularly mobile lives.[3]

Practitioners should also consider the taxpayer's duty of consistency when characterizing assets as community or separate. Where the taxpayer (or the couple) previously reported an asset as separate property or otherwise represented a particular ownership characterization on prior income, gift, or other tax filings, and the government relied on that representation, the estate or surviving spouse may be precluded from later adopting an inconsistent position to obtain a more favorable estate tax inclusion, deduction, or basis result. This risk is heightened in mobile client fact patterns, where titles, registrations, and state law characterizations may not line up neatly over time. At a minimum, the preparer should identify any prior reporting positions (including basis reporting) that might be inconsistent with the Form 706 characterization, and either conform the reporting or document the legal and factual basis for any change.

The determination of what constitutes community property of the decedent's will require looking beyond titles and account registrations. For example, real estate titled in the name of one spouse may nevertheless be characterized as community property if it was acquired using community

---

[3] Estate of Charania v. Shulman, 608 F.3d 67 (1st Cir. 2010), *aff'g in part,* and *rev'g in part,* 133 T.C. No. 7 (Sep. 14, 2009).

funds, with the intent to create community property.[4] Conversely, an account titled jointly may not be community property, unless it originated as one spouse's separate property, and local law requires a formal written agreement to effect a transmutation.[5] Assets acquired before marriage, gifts and inheritances received during marriage, and property acquired with traceable separate funds remain separate in most jurisdictions. Federal estate tax law does not create community property; it simply acknowledges the state law classification and applies § 2033 and § 2034 accordingly.

Particular care is needed where the decedent and his or her spouse have moved into or out of a community property state. "Quasi-community property" status may arise when spouses acquire property in a noncommunity property state but bring it into a community property jurisdiction. Such property may be treated as community at death even if it was not community when acquired. Some states apply quasi-community property rules only in divorce, others at divorce and death, and the executor must know which system the decedent's domicile used. The double step-up in basis under Internal Revenue Code § 1014(b)(6) does not apply to quasi-community property or to property held as joint tenants with right of survivorship acquired after 1976.[6]

Deductions, Funeral Expenses, Administration Expenses, and Debts

Community property classification also impacts the deductibility of expenses and debts under Schedule J and Schedule K. Because state law

---

[4] *See* CAL. FAM. CODE § 760; *In re* Marriage of Valli, 58 Cal. 4th 1396 (2014) (property acquired with community funds remains community property absent statutory transmutation); *In re* Brace 470 P.3d 15 (Cal. 2020) (title form alone insufficient to transmute).

[5] *In re* Marriage of Lafkas, 188 Cal. Rptr. 3d 484 (Cal. App. 2d Dist. 2015) held that a partnership "Modification and Extension" agreement listing "John and Jean Lafkas, husband and wife, as to 1/3 interest" did not satisfy Cal. Family Code § 852(a)'s "express declaration" requirement and therefore did not transmute the husband's premarital partnership interest into community property.

[6] Gerry Beyer, Tex. Tech Univ. Sch. of L., Session 12A: Community Property Tips and Traps for Lawyers in Common Law States: Strategies for Migrating Clients at the 47th Annual Notre Dame Tax & Estate Planning Institute (Oct. 22, 2021). Whether property held as community property with right of survivorship should receive a double step-up in basis is considered in Chapter 4.

governs which portion of an obligation is chargeable to the decedent's half of the community, the executor must consult the applicable state law before taking any deduction. Some states treat funeral expenses as chargeable entirely to the decedent's share of the community while others divide them equally for administrative expenses. Administration expenses, attorney fees, accountant fees, and personal representative commissions may be allocated in different proportions depending on whether the underlying work benefits the decedent's half of the community, the survivor's half, or the estate as a whole.[7]

Debts require similar care. A debt that was the decedent's separate obligation is deductible in full. A debt enforceable against the marital community may be deductible only to the extent attributable to the decedent's half, although some states allow full satisfaction of community debts from the decedent's estate. In every case, local law must be reviewed closely.

COMMUNITY PROPERTY AND EMPLOYEE BENEFIT PLANS

Overview of Community Property and Employee Benefits

As a general rule in a community property jurisdiction, earnings accumulated during marriage are classified as community property and are owned

[7] In community property estates, the deductibility of administration expenses on Form 706 generally turns on whether the expense is properly chargeable to and incurred for the benefit of the decedent's estate, rather than for the benefit of the surviving spouse. Because only the decedent's one-half interest in community property is includible in the gross estate, administration expenses attributable to the management, valuation, or settlement of community assets are typically deductible only to the extent allocable to the decedent's one-half community interest, unless local law provides otherwise. For example, appraisal expenses incurred to value community property commonly benefit both the estate and the surviving spouse's one-half interest; in such cases, it may be appropriate to deduct only one-half of the appraisal cost as an administration expense of the estate. Local law must be consulted carefully, however, as some jurisdictions permit specific categories of administration expenses to be charged in full against the community or the estate.

in undivided equal shares by both spouses.[8] Because retirement benefits are typically earned through labor during the marriage, most states treat a participant's accrued interest in a pension, profit-sharing plan, or similar employee benefit arrangement as community property to the extent it is derived from community earnings.[9] Although community property law defines ownership of the retirement benefit, those ownership rights do not alter a qualified plan's obligation to pay benefits strictly in accordance with its written terms and applicable federal law.[10] Thus, the community property characterization of the asset and the federal rules governing benefit distribution operate in parallel but sometimes conflicting spheres. This interaction is further complicated by ERISA's broad preemption clause and its anti-alienation provision.[11] Together, these clauses restrict the ability of a nonparticipant spouse (or even the spouse's heirs) to enforce community property interests directly against a qualified retirement plan.[12] Federal courts have held that these federal law–required provisions override state law community property interests when the state rule would alter the distribution structure mandated by ERISA.[13]

The Ninth Circuit and U.S. Supreme Court cases of *Ablamis* and *Boggs* marked a fundamental shift that took place in the years 1991 through 1997 from earlier cases that have allowed community property to be asserted

---

[8] *See, e.g.*, Estate of Austin, 206 Cal. App. 3d 1249 (Ct. App. 1988); Bowman v. Bowman, 171 Cal. App. 3d 148 (Ct. App. 1985); Snyder v. Snyder, 197 Cal. App. 3d 6 (Ct. App. 1987); T.L. James & Co. v. Montgomery, 332 So. 2d 834 (La. 1975); Allard v. Frech, 754 S.W.2d 111 (Tex. 1988); Farver v. Dep't of Retirement Systems, 97 Wash. 2d 344, 644 P.2d 1149 (1982).

[9] *Id.*

[10] *See* 29 U.S.C. §§ 1104(a), 1132(a) (ERISA mandates plan administration strictly under governing instruments); Estate of Austin, 206 Cal. App. 3d at 1253–54 (state law ownership does not compel payment contrary to plan terms).

[11] 29 U.S.C. § 1144(a) (ERISA preempts state laws "relating to" employee benefit plans); *id.* § 1056(d)(1) (anti-alienation rule).

[12] *Id.*

[13] Ablamis v. Roper, 937 F.2d 1450, 1454–62 (9th Cir. 1991) (ERISA preempts testamentary transfer of a nonparticipant spouse's community share); Boggs v. Boggs, 520 U.S. 833, 843–55 (1997) (ERISA preempts Louisiana community property rights of a predeceased spouse's heirs).

directly against qualified plans.[14] Following the decision in *Ablamis*, the Department of Labor repeatedly confirmed that ERISA prohibits probate-based attempts to assign or enforce community property claims against plans, concluding that Congress intended qualified domestic relations orders, and not testamentary transfers, to be the exclusive vehicle for assigning benefits to nonparticipants.[15]

Layered on top of these property law issues are the federal tax rules, which may treat a nonparticipant spouse as having an includible economic interest in a retirement benefit even when ERISA precludes that spouse (or the spouse's heirs) from enforcing ownership under state law.[16] In TAM 8943006, the IRS concluded that a deceased nonparticipant spouse's community property interest in her husband's qualified plan was includible in her gross estate under § 2039 even though ERISA prevented her from transferring that interest at death, a result reached by relying on the unreported lower court opinion in *Ablamis* and rejecting the contrary interpretation in *Allard*.[17]

Unlike qualified plans, IRAs are governed primarily by the Internal Revenue Code and are not subject to ERISA's anti-alienation or preemption rules.[18] Although § 408(g) directs that the technical requirements of IRA taxation be applied without regard to community property laws, the IRS held in the 1999 private letter ruling that § 408(g) does not displace state law for purposes of classifying an IRA as community or separate property.[19] Courts in multiple states have therefore concluded that IRAs funded

---

14 *Compare, e.g.*, Allard v. Frech, 754 S.W.2d at 114 (permitting heirs of a deceased nonparticipant to recover from plan), *with* Ablamis, 937 F.2d at 1457–62 (rejecting Allard's reasoning based on ERISA preemption).

15 DOL Adv. Ops. 90-46A and 90-47A (Dec. 4, 1990).

16 *See* I.R.C. § 2039(a)–(b) (estate inclusion for annuities derived from employer and employee contributions).

17 TAM 8943006.

18 I.R.C. § 408.

19 PLR 199937055 (classification determined under state law; § 408(g) affects only deduction and contribution mechanics). Note that private letter rulings are not precedential but provide us with a good view of the IRS's position on questions of the tax law.

with community earnings may themselves be community property.[20] Even when state law recognizes a community interest in an IRA, federal income tax rules may disregard that interest and impose tax consequences solely on the participant or the named beneficiary.[21] Similarly, the IRS has held that enforcing a nonparticipant spouse's or heir's community property rights through an assignment of an inherited IRA can cause immediate taxable income to the named beneficiary.[22]

Taken together, these authorities illustrate the central tension in this area: State law determines ownership, but federal law determines who can receive benefits and who bears the tax, and the two frameworks do not always align.[23] As a result, estate planners in community property jurisdictions must account for both the state law allocation of ownership and the federal law restrictions on benefit payment and taxation, particularly when addressing survivorship rights, beneficiary designations, marital trust funding, and taxable estate inclusion. This area of the law is extraordinarily dense, resting at the crossroads of federal benefit regulation, federal tax rules, and state community property doctrines that often point in different (and sometimes even conflicting) directions. This section aims to serve as a guide through these muddy and shifting waters, but because the terrain is highly nuanced and fact specific, careful and up-to-date research remains essential in every case.

Characterization of Pensions and IRAs as Community Property

In every community property jurisdiction, earnings accumulated during marriage are presumptively community property owned in equal, undivided shares by both spouses.[24] Because pension and retirement benefits are

---

[20] *See, e.g.*, Estate of MacDonald, 51 Cal. 3d 262, 794 P.2d 911 (1990) (transmutation and characterization principles apply); Succession of Egan, 543 So. 2d 940 (La. Ct. App. 1989); Succession of McVay, 476 So. 2d 1070 (La. Ct. App. 1985).

[21] Bunney v. Comm'r, 114 T.C. 259, 267–69 (2000).

[22] PLR 201623001.

[23] *Boggs*, 520 U.S. at 844–55.

[24] *See, e.g.*, Estate of Austin, 206 Cal. App. 3d 1249 (Ct. App. 1988); Bowman v. Bowman, 171 Cal. App. 3d 148 (Ct. App. 1985); Snyder v. Snyder, 197 Cal. App. 3d 6 (Ct. App. 1987); T.L. James & Co. v. Montgomery, 332 So. 2d 834 (La. 1975);

typically earned as a form of deferred compensation for labor performed during marriage, courts consistently treat the participant spouse's accrued interest in a qualified retirement plan as community property to the extent the benefit was earned with community labor.[25] This state law characterization applies broadly across different types of qualified retirement arrangements. Defined benefit pensions, defined contribution plans, and similar employer-sponsored benefit programs are generally treated as community assets to the extent they accrue during the marriage, even where part of the benefit reflects premarital or postmarital service that requires allocation or apportionment under state law formulas.[26]

There is also significant authority holding that individual retirement accounts (IRAs) may be characterized as community property when funded with community earnings, despite being individually titled.[27] The Internal Revenue Code provision governing IRAs, § 408(g), specifies that the technical requirements of IRA qualification are applied "without regard to any community property laws."[28] However, the IRS has clarified that § 408(g) does not preempt state community property law for purposes of determining ownership of an IRA; rather, it is directed at the computation of contribution deductions and eligibility for IRA participation.[29] Thus, while federal law controls how IRA distributions are taxed, it does not displace state law principles governing whether the underlying account is community or separate property.

A community spouse's state law ownership interest in a qualified retirement plan or an IRA does not compel the plan administrator or IRA

Allard v. Frech, 754 S.W.2d 111 (Tex. 1988); Farver v. Dep't of Retirement Systems, 97 Wash. 2d 344, 644 P.2d 1149 (1982).

25 *Id.*

26 Estate of Austin, 206 Cal. App. 3d at 1253–54 (time-rule apportionment); *Farver*, 97 Wash. 2d at 348–49 (Washington apportions pension rights based on periods of service); *T.L. James*, 332 So. 2d at 851–52 (Louisiana recognizes spouse's vested interest in retirement contributions accrued during marriage).

27 Estate of MacDonald, 51 Cal. 3d 262, 794 P.2d 911 (1990).

28 I.R.C. § 408(g).

29 PLR 199937055 (state law determines classification of IRA; § 408(g) affects only contribution rules); H.R. Rep. No. 93-779, at 363 (1974) (community property laws disregarded for purposes of IRA contribution deductions).

custodian to distribute benefits in a manner inconsistent with governing federal law or the controlling plan or account documents.[30] For qualified plans, ERISA requires fiduciaries to administer benefits strictly in accordance with the written plan instrument, even when community property principles would allocate ownership differently between the spouses.[31] For IRAs, which are not governed by ERISA, distribution rights and the identity of the distributee are determined under the Internal Revenue Code and the IRA custodial agreement, rather than by state community property law.[32]

As a result, while characterization of pensions and IRAs as community property is often relatively straightforward under state law, the enforceability and tax treatment of those community interests are heavily shaped by federal regimes such as ERISA, the Internal Revenue Code, the Retirement Equity Act, and federal survivor-annuity rules. Understanding that community property characterization and federal benefit-distribution and tax rules operate independently, and often inconsistently, is essential before advising on spousal rights, beneficiary designations, or estate and gift tax consequences involving retirement benefits.

Ablamis v. Roper

In *Ablamis v. Roper*, the Ninth Circuit held that a deceased nonemployee spouse could not use a testamentary transfer under state community property law to control one-half of the surviving employee-spouse's pension benefit payable under an ERISA plan.[33] *Ablamis* reasoned that, even if state law recognizes that retirement benefits earned during marriage create a present community property interest, ERISA restricts the plan's ability to recognize or honor state law transfers that operate outside ERISA's limited statutory exceptions.[34] *Ablamis* has been followed in later cases rejecting probate-based redirection of ERISA plan benefits, including in contexts

---

[30] 9 U.S.C. § 1104(a) (ERISA fiduciaries must follow plan documents); Estate of Austin, 206 Cal. App. 3d 1249, 1253–54 (1988) (state law characterization does not alter the plan's payment obligations); I.R.C. § 408 (IRA structure and distribution rules).

[31] 29 U.S.C. § 1104(a); *Estate of Austin*, 206 Cal. App. 3d at 1253–54.

[32] I.R.C. § 408(g); Bunney v. Comm'r, 114 T.C. 259, 267–69 (2000).

[33] Ablamis v. Roper, 937 F.2d 1450 (9th Cir. 1991).

[34] *Id.*

involving intestate succession.[35] The Department of Labor has likewise concluded, in advisory opinions addressing probate court orders, that Congress intended QDROs (rather than testamentary transfers) to be the exclusive ERISA-compliant mechanism for assigning plan benefits to a nonparticipant spouse or dependent.[36] In this sense, *Ablamis* functions as a practical limit on the reach of community property law: State law may characterize part of the retirement benefit as community property, but ERISA can disable probate and inheritance mechanisms that would otherwise transit that interest at the nonparticipant spouse's death.

Boggs v. Boggs

In *Boggs v. Boggs*, the U.S. Supreme Court held that ERISA preempted Louisiana community property law to the extent that the state law would require heirs of a first dying spouse to assert a community property interest in the surviving participant's pension profits.[37] *Boggs* emphasized the conflict between ERISA's protections for plan participants and surviving spouses, and state law rules that would permit heirs of a predeceased spouse to divert benefits away from ERISA's federally protected survivor-benefit framework.[38] *Boggs* also treated the qualified domestic relations order (QDRO) provisions as a critical signal of congressional intent: ERISA confers beneficiary-like status only on a limited class of persons via QDROs, and Congress did not extend comparable rights to a predeceased spouse's heirs.[39] For community property purposes, the key takeaway is that an heir or estate of a predeceased nonparticipant spouse generally cannot enforce the spouse's "one-half" community interest directly against an ERISA plan, because ERISA's remedial structure does not recognize that state law pathway.[40]

---

35 Meek v. Tullis, 791 F. Supp. 154 (W.D. La. 1992).

36 DOL Advisory Opinions 90-46A and 90-47A (Dec. 4, 1990).

37 Boggs v. Boggs, 520 U.S. 833 (1997).

38 *Id.*

39 *Id.*

40 *Id.*

Egelhoff and the "Plan Administration" Rationale

The Supreme Court's reasoning in *Boggs* aligns with later ERISA preemption jurisprudence emphasizing that state laws cannot require plan administrators to alter plan distribution outcomes based on external, state law rules.[41] In *Eglhoff v. Egelhoff*, the Court held that ERISA preempted a state statute that would have changed the recipient of ERISA plan benefits based on divorce, because such a statute interfered with uniform plan administration by imposing state law beneficiary rules.[42] For community property planners, *Egelhoff* reinforces that ERISA can preempt state rules that would force plan administrators to change who gets paid under the plan's federally governed distribution mechanics.[43]

Practical Consequences for Community Property Enforcement

Because probate mechanisms and post-death community claims may be blocked by ERISA preemption, a spouse seeking to "lock in" a community property share of a qualified plan generally must rely on the QDRO framework or other ERISA-compliant mechanisms while the relevant domestic relations context is still available.

In particular, where the nonparticipant spouse's primary concern is survivorship risk (i.e., the spouse may predecease the participant and thereby lose effective access to the community share), one planning alternative is to take a distribution under a QDRO while the participant is alive and eligible, so the spouse can hold the proceeds separately. This approach is conceptually consistent with the observation that, by taking a distribution under a QDRO (when permitted), the nonparticipant spouse can preserve economic control even if the spouse dies before the participant begins receiving benefits.

---

41 Egelhoff v. Egelhoff, 532 U.S. 141 (2001).

42 *Id.*

43 *Id.*

Estate Tax Inclusion of Community Interests in Qualified Plans

Even when ERISA prevents a nonparticipant spouse (or the spouse's heirs) from enforcing a community interest against a qualified plan, federal transfer tax rules can still treat the spouse as holding an includible interest for estate tax purposes in certain circumstances.

Section 2039 of the Internal Revenue Code generally requires inclusion in a decedent's gross estate of the value of an annuity or other payment receivable by a beneficiary by reason of surviving the decedent to the extent that the value of the benefit is attributable to contributions made by the decedent or the decedent's employer.[44] The statute measures inclusion by reference to the "purchase price" of the annuity contract, providing that only the portion of the benefit attributable to amounts contributed by or on behalf of the decedent is includible.[45] Because community property law treats earnings during marriage as owned equally by both spouses, one-half of the consideration used to acquire the annuity is treated as having been furnished by the decedent spouse, and one-half is considered as owed by the surviving spouse.[46] As a result, when a community-funded annuity will pay survivor benefits after the death of the first spouse, only the decedent's one-half community interest is includible in the decedent's gross estate under § 2039.[47]

In TAM 8943006, the IRS concluded that a deceased nonparticipant spouse's community property interest in the employee spouse's qualified plan was includible in the nonparticipant spouse's gross estate under § 2039, even though ERISA prevented the spouse from transferring that interest at death.[48] The deeper problem exposed by the TAM is the uneasy gap between state law ownership concepts and federal control over benefit payment, and how that gap should be treated for estate tax inclusion under

[44] I.R.C. § 2039(a).

[45] *Id.* § 2039(b).

[46] Poe v. Seaborn, 282 U.S. 101 (1930) (community ownership of marital earnings).

[47] I.R.C. § 2039(b).

[48] TAM 8943006.

§ 2039.[49] The IRS recognized that, under Louisiana community property law, the nonparticipant spouse would ordinarily be viewed as owning a one-half community interest in the pension benefit attributable to marital labor.[50] At the same time, however, the memorandum accepted that ERISA's anti-alienation rules and the post-ERISA narrowing of testamentary access to qualified plan benefits effectively prevented that interest from being passed to heirs through a will or probate process.[51] Rather than allowing the decedent's attempted testamentary transfer to children to control, the IRS treated the plan's federally mandated joint-and-survivor annuity structure as causing the decedent spouse's interest to pass automatically to the surviving participant spouse by operation of law.[52] In practical terms, the TAM highlights a central tension in this area, in that ERISA can block heirs from enforcing a community property claim, yet federal transfer tax law may still treat the nonparticipant spouse as having owned an includible annuity interest at death.[53]

PLR 201623001

PLR 201623001 illustrates the particularly harsh interaction between community property law and the federal income tax rules governing inherited IRAs.[54] In that ruling, the decedent named a child, rather than the surviving spouse, as beneficiary of several IRAs funded with community earnings.[55] After death, the surviving spouse asserted a state law claim to her one-half community interest, and a state court approved a settlement ordering that a portion of the inherited IRA be "assigned" to the spouse as a

---

49 *Id.*

50 *Id.*

51 *Id.*

52 *Id.*

53 *Id.* Critics argue that § 2039 inclusion is difficult to justify on policy grounds when the decedent spouse's heirs receive nothing, and the decedent lacked any real power to redirect the benefit at death. *See* Edward A. Zelinsky, *Transfer Taxation Without Transfers: Reflections on Employer-Provided Death Benefits, Section 2039, Disclaimers, New Forms of Wealth, and the Evolution of the Federal Estate Tax*, 58(4) TULANE L. REV. (1984).

54 PLR 201623001.

55 *Id.*

spousal rollover IRA.[56] The IRS declined to determine whether the spouse held a valid community property interest under state law, but held that § 408(g) requires the IRA distribution and rollover rules to be applied without regard to community property law.[57] Because the child was the named beneficiary, the account was treated as an inherited IRA for the child, and the surviving spouse could not be treated as a "payee" eligible to complete a spousal rollover under § 408(d)(3).[58]

LIFE INSURANCE

The application of community property law to life insurance poses unique challenges in estate planning and Form 706 preparation because ownership, funding, and beneficiary designations can have results that are separate and apart from what would typically be expected.

For example, when one spouse owns a life insurance policy and pays all of the premiums, the other spouse may be considered to own half of the policy, and to have made a gift equal to one-half of the policy proceeds when the insured/owner spouse dies.

Under general community property principles, when insurance premiums are paid with community funds, both spouses own an undivided one-half interest in the policy and its proceeds. As a result, determining which portion of the proceeds is includible in the decedent's gross estate and whether any portion constitutes a taxable gift from the surviving spouse depends on both the form of ownership and the beneficiary designation.

Generally, insurance proceeds on the decedent's life that are payable to the estate or the executor of the estate are included in the decedent's gross estate.[59] However, where the policy is community property, only the decedent's one-half share of the proceeds would be includible on Schedule D of Form 706.[60] This inclusion rule may appear favorable, but it can trigger

---

[56] *Id.*

[57] *Id.*

[58] *Id.*

[59] I.R.C. § 2042

[60] Rev. Rul. 2003-40; § 20.2042-1(b)(2) (highlighting that if the proceeds of an insurance policy are community assets under the local community property law and, as a result, one-half of those proceeds belong to the decedent's surviving

unintended gift tax consequences. When a life insurance policy purchased with community funds designates someone other than the surviving spouse as beneficiary, the surviving spouse is deemed to have transferred their one-half community interest to that third party.[61] This will constitute a gift for federal tax purposes as if one-half of the death benefit was transferred by the surviving spouse to the beneficiary of the policy.

The Fifth Circuit's decision in *Estate of Cavenaugh v. Commissioner* is an instructive case when addressing the intersection of community property law and federal estate tax valuation in the context of life insurance policies.[62] The court emphasized that the inclusion of life insurance proceeds in the gross estate depends on the decedent's incidents of ownership at death and the community property character of the policy under state law.[63]

---

spouse, then only one-half of the proceeds are considered to be receivable by or for the benefit of the decedent's estate). However, a thorough review of the decedent's domiciliary state law is essential when preparing Form 706. In some jurisdictions, the entirety of a policy's proceeds may be includible in the decedent's gross estate rather than only one-half, depending on the state's management and control provisions. Because each community property state's statutes and public policy differ, it is critical to understand the governing state's specific rules before determining inclusion and valuation.

[61] This principle is best understood through an example. When community funds are used to purchase a life insurance policy, the policy is generally classified as community property. Each spouse is therefore treated as owning an undivided one-half interest in the policy. If the insured spouse dies and the policy proceeds are payable entirely to the surviving spouse, there is no adverse tax consequence. The decedent's one-half share is included in the gross estate, while the surviving spouse's one-half share represents their own property and does not constitute a taxable gift. The analysis changes, however, when the beneficiary designated under the policy is someone other than the surviving spouse. In that case, only one-half of the proceeds (the decedent's share) is included in the decedent's gross estate. The remaining one-half, belonging to the surviving spouse, has been transferred to a third party, and that transfer is treated as a taxable gift from the surviving spouse to the recipient of the proceeds.

[62] Estate of Cavenaugh v. Comm'r, 51 F.3d 597 (5th Cir. 1995).

[63] *Id.* at 605.

In *Cavenaugh*, the decedent, Herbert R. Cavenaugh, and his wife were residents of Texas, a community property state.[64] During their marriage, several life insurance policies were purchased on Mr. Cavenaugh's life using community funds, and he was the owner, with his wife being named as the beneficiary.[65] Mrs. Cavenaugh died and was survived by Mr. Cavenaugh. At issue was whether the entire proceeds of the policies were includible in Mr. Cavenaugh's gross estate under § 2042(2), or whether only his one-half community share was subject to inclusion.[66]

The Fifth Circuit began by reaffirming that ownership of property for federal estate tax purposes is determined under state law.[67] Under Texas community property principles, each spouse owns an undivided one-half interest in community assets, including insurance acquired and maintained with community funds.[68] Accordingly, Mr. Cavenaugh possessed incidents of ownership only in his one-half share of the policies, while his wife owned the remaining one-half outright.[69] Two complicating facts intervened, the wife's death in 1983 and the insured's personal renewals in 1984, 1985, and 1986.[70] First, the IRS contended that the community property interest expired with the last term paid from community funds upon Mrs. Cavenaugh's death; second, it argued that any community claim was capped at one-half of cash surrender value, which was zero; and third, it asserted that the lack of monetary value at the wife's death extinguished her interest, eliminating the need for any form of partition.[71]

Texas law disproved these theories. Absent a partition before the insured's death, the deceased spouse's community interest is not extinguished, and the policy retained its community status through maturity, rendering all of the death proceeds to community property.[72] The court cited previous decisions showing that dissolution of the marital community

---

64 *Id.* at 599.

65 *Id.*

66 *Id.* at 602.

67 *Id.*

68 *Id.*

69 *Id.*

70 *Id.*

71 *Id.*

72 *Id.* at 602–03.

by death does not automatically divest either spouse's interest; in fact, it is best understood as tenancy in common until payout.[73]

The court also distinguished cases involving federal employment benefit plans that preempt state community claims, noting that previous cases turned on a statutory assignment of interests to the widow, not on the absence of cash value.[74] Looking closely at the term life contract, the court found that the community purchased more than a bare one-year risk because the policy carried guaranteed renewal rights for up to 21 years at stated rates without proof of insurability, an automatic conversion right, incontestability after two years, elimination of the suicide exclusion, and dividend features that increased with continued coverage.[75] These embedded options and protections were not trivial, and the bundle of contractual rights was found to be tied to the later renewals back to the original community acquisition.[76] The Fifth Circuit held the Tax Court erred in including 100 percent of the term proceeds of Mr. Cavenaugh's estate, and directed a recomputation to attribute one-half of the death proceeds to Mr. Cavenaugh's estate and one-half to the unpartitioned community interest of Mrs. Cavenaugh.[77]

The *Cavenaugh* decision underscores the necessity of confirming that a life insurance policy truly retains its community property character before relying on a 50 percent inclusion ratio for estate tax purposes. The Fifth Circuit's analysis depended heavily on the unbroken community nature of the asset: namely, that all premiums were paid from community funds, with no subsequent infusion of separate property. Had separate funds been used to maintain or renew the policy, the community character could have been altered or lost entirely under Texas's inception-of-title doctrine, jeopardizing the estate's ability to limit inclusion to one-half of the proceeds. Practitioners must therefore ensure that premium payments are properly traced and documented, and that any change in the source of payment is reflected through a formal partition or reimbursement agreement (for example, where premiums are thereafter paid by one spouse's separate funds or by a

---

73 *Id.* at 603.

74 *Id.*

75 *Id.* at 604.

76 *Id.*

77 *Id.* at 605.

third party under an arrangement that allocates policy benefits), or risk the Service asserting that the policy became entirely the decedent's separate property.

Beyond tracing, *Cavenaugh* highlights the broader estate-planning risk of casual premium practices in community property jurisdictions. A policy initially acquired with community funds may later be maintained with separate property after the death of a spouse or following a marital agreement, creating a hybrid ownership interest that complicates both estate inclusion and gift tax exposure. Without clear evidence that community status continued uninterrupted, the Commissioner may argue for full inclusion under § 2042(1) or (2), asserting that the decedent's "incidents of ownership" extended to the entire contract. For this reason, practitioners should treat life insurance as an actively managed community asset, not a static one, and periodically verify the character of the funds used to sustain it, ensuring the estate's inclusion position can withstand IRS scrutiny.

The Internal Revenue Service's position in Revenue Ruling 80-242 provides essential guidance when a life insurance policy on the decedent's life is partly funded with community funds but originated as the decedent's separate property.[78] In that ruling, the decedent, a Texas resident, had acquired a $100,000 whole-life policy before marriage, paying $3,000 in premiums with separate funds.[79] After marriage, $12,000 of additional premiums were paid from community property.[80] At death, the insured retained all incidents of ownership, and the surviving spouse was the designated beneficiary.[81]

Under Texas law, a life insurance policy acquired before marriage remains the insured's separate property,[82] and subsequent payment of premiums from community funds does not transmute the policy into community property; rather, it gives rise to a right of reimbursement in favor of the community.[83] Consistent with that principle, the Service concluded that the proceeds belonged to the insured's separate estate, but that the community

---

78 Rev. Rul. 80-242.

79 *Id.*

80 *Id.*

81 *Id.*

82 *Id.*

83 *Id.*

was entitled to reimbursement for the $12,000 in community premiums paid.[84] Accordingly, the amount includible in the decedent's gross estate under § 2042(2) was limited to the face amount of the proceeds, reduced by the community's reimbursement claim.[85] In this case, $88,000 was includible under § 2042(2), and one-half of the $12,000 reimbursement ($6,000) was includible under § 2033 as the decedent's community interest.[86]

The ruling clarified an important procedural distinction as well. Although the community's right of reimbursement reduced the includible portion of proceeds under § 2042, it did not generate a deductible claim under § 2053.[87] Because the reimbursement right attaches to the policy proceeds rather than to the decedent's estate, it is satisfied before the estate ever receives the proceeds, precluding any deduction under §§ 20.2053-4 and 20.2053-7 of the Treasury Regulations.[88] This analysis effectively overruled the earlier Revenue Ruling 54-272, which had required full inclusion of proceeds purchased in part with community funds.[89]

This revenue ruling illustrates how careful tracing of premium sources can materially affect estate inclusion. When a separately owned policy is maintained with community funds, the result is not a shift in ownership but an equitable adjustment at death through reimbursement. If, by contrast, all premiums are paid with community funds, the outcome reverts to the framework of *Estate of Cavenaugh v. Commissioner*, where only one-half of the proceeds are includible. In either situation, documentation of premium payments and clear delineation of the policy's origin are indispensable to defending the estate's position under § 2042.

---

84 *Id.*

85 *Id.*

86 *Id.*

87 *Id.*

88 *Id.*

89 *Id.*

SINGLE-MEMBER LLCS OWNED BY SPOUSES IN A COMMUNITY PROPERTY STATE

Under federal income tax law, a limited liability company (LLC) with only one member is generally disregarded as an entity separate from its owner, unless it elects to be treated as a corporation under the "check-the-box" regulations.[90] In community property states, however, an apparent tension arises where both spouses are members of the same LLC. Because state law typically grants each spouse an undivided one-half ownership interest in community property, the LLC appears to be a multimember entity, potentially precluding disregarded treatment.

Revenue Procedure 2002-69 resolves this uncertainty by providing that an LLC or other check-the-box eligible entity wholly owned by a married couple as community property may elect either to be treated as a disregarded entity or as a partnership for federal tax purposes.[91] The IRS recognizes both options as consistent with the check-the-box regulations, provided that (1) the entity is wholly owned by the spouses as community property under state law, (2) no other person holds an interest, and (3) the spouses treat the entity consistently for all federal tax purposes.[92]

The Revenue Procedure likely arose because of inconsistent treatment among community property states. Some taxpayers could argue that

---

[90] Treas. Reg. § 301.7701-3(b)(1)(ii).

[91] Rev. Proc. 2002-69, 2002-2 C.B. 831. For the same reasons, an LLC owned by husband and wife as tenancy by the entireties under state law should also qualify to check the box as a disregarded entity. *See* Gassman & Ketron, *Yes, It Is Usually Safe to Consider an LLC Owned as TBE as Disregarded for Income Tax Purposes*, THE THURSDAY REPORT (Dec. 11, 2014) https://gassmanlaw.com/thursday-reports/the-thursday-report-12-11-14/. Of course, that a TBE LLC checking the box to be treated as disregarded will be respected by the IRS is not certain. Additionally, Rev. Proc. 84-35 provides a presumption of reasonable cause for abating the § 6698 failure to file penalty that would otherwise occur for the failure to file for certain "small partnerships" if conditions are met (including that the partnership have no more than ten partners all of whom are natural persons or the estate of natural persons and that the partners seeking abatement from the penalty reported their share on timely filed Form 1040s.).

[92] *Id.*

community ownership made the entity multimember by definition, while others treated it as single member for simplicity. The IRS acknowledged that both positions had support under existing regulations, and therefore permitted either treatment as a matter of administrative convenience and fairness.

The significance of Revenue Procedure 2002-69 is that it preserves the flexibility of disregarded entity treatment for married taxpayers in community property states without requiring formal restructuring. For example, a married couple who jointly operate a business through an LLC in Texas or California may report its income directly on Schedule C as a sole proprietorship, provided they both consent, and no third party owns an interest. This approach avoids the need to file a partnership return and simplifies accounting, while remaining consistent with state law classification of ownership.

Practitioners should note that this rule is unique to community property jurisdictions and does not extend to joint ownership by unmarried individuals or spouses in common law property states. Furthermore, if the entity elects corporate treatment under the check-the-box rules, or if either spouse becomes ineligible for community property status (for example, by divorce or change of domicile), the entity's classification must be reevaluated at that time.

For estate tax purposes, Form 706 reflects state law ownership rather than federal income tax classifications. Even if a married couple elects under Revenue Procedure 2002-69 to treat their community-owned LLC as a disregarded entity for income tax purposes, the ownership interest remains community property under state law. Accordingly, only one-half of the entity's value is includible in the first dying spouse's gross estate under § 2033. Schedule F should therefore describe the asset as a "one-half community property interest in [LLC name]" and report the fair-market value of that one-half interest as of the date of death. This approach keeps the estate's reporting consistent with the decedent's actual property rights while avoiding any implication that the entity was solely owned.

In practice, preparers should also ensure that valuation documentation supports the inclusion of only the decedent's community share. This includes confirming that no separate-property funds were contributed to the LLC and that the entity's income, assets, and distributions were consistently treated as community during life. Where the spouses file joint returns treating the entity as disregarded, that characterization may be referenced in the return's explanatory attachments, but it should not override the state law description of ownership on Schedule F of the Form 706. In short, the preparer's task is to harmonize the federal estate tax reporting requirements with the underlying state property law, preserving consistency while preventing inadvertent overinclusion in the gross estate.

From a valuation standpoint, the decedent's one-half community interest in the LLC should generally be analyzed as a noncontrolling, nonmarketable interest for purposes of § 2031.[93] Even if the entity was treated as a disregarded entity during life, that classification does not alter the state law fact that each spouse owned only an undivided one-half interest. Because neither spouse alone possessed unilateral control over the entity, the decedent's estate may be entitled to apply discounts for lack of control and lack of marketability in determining the fair market value of the included interest. Such discounts should be supported by a qualified appraisal that considers the LLC's operating agreement, transfer restrictions, and the limited liquidity typical of closely held business interests, and will result in a tax basis of less than 50 percent of the value of the entity.[94]

SECTION 2032A AND COMMUNITY PROPERTY

The interaction between § 2032A and community property law is a very nuanced area of estate taxation. Section 2032A allows an executor to elect

---

[93] *See* Estate of Bright v. United States, 658 F.2d 999 (5th Cir. 1981) (holding that a decedent's one-half community property interest must be valued independently under § 2031, and rejecting the government's "unity of interest" argument that a married couple's combined ownership should be treated as a single controlling block; instead, each spouse's share is valued from the standpoint of a hypothetical willing buyer and seller, without assuming cooperation between spouses). The court's reasoning establishes that a one-half community interest may be treated as a noncontrolling, nonmarketable interest for valuation purposes, even when the surviving spouse owns the remaining half. *See also* Propstra v. United States, 680 F.2d 1248, 1252 (9th Cir. 1982) (extending *Bright* to fractional ownership of real property and holding that valuation should reflect the decedent's undivided interest rather than the value of the whole property, thereby permitting discounts for lack of control and lack of marketability).

[94] *See Propstra*, 680 F.2d at 1252.

special use valuation for qualified real property used in farming or other closely held business activities, permitting valuation based on the property's actual use rather than its fair market value.[95] This provision is designed to alleviate liquidity pressures on family-owned farms and businesses by ensuring that estate tax liability reflects the property's productive value rather than its resale market potential.

When qualified real property is held as community property, § 2032A(e)(10) directs that the surviving spouse's community interest be "taken into account to the extent necessary to provide a result which is consistent with the result which would have been obtained had the property been common law property."[96] Congress intended that decedents in community property jurisdictions would receive treatment equivalent to those in common law jurisdictions. To achieve this parity, the statute provides that the decedent's community property interest is to be treated as if owned by the decedent individually.[97] This approach prevents the artificial reduction of the § 2032A limitation merely because the property is subject to the community property system.[98]

The IRS formalized this interpretation in Revenue Ruling 83-96. In that ruling, the decedent, a Texas resident, died owning a community property interest in a farm for which the executor elected special use valuation under § 2032A.[99] The Service held that the full limitation on the allowable decrease in value under § 2032A(a)(2) applies to the decedent's one-half community property interest, even though the decedent made no contribution toward the purchase of the property.[100] The ruling reasoned that § 2032A(e)(10) requires treating the decedent's community property interest as if owned individually, thereby entitling the estate to the same valuation benefit as if the decedent had owned the property as a tenant in common.[101] The Service further explained that, for federal estate tax purposes, the community property system most closely parallels a tenancy

---

95 I.R.C. § 2032A(a)(1).

96 *Id.* § 2032A(e)(10).

97 *Id.*

98 Rev. Rul. 83–96, 1983–1 C.B. 225.

99 *Id.*

100 *Id.*

101 *Id.*

in common because each spouse owns an undivided one-half interest without survivorship rights, and the amount contributed by each spouse toward acquisition is irrelevant to the amount includible in the gross estate.[102]

The Service also acknowledged an alternative rationale, that community property ownership resembles a tenancy by the entirety or joint tenancy, where equal ownership is presumed regardless of contribution.[103] Under either analogy, the outcome is the same: The full special use valuation limitation applies to the decedent's one-half interest.[104] Revenue Ruling 83-96 thus clarifies that a decedent's lack of contribution toward acquisition of community property does not diminish the estate's ability to claim the maximum § 2032A reduction.[105] This reasoning applies equally to later statutory amendments adjusting the limitation amount, confirming that community property estates are not disadvantaged by their ownership form.[106]

The § 2032A election is made on a timely filed Form 706, but the election is not effective unless the return includes the statutorily prescribed notice of election. Treasury regulations require that the notice include a comprehensive statement of the property to which special use valuation applies, the identity of qualified heirs, and the method by which the property's special use value was determined.[107] In practice, preparers generally attach a detailed rider or schedule entitled "Notice of Election Under I.R.C. § 2032A," signed under penalties of perjury by the executor or other signer of the Form 706. This statement typically restates the decedent's ownership interest, describes the nature and location of the property, identifies each qualified heir by name and relationship, explains the method used to determine the special use value (including capitalization rate and comparable rentals), and incorporates a statement of material participation. Failure to include this statement or to provide sufficient detail may invalidate the 2032A election even if the Form 706 box is checked.

---

102 *Id.*

103 *Id.*

104 *Id.*

105 *Id.*

106 *Id.*

107 Treas. Reg. § 20.2032A-8(a)(3).

Chapter 11

Estate Planning Strategies with Community Property and Practical Points of Consideration

JOINT REVOCABLE TRUSTS

Joint revocable trusts have long been the dominant trust vehicle for married couples in community property jurisdictions. These trusts first gained traction because they allowed spouses to combine two distinct legal and tax benefits: the statutory benefits of community property ownership (particularly the full basis adjustment under § 1014(b)(6)) and the administrative convenience, privacy, and continuity that a revocable trust offers. By placing the community property into a joint trust, couples preserved its character for both state law and federal tax purposes while avoiding probate on trust assets and simplifying postmortem management.

Community property contributed to a joint revocable trust will continue to be treated as community property for federal tax purposes under

Internal Revenue Code § 1014(b)(6) as long as it is considered community property under state law.[1]

Joint revocable trusts have also been used in noncommunity property states over the years, because some practitioners believe that their clients will be better served or will find their estate plan easier to understand when it is incorporated into a single trust.[2] As Howard Zaritsky notes, "It is difficult to understand how the incorporation of both spouses' estate planning choices into a single revocable trust would be inherently simpler and more understandable than would be the same plan as incorporated into two separate revocable trusts, but such is the view of some practitioners."[3]

Assigning community property to a revocable trust will not change its character, even if it is to a trust that is purported to be owned by one spouse or the other. For example, in *Katz v. United States*, the assignment of a husband and wife's community property to the husband's revocable trust did not convert the property to the separate property of the husband.[4] There, the court held that the statutory presumption under California law that property acquired by spouses during marriage is community property was not overcome by the assignment of the community property to the revocable trust.[5]

Unlike the "his and hers" separate revocable trusts that predominate in noncommunity property jurisdictions, most spouses who have previously done estate planning before moving from a community property jurisdiction will have a joint revocable trust in place.

The typical joint revocable trust for community property clients will provide for a three-trust plan to go into effect after the death of the first dying spouse:

- Survivor's Trust (Trust A)

  This trust receives the surviving spouse's one-half share of the community property, together with any of his or her separate

[1] Rev. Rul. 66-283, 1966-2 C.B. 297 (explaining that "[f]or purposes of section 1014(b)(6) of the Code, H and W are considered as continuing to own the property transferred by them to the revocable trust as their community property").

[2] Zaritsky, Tax Planning for Family Wealth Transfers at Death, The Joint Revocable Trust, WGL-TPFWTD ¶ 4.07. Zaritsky's treatise is by far the most exhaustive in its discussion of joint revocable trust planning.

[3] *Id.*

[4] Katz v. United States, 382 F.2d 723, 728 (9th Cir. 1967).

[5] *Id.*

property that had been contributed to the joint trust. The survivor's trust remains fully revocable and amendable by the surviving spouse and will be includible in the survivor's gross estate.

- The Decedent's Trust (Trust B)

  The first dying spouse's one-half share of the community property is allocated to a separate, irrevocable trust for the benefit of the surviving spouse and descendants. This trust will generally be structured as a credit shelter trust, using, to the fullest extent possible, the decedent's applicable federal state and gift tax exclusion amount or state estate tax exemption amount. Income from Trust B may be payable to the survivor, and the trustee will have discretion to make distributions limited by an ascertainable standard, so that the asset will be excluded from the survivor's taxable estate.

- The Marital (QTIP) Trust (Trust C)

  If Trust B would exceed the first dying spouse's applicable estate and gift tax exclusion amount, then a third trust is created for any excess over the decedent's applicable exclusion. This QTIP trust provides income to the surviving spouse for life. At the survivor's death, the remaining assets of the QTIP are included in the surviving spouse's gross estate, ensuring deferral (but not elimination) of estate tax, and will therefore receive a new fair market value income tax basis at the death of the surviving spouse.

This three-trust division preserves the principal tax advantages of community property while providing for both estate-tax planning and post-mortem administration. Because community property receives a full basis adjustment at the first death, all three trusts begin with assets having an income tax basis equal to their fair market value on the date of the decedent's death, so that the survivor or trustee can diversify without immediate income tax cost. The survivor's half, remaining in the survivor's trust, and the QTIP trust assets will, in turn, receive a second basis adjustment at the survivor's later death.

The joint revocable trust requires careful drafting of the surviving spouse's rights upon the first spouse's death. If the surviving spouse loses the ability to revoke or amend the trust as to their own contributed share (or deemed contributed share), the survivor may be treated as having made a completed gift to the remainder beneficiaries at the first death. Conversely, if the survivor retains too much control, the intended credit shelter structure may collapse and result in inclusion of the entire trust at the survivor's death.

The Uniform Trust Code, as adopted by many of the states, provides that, with respect to community property held by a joint revocable trust, the trust can be revoked by either spouse acting alone, but can be amended only by joint action of both spouses. With respect to property other than community property that is held by a joint revocable trust, the Uniform Trust Code provides that the trust may be revoked or amended by either grantor as to the portion of the trust attributable to that spouse's contribution.[6]

If the surviving spouse's ability to revoke or amend the joint revocable trust ceases at the first spouse's death, the surviving spouse may be treated as having made a completed gift of the portion of the trust attributable to his or her own contributions.[7] The theory is that the surviving spouse's initial transfer to the trust becomes complete for gift tax purposes once the right to undo or reclaim that transfer is eliminated. This result is avoided, however, if the surviving spouse remains the sole beneficiary of the trust after the first death and holds a testamentary power of appointment over the trust assets, in which case the survivor has not truly parted with dominion and control.[8] Alternatively, the surviving spouse could have the right to veto distributions and a testamentary power of appointment to keep the gift incomplete, even when it may benefit one or more individuals other than the surviving spouse.[9]

---

[6] ZARITSKY, *supra* note 2, citing: UNIF. TRUST CODE § 602(b); ALA. CODE § 19-3B-602; ALASKA STAT. § 13.36.340; ARIZ. REV. STAT. § 14-10602; ARK. CODE § 28-73-602; COLO. REV. STAT. § 15-16-702; DC CODE § 19-1306.02; FLA. STAT. § 736.0602; IND. CODE § 30-4-3-1.5; KAN. STAT. § 58a-602; ME. REV. STAT. tit. 18-B, § 602; MASS. GEN. LAWS tit. 203A, § 602; MO. REV. STAT. § 456.6-602; MONT. CODE § 72-38-602; N.D. CENT. CODE § 59-14-02; NEB. REV. STAT. § 30-3854; NH REV. STAT. § 564-B:6-602; NM STAT. § 46A-6-602; N.C. GEN. STAT. § 36C-6-602; OHIO REV. CODE § 5806.02; ORE. REV. STAT. § 130.505; 20 PA. CONS. STAT. § 7752; S.C. CODE § 62-7-602; TENN. CODE § 35-15-602; UTAH CODE § 75-7-605; VA. CODE § 64.2-751; VT. STAT. tit. 14, § 602; WASH. REV. CODE § 11.103.030; W. VA. CODE § 44D-6-602; WYO. STAT. § 4-10-602.

[7] *Id.* at 4.07[2][b][ii], citing Treas. Reg. § 25.2511-2(b).

[8] *Id.* citing Treas. Reg. § 25.2511-2(b).

[9] "[T]he retention of a testamentary power to appoint the remainder of a trust is considered a retention of dominion and control over the remainder. Accordingly . . . we conclude that the retention of this power causes the [] transfer to Trust to be incomplete with respect to the remainder interest in Trust." IRS,

> The amount of the gift caused by the surviving spouse's loss of the power to revoke or amend the joint revocable trust at the first spouse's death would likely be valued at the full amount of the share of the trust attributable to the surviving spouse's contributions to the trust, with no reduction for the value of any life estate or possibility of discretionary distributions to which the surviving spouse may be entitled.[10]

Noncommunity property practitioners who find themselves advising clients with community property should, where possible, coordinate with counsel familiar with community property principles. Indeed, associating with counsel who is licensed in the state whose community property regime applies is not merely prudent but may be necessary to avoid the unauthorized practice of law in that jurisdiction. In many cases, the practitioner can accommodate the clients' wishes most efficiently by maintaining the clients' existing joint revocable trust with community property, or what was community property maintained thereunder, and establishing separate revocable trusts for each of the clients using their normal forms to hold the property thereafter acquired while the couple is domiciled in the noncommunity property state. Alternatively, if no previously established joint revocable trust exists, the practitioner may establish a joint revocable trust specifically to hold the community assets, and then use the practitioner's standard revocable trusts for each spouse to hold separate property and to receive the respective shares at the first spouse's death.

It is therefore not unusual to have a community property joint trust that remains intact but is amended to provide that the share of the surviving spouse will pass to a separate revocable trust of the surviving spouse on the first death, and the share of the first dying spouse to pass from the joint

---

Private Letter Ruling 201525003, at 7-8 (2015). "In this case, Grantor retained the Grantor's Sole Discretionary Veto Powers to veto discretionary distributions. . . . Grantor also retained the Grantor's Sole Objective Veto Powers and Grantor's Consent Veto Power to veto quarterly distributions to Grantor's Charities. Pursuant to these powers, at the time of the [] transfer to Trust, Grantor retained the right to veto any distributions of income and principal to any one or more of Grantor's Charities during her lifetime . . . [a]ccordingly. . . . [W]e conclude that the retention of these veto powers causes the [] transfer to Trust to be an incomplete gift of the lifetime interests in Trust." *Id.*

[10] *Id.* citing I.R.C. § 2702.

community property trust to the separate revocable trust of the first dying spouse, which may have modernized and more up-to-date language with reference to how the first dying spouse wishes to have the credit shelter trust and any QTIP trust or outright marital deduction trust pass.

The system allows the lawyer in the noncommunity property state, when dealing with clients who have moved from a community property state, to implement trusts that accommodate the law and customary drafting practices of the noncommunity property state without dismantling the couple's preexisting joint revocable trust, which continues to hold the community property the spouses acquired while domiciled in a community property state before relocating. This coordinated structure may be thought of as a legacy joint community property trust with separate revocable trusts for thereafter-acquired separate property.

COORDINATING A JOINT REVOCABLE TRUST WITH SEPARATE REVOCABLE TRUSTS IN A NONCOMMUNITY PROPERTY STATE

Clients who relocate from a community property jurisdiction to a noncommunity property state often arrive with a joint revocable trust already in place. Where that trust was historically funded with community property, the trust can be maintained to preserve § 1014(b)(6) treatment and maintain the community property character despite the change in domicile. Noncommunity property practitioners need not dismantle or redraft the structure entirely. As mentioned earlier, in many cases the most prudent and efficient approach is to retain the existing joint revocable trust and then supplement the plan by creating separate revocable trusts for each spouse for administration and dispositive planning.

Under this approach, the joint revocable trust continues to hold the community property, preserving its characterization, while each spouse's separate revocable trust can hold (or later receive) that spouse's separate property and any share distributed to that spouse at the first death. To facilitate this coordination, the joint trust may be amended or restated to include powers allowing each spouse during their joint lifetimes to revoke or withdraw the portion of the trust attributable to that spouse's own separate property contributions and direct that portion into his or her individual revocable trust.

At the first spouse's death, the joint revocable trust will typically divide into the three-trust framework described previously: a survivor's trust for the surviving spouse's one-half share, a credit shelter trust for the first dying spouse's share (referred to in some community property states as a "family trust"), and a QTIP trust for any excess over the amount of the first dying spouse's remaining estate tax exemption. The instrument may then provide that the survivor's trust may be merged or distributed in kind into the surviving spouse's separate revocable trust. The joint revocable trust will continue to hold the community property that the married couple owned before moving to the common law state. Each spouse's separate revocable trust will hold that spouse's separate property, and, after the first death, the portion allocated to the surviving spouse. In that manner, the surviving spouse receives the A share, and the deceased spouse's share is administered under the B share. This approach preserves administrative simplicity without changing beneficial interests or the intended income and estate tax results. By contrast, the credit shelter trust and QTIP trust should generally remain irrevocable and should not be merged into the surviving spouse's revocable trust, to avoid unintended estate tax inclusion or loss of QTIP qualification.

THE VARIABLE VALUE OF THE DOUBLE STEP-UP IN BASIS

The theoretical allure of community property trust planning is the full basis adjustment under § 1014(b)(6) at the first spouse's death. But the actual value of this benefit depends heavily on the spouses' relative life expectancies and whether a step-up is needed to provide for the surviving spouse to be able to unlock appreciated assets for support and otherwise. For a married couple, both aged 85 with similar health profiles, the period between deaths may be relatively short. The survivor is likely to die not long after the first spouse, at which point the survivor's remaining assets, to the extent included in their gross estate, will receive a second basis adjustment. In such cases, even if the couple never held their assets as community property, the survivor's estate would still effectively obtain a full basis step-up at the second death. Thus, in marriages where life expectancies are similar, the incremental benefit of the § 1014(b)(6) double step-up may be economically modest, and creating community property through the use of an elective community property trust may add complexity without meaningful tax advantage.

By contrast, the timing of the basis adjustments becomes highly valuable in marriages where there is a significant age or health differential. For example, consider a married coupled varying in age by 15 years. In that scenario, placing low-basis appreciated assets into a community property trust allows the entire asset to step up to fair market value at the first death under § 1014(b)(6). The surviving spouse may then sell, diversify, or reposition those assets without current capital gain recognition and continue to hold the assets for decades. Accordingly, the community property trust is most compelling where life expectancies diverge, investment horizons are long, and appreciation potential is significant.

While the income tax treatment of community property can be favorable, it is not universally advantageous. In many cases, spouses may prefer not to hold assets as community property due to creditor protection concerns, marital control considerations, or exposure to claims in the event of divorce. For migrating spouses, it is necessary to weigh the income tax value of § 1014(b)(6) against the legal protections available under other forms of ownership, such as tenancy by the entireties (TBE).

Asset ownership in TBE form typically protects the property from the creditors of only one spouse, because neither spouse individually owns a severable interest. Several states, such as Florida, Delaware, Wyoming, and Pennsylvania, provide for full protection of TBE assets when only one spouse has a judgment against him or her while other TBE states have more limited creditor protection or none at all for TBE assets. A judgment creditor of husband alone, or wife alone, generally cannot force the sale of TBE property so long as the other spouse is not a joint debtor.

By contrast, community property lacks this protection. Each spouse is deemed to own an undivided one-half interest in community assets. Therefore, a creditor of either spouse may generally reach that spouse's one-half interest in the community assets, and in some jurisdictions may reach the entire asset under a "management" theory, or if the debt relates to benefits to the community.[11] Thus, the planning questions become practical and client specific. Does the tax value of the § 1014(b)(6) full basis adjustment exceed the asset protection value of TBE? Does the estate tax inclusion required to secure the full basis adjustment inadvertently create or increase

---

[11] See Chapter 5 for the in-depth discussion on creditor rights in community property.

an estate tax liability at either spouse's death? And more broadly, does the couple's overall net-worth trajectory suggest that estate tax exposure associated with inclusion is likely to outweigh, match, or fall well below the capital gains savings produced by the step-up?

These are not theoretical concerns. For clients who are below or near the federal estate tax exemption (or who reasonably expect to remain so), the income tax savings from the full step-up may be large and economically decisive. For clients whose combined estate may exceed the exemption, the full basis adjustment under § 1014(b)(6) must be weighed carefully. Because the full step-up requires that at least one-half of the whole of the community property be includible in determining the value of the decedent's gross estate, the community property trust approach can, in certain cases, substitute a potentially modest capital gains liability for a materially larger estate tax exposure. Where projected estate tax liability exceeds the capital gains savings associated with the full step-up, it will often be more prudent to avoid community property treatment or instead craft an estate plan designed to keep future appreciation outside both spouses' taxable estates.

TRAPS FOR THE UNWARY IN PLANNING FOR MIGRATING SPOUSES

Accidentally Contributing Community Property to a SLAT

When spouses who formerly lived in a community property state undertake new estate planning in a noncommunity property state, the most significant risks often arise not from what planners do intentionally, but from what they do inadvertently. This can include accidental use of community property to fund irrevocable trusts, such as spousal lifetime asset trusts (SLATs). If the assets used to fund the SLAT are community property at the time of funding, both spouses are treated as having contributed to the trust. In such a case, the beneficiary spouse is treated as a deemed contributor to the SLAT to the extent of his or her one-half community interest. Of course, a spouse cannot make a completed gift to a trust of which the same spouse is also the primary beneficiary without triggering self-settled trust risks, including creditor access concerns and inclusion of the SLAT assets in the beneficiary spouse's gross estate under §§ 2036 and 2038 if creditors of the beneficiary spouse can reach into the trust.

To avoid this result, the spouses should first execute a partition or transmutation agreement that converts the community property into two separate one-half interests, with each spouse receiving separate property of equal value. A properly drafted 50/50 partition is not a taxable gift, because each spouse retains precisely the economic interest they held before the partition.

If the spouses were to transmute all of the community property into the name of one spouse who will then contribute to the SLAT, the noncontributing spouse who has given up his or her community property interest via the transmutation will be deemed to have made a gift of his or her one-half community interest to the other spouse. Of course, assuming both spouses are U.S. citizens, the deemed gift will qualify for the § 2523 unlimited marital deduction, and there will be no gift tax imposed at the time of the transmutation. The real hazard with this approach lies in who is treated as the "transferor" of the assets to the SLAT. The IRS may still treat the nongrantor spouse as a transferor under a step-transaction analysis if the spouse's former one-half interest is later contributed to a SLAT from which that spouse may benefit. If there were a deemed gift to the contributing spouse immediately before funding the SLAT, this would appear to be an indirect funding of the SLAT by the beneficiary spouse.

Thus, the advisable method for funding a SLAT in this situation is to first partition the community property into separate but equal one-half shares, allow some time to pass, and only then have the settlor spouse alone contribute their separate one-half share to the SLAT, or assets that might be exchanged at arm's length.

Chapter 12

But Is the JEST (Joint Exempt Step-Up Trust) Superior to the Community Property Trust? Take a Serious Look at This Planning Tool

The joint exempt step-up trust, or the JEST, is a joint revocable trust established by a married couple. Under a JEST, the first dying spouse has the testamentary power to appoint all of the trust assets to creditors of his or her estate, which causes all assets of the trust to be included in his or her estate for federal tax purposes so that such assets may receive a new fair market value income tax basis under Code § 1014, and be considered to be the assets of the first dying spouse for purposes of funding a credit shelter trust.[1]

---

[1] A power of appointment exercisable in favor of the decedent, his estate, his creditors, or the creditors of his estate constitutes a general power of appointment

Three private letter rulings (PLRs) and a technical advisory memorandum (TAM) published in 1999 and 2000 help to support this proposition, although there is a risk that the IRS might not follow these nonprecedential pronouncements and take the position that the transfer of assets considered as owned by the surviving spouse to a credit shelter trust might be characterized as a gift by the surviving spouse.[2] One of these private letter rulings was applied where each spouse had a separate revocable trust, and each spouse had a power of appointment over the assets of the revocable trust of the other spouse. This technique may work as well as a JEST, but is often considered to be confusing by clients and many advisors.[3] This risk of a gift being made by the surviving spouse on the first death is ameliorated by the design of the JEST, which contains provisions that the assets that were contributed to the trust by the surviving spouse and held in a separate credit shelter trust may not benefit the surviving spouse unless certain events occur that are outside of the control of the surviving spouse, and the surviving spouse is not a beneficiary unless or until such spouse is added by a committee of independent trust protectors serving in a nonfiduciary capacity.[4]

Further, the JEST may be structured so that the separate credit shelter trust is deemed funded by the surviving spouse and constitutes an incomplete gift for gift tax purposes. This is accomplished by giving the surviving spouse the power to direct how assets may pass among the spouses'

---

under I.R.C. § 2041(b)(1), causing the subject property to be included in the decedent's gross estate under I.R.C. § 2041(a)(2), and thereby qualifying such property for a stepped-up fair market value income tax basis under I.R.C. § 1014(b)(9).

[2] Alan Gassman, Christopher Denicolo & Kacie Hohnadell, *JEST Offers Serious Estate Planning Plus for Spouses—Part 1*, 40 EST. PLAN. 3, 3–11 (2013); *see also* Susan L. Racey, *Joint Revocable Trusts*, 20 OHPRLF 77 (2008).

[3] *Power of Appointment, Legal Information Institute*, CORNELL UNIV. L. SCH. (June 2022), https://www.law.cornell.edu/wex/power_of_appointment.

[4] *Joint Exempt Step-Up Trust*, ULTIMATE EST. PLANNER, https://ultimateestateplanner.com/products/joint-exempt-step-trust-legal-document-form-jest/ (last visited July 18, 2023).

common descendants or otherwise upon death and requiring the surviving spouse's consent to any distribution from such separate credit shelter trust.[5]

The three PLRs and the TAM that concluded that a credit shelter trust could be funded with assets considered as owned by the surviving spouse also concluded that those assets would not receive a new income tax basis on the first death, based upon the assertion that the arrangement constitutes a gift by the surviving spouse to the first dying spouse immediately before death, which is then inherited by the surviving spouse, thus triggering the Internal Revenue Code § 1014(e) one-year rule.[6]

The PLRs and TAM, however, failed to point out that while § 1014(e) applies when an asset is gifted to a decedent who devises it back to the donor upon death, it does not necessarily apply in a situation where the assets are left to an irrevocable trust that may benefit the donor, so § 1014(e), by the view of the authors, should not apply. The statute simply says that it must come back to the donor upon death, and does not seem to support the conclusion that a transfer back to a trust that benefits the donor would be sufficient to trigger the statute.[7]

A properly drafted JEST may therefore contain provisions that would make it unlikely or potentially even impossible for the surviving spouse to benefit from the credit shelter trust that is funded with the assets considered to have been held by the surviving spouse. Section 1014(e) should not be implicated if the surviving spouse cannot benefit from assets that he is considered to have contributed to the trust, therefore allowing for a step-up in basis as to such assets on the first dying spouse's death. This is why a JEST will typically provide that the surviving spouse will not be a beneficiary of the credit shelter trust established and funded with the assets of the surviving spouse on the first dying spouse's death unless or until any and all other trusts for the surviving spouse have been completely spent, and trust protectors acting in a nonfiduciary capacity, or the holder of a power of

---

[5] H. Zaritsky & Farhad, Tax Planning for Family Wealth Transfers at Death: Analysis with Forms § 4.07[3][b][iii] (Thomson Reuters/Tax & Accounting 2014, with updates through July 2023) (providing an additional discussion on JESTS).

[6] I.R.C.§ 1014.

[7] *See* Alan S. Gassman et al., *Gassman, Ellwanger & Hohnadell: It's Just a JEST, the Joint Exempt Step-Up Trust*, Steve Leimberg's Est. Planning Newsletter, https://leimbergservices.com/newsletters/view.cfm?linkid=4590#_ednref1 (Apr. 3, 2013).

appointment without a fiduciary duty to exercise it, may add the surviving spouse to the trust.

As a practical matter, assets held under a JEST might be sold to avoid capital gains taxes shortly after the death of the first spouse, and the surviving spouse would not be added to or considered to be a beneficiary of the JEST credit shelter trust unless or until it is clear that the income tax return for the tax year of the sale would not be audited, or that the audit would not be complete.

The JEST is clearly more complicated than the community property trust from the point of view of the drafter and for tax administration purposes, but should allow for the funding of a credit shelter trust from all assets of the JEST, not just half, and assets under the JEST may be much better protected from creditors. For example, the JEST might provide that 5 percent of its assets are held as assets of one spouse, and 95 percent are held as assets of the other spouse, notwithstanding that the spouse having 5 percent ownership may still have a testamentary power of appointment to allow the other 95 percent of assets to fund a credit shelter trust on the first death. A creditor of that spouse would only be able to reach 5 percent of the JEST assets.

Chapter 13

Conclusion

The landscape of American marital property law is far more complex than the simple binary of "community property" versus "separate property" suggests. As this book has demonstrated, the reality facing estate planning practitioners is one of layers, exceptions, permutations, and—above all—movement. Clients relocate across state lines for career opportunities, lifestyle changes, and family reasons. They acquire property in multiple jurisdictions. They marry, divorce, and remarry. Each of these events carries the potential to alter the character, ownership, and tax treatment of their assets in ways that are neither obvious nor intuitive.

For practitioners in noncommunity property states, the temptation has long been to treat community property as a specialized subject relevant only to colleagues in Arizona, California, Idaho, Louisiana, Nevada, New Mexico, Texas, Washington, and Wisconsin. That temptation must be resisted. With California and Texas together accounting for nearly one-quarter of the nation's population, and with sustained migration patterns bringing former community property residents to states like Florida, the Carolinas, and beyond, a rudimentary competency in community property law is no longer optional; it is essential. The arrival of elective community property trust statutes in Alaska, South Dakota, Tennessee, Kentucky, and Florida has only broadened the need for fluency in this area, offering planning opportunities and pitfalls in equal measure. As always, practitioners should consult with counsel licensed in each community property state whose law is involved in a particular estate plan to ensure that planning decisions reflect the current law of the relevant jurisdiction.

THE CORE LESSONS

Throughout this book, we have returned to several foundational principles that bear repeating as we close:

State law defines property rights, while federal law applies tax consequences to those rights. This principle, articulated by the Supreme Court and reaffirmed countless times by the IRS and lower courts, is the bedrock of all community property tax planning. The Internal Revenue Code does not create or destroy community property—it simply respects (or, in some cases, disregards for specific purposes) the ownership interests that state law has already established. Understanding this hierarchy is essential to navigating conflicts of law, basis planning, and estate inclusion questions.

Community property ordinarily retains its character after a change of domicile, absent affirmative action by the spouses, subject to possible issues of transmutation, including inadvertent transmutation, under applicable state law. The doctrine of partial mutability teaches that movable property acquired while domiciled in a community property state remains community property even after the couple relocates to a separate property state. This principle is widely recognized but inadequately understood. It means that practitioners must affirmatively inquire into their clients' residential history; trace the origin of significant assets; and help clients decide whether to preserve, partition, or transmute community property interests in light of their current and future planning goals.

The "double step-up" in basis under § 1014(b)(6) is one of the most significant tax advantages of community property ownership. At the death of the first spouse, both halves of community property—the decedent's share and the survivor's share—receive a new fair market value basis, effectively eliminating all built-in capital gains. This benefit is not a loophole; it is a deliberate congressional choice made in 1948 to equalize the tax treatment of married couples across community property and common law states. For couples with substantial appreciated assets and disparate life expectancies, the value of this provision can be measured in the hundreds of thousands or even millions of dollars of avoided capital gains tax.

Elective community property trusts offer the prospect of a full step-up in basis, but practitioners must understand the legal foundation that supports them. Alaska, South Dakota, Tennessee, Kentucky, and Florida have each enacted statutes allowing married couples to opt in to community property treatment by transferring assets to a qualifying trust. These statutes are drafted to vest each spouse with a present, undivided one-half interest in trust property, mirroring the ownership structure that defines community property in every jurisdiction that recognizes it. Yet the IRS has expressed doubt, most notably in Internal Revenue Manual 25.18.1.2.3 and Publication 555 dated December 2024, about whether such opt-in trusts will be respected for federal tax purposes, citing the U.S. Supreme Court's 1944 decision in *Commissioner v. Harmon.*

We have argued at length that *Harmon* is distinguishable, that its reasoning has been overtaken by subsequent statutory changes, and that a properly drafted community property trust under a properly drafted state statute should be effective to secure the § 1014(b)(6) step-up. But candor requires acknowledgment: No published ruling or court decision has definitively resolved this question, and practitioners who recommend community property trusts should explain this uncertainty to their clients.

Creditor protection often cuts against community property planning. One of the recurring tensions in this book has been the trade-off between income tax efficiency and asset protection. In many separate property states, property held as tenants by the entirety is shielded from the creditors of either spouse acting alone, and some couples will be well advised to keep most of the otherwise exposed assets in the name or under a revocable trust of the spouse who has lower creditor risk. Also, one spouse may place noncommunity property into the name of another spouse. It should not be subject to creditor claims against the non-owner spouse in a noncommunity property state. Many planners therefore have their community property married clients transmute out of community property status and place assets in the name of the spouse who is less at risk for creditor protection purposes.

Community property law offers no equivalent protection; each spouse's creditors can generally reach that spouse's undivided one-half interest in community assets. For clients facing professional liability, business risk, or other creditor exposure, the choice between TBE ownership and community property treatment is not a tax question—it is a risk management question that must be evaluated in light of the client's specific circumstances and the applicable state's creditor rights laws.

Divorce and death are governed by different legal frameworks, even within the same marital property regime. Equitable distribution at divorce and elective share protections at death are not simply the "separate property equivalents" of community property division—they are distinct bodies of law with their own histories, policies, and outcomes. As Chapter 3 demonstrated, most community property states have themselves adopted equitable distribution principles at divorce, diverging from the strict 50/50 division that traditionally defined community property at death. Understanding these distinctions is critical for practitioners advising clients on premarital agreements, postnuptial agreements, and estate plans that must account for both dissolution of marriage and survivorship scenarios. For example, it can make good sense to put assets, or perhaps a nonvoting member interest, in an LLC that owns assets into the name or revocable trust of the spouse who is less likely to have liability issues to both protect the assets from judgments against the other spouse, and also enable those assets to pass into one or more trusts that can benefit the surviving spouse who is at higher risk without being subject to his or her creditor claims.

The Myth of "Traditional" Community Property

One of the most significant insights to emerge from this book's comprehensive examination is that the very notion of "traditional" or "legal" community property, invoked by the IRS in questioning elective regimes by citation to *Harmon*, is something of an illusion. The Internal Revenue Manual's suggestion that elective community property systems cannot be respected for federal tax purposes because they lack the "traditional" character of the eight original community property states rests on an assumption that does not withstand scrutiny.

What, exactly, is "traditional" about the traditional community property states? As we explored in Chapters 3 and 5, and Appendix A, the answer is very little, beyond their age.

Consider the treatment of community property at divorce. California, Louisiana, and New Mexico continue to require an equal 50/50 division of community assets upon dissolution of marriage, consistent with the theoretical underpinnings of community property as a marital partnership. But Arizona, Idaho, Nevada, Texas, and Washington—five of the eight "traditional" states—have adopted equitable distribution principles that permit courts to divide community property unequally based on need, ability to work, health, fault, and other factors. In practice, these states' divorce outcomes often more closely resemble those in common law equitable distribution jurisdictions than those in their sister community property states.

Now turn to creditor rights. In Arizona, New Mexico, and Washington, courts apply a "community debt" framework that presumes that obligations incurred during marriage benefit the community and may be satisfied from community assets. California, Nevada, Idaho, Louisiana, and Texas, by contrast, follow a "managerial" system in which liability turns on which spouse has management and control over the property. Within the managerial states, the rules diverge further: California ties liability to statutory management authority; Louisiana allows community property to satisfy either spouse's debts but grants reimbursement rights; Texas distinguishes sole-management from joint-management community property and applies different creditor-access rules to each.

Even the classification of income from separate property during marriage, a bedrock question of what is and is not community, produces a clean split. Arizona, California, Nevada, New Mexico, and Washington treat income from separate property as remaining separate. Idaho, Louisiana, and Texas treat such income as community property.

The same fragmentation appears in rules governing management and control, transmutation formalities, the treatment of quasi-community property, and even the definition of what constitutes "community property" in the first place. Some states permit oral or implied transmutations; others require express written declarations. Some apply quasi-community property rules at both divorce and death; others apply them only at divorce. Some allow community property to be held with a right of survivorship; others do not.

These "traditional" states do not share a uniform body of substantive rules. What they share is *history*—most adopted community property principles in the nineteenth century as part of their civil law inheritance from Spain, Mexico, or France—and *federal recognition*, which they obtained because they were already in place when the Supreme Court decided *Poe v. Seaborn* in 1930.

The IRS's reliance on *Commissioner v. Harmon* to question elective community property regimes rests on a similar misconception. *Harmon* was decided in 1944, in the middle of the Supreme Court's long struggle to reconcile the assignment-of-income doctrine with the realities of community property ownership. As we demonstrated in Chapter 8, Justice Douglas's dissent in *Harmon* exposed the majority's reasoning as formalistic and unsustainable: The distinction between "legal" and "consensual" community property systems cannot be maintained when both vest each spouse with a present, undivided one-half interest in marital acquisitions. Douglas argued that *either* the Court should apply *Poe v. Seaborn* uniformly to any state that substantively creates community ownership, *or* it should abandon *Seaborn* altogether and embrace a uniform assignment-of-income rule under *Lucas v. Earl.* The majority chose neither path, and instead drew a line that turned on whether a state's regime was "traditional."

Congress resolved this tension four years later. The Revenue Act of 1948 adopted income splitting for all married couples and enacted § 1014(b)(6) to provide a full basis adjustment for community property at the first spouse's death. The legislative history is unambiguous: Congress intended to equalize the federal tax treatment of married couples *across* jurisdictions, removing the distortions created by state law differences in marital property regimes. Section 1014(b)(6) refers simply to property held "under the community property laws of any State," without qualification or limitation. It does not require that those laws be "mandatory," "traditional," or of any particular vintage. It asks only whether, under applicable state law, the property is community property and whether at least one-half of the community interest is includible in the decedent's gross estate.

The IRS's insistence that elective regimes cannot qualify under § 1014(b)(6) because they are not "traditional" may therefore invert the statutory framework. State law defines the property interest. Federal law applies the tax consequence. If Alaska, South Dakota, Tennessee, Kentucky, or Florida enacts a statute that vests each spouse with a present, undivided one-half interest in property transferred to a qualifying trust—and if that statute operates with the same incidents—the same rules of ownership, management, and disposition as community property in California or Texas—then the property *is* community property for purposes of § 1014(b)(6). The fact that the couple *elected* into the regime rather than being automatically subject to it is a distinction without a difference, just as Justice Douglas argued in 1944.

The IRS's position in Internal Revenue Manual 25.18.1.2.3, if taken to its logical conclusion, would produce absurd results. Suppose Louisiana amended its Civil Code to make community property treatment elective rather than mandatory, while leaving all other substantive rules unchanged. Would the IRS then refuse to recognize Louisiana community property for purposes of § 1014(b)(6)?

The answer, of course, is that these hypotheticals expose the incoherence of the "traditional versus elective" or "legal versus consensual" distinctions. The proper inquiry is whether state law has created an ownership interest that federal tax law is required to respect. If it has, then the tax consequences follow from the Code, not from the IRS's view of which state systems are sufficiently venerable.

Practical Takeaways for the Practitioner

As you close this book and return to your practice, we offer the following practical guidance:

Always take a property characterization history. Your intake questionnaire should ask not only where the client currently lives but also where the client has lived during the marriage, where significant assets were acquired, and whether any formal agreements (premarital, postnuptial, partition, or transmutation) have been executed. For clients who have lived in multiple states, consider preparing a timeline that maps asset acquisition to periods of domicile in community property versus separate property jurisdictions.

Do not assume that title controls ownership in community property states. An account titled in the husband's name alone may still be community property if funded with community earnings. Real estate titled jointly may be separate property if acquired with separate funds and properly documented.[1] The operative question is not "whose name is on the account?" but "what was the source of the funds, and what does state law say about the character of property acquired with those funds?"

---

[1] Because community property states do not rely on title theory, extra steps must be taken to ensure property acquired during the marriage is held to be separate property in that jurisdiction in spite of title saying otherwise.

Consider preserving community property character when clients move from community property states to separate property states. For clients relocating from California, Texas, or another community property jurisdiction to a separate property state, consider establishing a joint revocable trust to hold the community property and preserve its character. Attach a schedule identifying the community assets and include express language in the trust instrument affirming that the property will retain its community character notwithstanding the change in domicile. If the client's new state has adopted the Uniform Disposition of Community Property Rights at Death Act (UDCPRDA) or its successor, the Uniform Community Property Disposition at Death Act (UCPDDA), confirm that the statute will preserve the client's testamentary rights at death—but do not rely on the statute alone to maintain community status during the life of the marriage.

Use transmutation and partition agreements strategically. Where clients wish to convert community property to separate property (or vice versa), a written transmutation or partition agreement is essential. The agreement should be explicit, signed by both spouses, and recorded if it affects real property. A court order may be required to bless the agreement if the couple resides in Louisiana or legal counsel wants to be absolutely sure of the enforceability of the transmutation. Where the goal is to preserve community property character in a separate property state, consider an agreement to be signed by both spouses that reaffirms the community nature of the property and documents the spouses' intent to maintain community ownership despite the change in domicile.

Evaluate community property trust planning carefully and disclose the risks. For clients in Alaska, South Dakota, Tennessee, Kentucky, or Florida who are interested in obtaining a full step-up in basis, the community property trust is a powerful tool, but it is not without controversy. Walk the client through the mechanics of the trust, the requirements under state law, the uncertainty surrounding IRS recognition, and the creditor exposure that community property entails. Provide the disclosure in writing, and ensure the client understands that the full step-up in basis is a benefit that *should* be available under a proper reading of § 1014(b)(6) and the 1948 legislative history, but that the IRS has not formally blessed elective regimes, and a risk of challenge exists. The joint exempt step-up trust is discussed in Chapter 12 as an alternative to community property trusts and may become more popular if and when community property begins to become attacked by or challenged by the Internal Revenue Service. While the JEST does not offer a guaranteed step-up in basis and remains largely untested in reported cases or authoritative guidance, the two private letter rulings and TAM seem to indicate that up to all of the trust assets could be used to fund a credit shelter trust on the first death, and there is certainly support for the proposition that a step-up occurs.

Stay current with developments in this area. Community property law is not static. State legislatures continue to refine their community property statutes, elective community property trust states are still working through implementation questions, and the IRS may issue additional guidance (whether through revenue rulings, private letter rulings, or updated publications) that clarifies or changes the federal tax treatment of elective regimes. Subscribe to trusted treatises, attend continuing education programs, and monitor developments in the states where your clients have lived or acquired property. When a client's estate plan involves community property from one or more states, practitioners should consult with counsel who are familiar with the community property laws of each relevant jurisdiction to ensure that the plan is properly designed and executed.

A FINAL WORD

Community property law is, at its heart, a law of partnership. It rests on the principle that marriage is an economic as well as an emotional union, and that both spouses contribute to the accumulation of wealth during the marriage, whether through paid labor, unpaid labor, or the countless other forms of support and sacrifice that sustain a household. The community property law's recognition of each spouse's equal ownership interest in marital acquisitions is a statement of values.

One of the central arguments we have advanced in this book is that the IRS's position on elective community property trusts, grounded in a mechanical reading of *Harmon* and an appeal to "tradition," cannot withstand scrutiny. We have walked carefully through the development of the equitable distribution system, the patchwork of creditor right rules, the divergent treatment of income from separate property, and the varying requirements for transmutation and management. We have shown that the eight "traditional" community property states are united by little more than their age, and that their substantive rules differ as much from each other as they do from elective regimes.

We have traced Congress's response in the Revenue Act of 1948, which was designed to eliminate discrimination and to equalize federal tax treatment by keying tax consequences to state-defined property rights. And we have shown that § 1014(b)(6), by its plain terms, applies to property held "under the community property laws of any State," without requiring that those laws be mandatory, ancient, traditional, or legal, as opposed to consensual or elective.

The IRS's insistence that elective community property trusts cannot qualify for the full step-up in basis is a position unsupported by statute, legislative history, or sound tax policy. It is a relic of a pre-1948 jurisprudence that Congress deliberately overrode. It rests on an illusory dichotomy between "legal" and "consensual" community property systems.

We do not pretend that this question has been definitively settled by the courts or the Service. We acknowledge the risk, and we recommend that practitioners disclose that risk to clients. But we also believe, on the basis of careful analysis of the applicable statutory schemes and legislative history, that a properly drafted community property trust under a properly drafted state statute should be effective to secure the advantages of § 1014(b)(6), and that the IRS's contrary position is both legally and practically indefensible.

The fact that no case or ruling has yet confirmed this position does not mean the planning is unsound—it means the question is unresolved, and in that space between statute and administration lies opportunity. Where the code is clear, where state law is carefully drafted, and where the ownership structure mirrors that of the "traditional" community property states, practitioners should be prepared to assert the position, document the analysis, and defend the result. That is the nature of sophisticated tax planning in areas where the law has outpaced administrative guidance.

This book was written to equip you for that work. We hope it has succeeded. We hope that you will return to it when a new client walks into your office with a California deed, a Texas bank account, or a Florida community property trust. We hope that you will use it to avoid mistakes, to spot opportunities, and to serve your clients well.

Above all, we hope that you will come away from this book with a deeper appreciation for the complexity and the enduring relevance of community property law in modern American estate planning. It is a field that rewards careful study, disciplined analysis, and a willingness to look beyond the surface of title documents and account registrations to the underlying property rights that state law has created.

The migration patterns that define contemporary American life ensure that community property issues will only become more common in the years ahead. Clients will continue to move from California to Florida, from Texas to the Carolinas, from Washington to Tennessee, and back again. They will bring with them community property acquired decades earlier, now layered into joint brokerage accounts, family LLCs, or revocable trusts drafted without regard to the property's original character, and they will ask you whether their estate plan is "in order." Your answer may often depend not on what the account statement says today, but on what the law said 15 years ago in a state 1,500 miles away.

Appendix A

KEY:
CP = Community Property
SP = Separate Property

COMMUNITY PROPERTY AND COMMUNITY PROPERTY–TRUST STATES CHART

State	**Does the community property system apply automatically or by election?**	**Generally, can a postmarital creditor of only one spouse reach all of the community property to satisfy the debt?**	**Does community property include the income from, or the growth on, separate property?** Cite: M. Read Moore, *Coming Soon To Your State: Community Property.* See J. Thomas Oldham, *Separate Property Businesses That Increase in Value During Marriage,* 1990 WIS. L. REV. 585 (1990) for an interesting discussion on this issue.	**Is the community property divided equally upon divorce?** Cite: Brett R. Turner, *Equitable Distribution of Property*; William A. Reppy, Jr., *Major Events in the Evolution of American Community Property Law and Their Import to Equitable Distribution States*, 23 FAM. L.Q. 163, 163–92 (1989).	**Is a quasi-community property statute or Uniform Act in place to treat noncommunity property as community property when the couple has moved to the subject community property state?** Cite: Kenneth W. Kingma, *Property Division at Divorce or Death for Married Couples Migrating Between Common Law and Community Property States*, 35 ACTEC J. 74 (2009).
Arizona	Automatic. Spouses can opt out by marital property agreement.	No. The creditor of only one spouse cannot generally reach all CP to satisfy the debt unless the debt qualifies as a community debt. *State ex rel. Indus. Comm'r of Arizona v. Wright*, 43 P.3d 203 (Ariz. App. 1st Div. 2002) ("As a general proposition, we agree that a creditor cannot reach marital CP to satisfy a separate obligation incurred by either spouse after marriage."); however, Arizona has a strong presumption that debts arising during marriage are community in nature, absent clear and convincing evidence to the contrary. *Id.*	No—if the income or growth is primarily attributable to the inherent qualities of the SP, such property will remain SP. However, if the income or growth is primarily attributable to the labor, skill, or management of either spouse during the marriage—the income/growth will generally be CP. *Rueschenberg v. Rueschenberg*, 219 Ariz. 249 (App. 2008). But see *Morris v. Morris*, No. 1 CA-CV 19-0028 FC, 2020 WL 3250861 (Ariz. App. 1st Div. Apr. 9, 2020).	No. Divided on equitable basis. ARIZ. STAT. § 25-318. However, the Ariz. Supreme Court has interpreted the statute as requiring a substantially equal distribution of community assets in the absence of a compelling reason to the contrary. *Kelly v. Kelly*, 9 P.3d 1046, 1048 (Ariz. 2000), as amended (Oct. 11, 2000).	Yes, for divorce purposes. ARIZ. STAT. § 25-318(A). No, upon death. At death, the character of property is determined under the conflict of laws approach (i.e., movables determined by marital domicile at time of acquisition and immovables determined by situs of real property). *Rau v. Rau*, 6 Ariz. App. 362, 432 P.2d 910 (1967).

COMMUNITY PROPERTY AND COMMUNITY PROPERTY-TRUST STATES CHART *(Continued)*

California	Automatic. Spouses can opt out by marital property agreement.	Yes, the community estate is liable for debts incurred by either spouse before or during the marriage, regardless of which spouse has the management and control of the property and regardless of whether one or both spouses are parties to the debt or to a judgment for the debt. CAL. FAM. CODE § 910. But see CAL. FAM. CODE § 911 exempting earnings of a married person for premarital debts of the other spouse as long as the other spouse does not have a right of withdrawal over the account in which the earnings are deposited, and the earnings remain uncommingled.	No. Income generated on SP generally retains its character as SP. But fruits of the community's expenditures of time, talent, and labor are CP. *Patrick v. Alacer Corp.*, 136 Cal. Rptr. 3d 669 (Cal. App. 4th Dist. 2011); *In re Marriage of Dekker*, 21 Cal. Rptr. 2d 642 (Cal. App. 4th Dist. 1993).	Yes, unless there is a written agreement, oral stipulation in open court, or other statutory provision that allows for a different division. CAL. FAM. CODE § 2550. "[U]nlike virtually every other state, California has restricted judicial authority by requiring trial courts to divide the community estate equally between the parties." *In re Marriage of Cream*, 16 Cal. Rptr. 2d 575 (Cal. App. 1st Dist. 1993).	Yes. on divorce. Yes, on death. Yes, California recognizes quasi-CP at both divorce and death. CAL. CIV. CODE § 2550 (as to divorce), and CAL. PROB. CODE § 101 (as to death).
Idaho	Automatic. Spouses can opt out by marital property agreement.	Yes, and a postmarital debt does not need to be for the benefit of the community in order for the community to be liable. IDAHO CODE § 32-906; *Credit Bureau of E. Idaho, Inc. v. Lecheminant*, 235 P.3d 1188 (Idaho 2010).	Yes, unless the conveyance by which the property is acquired or a written agreement between the spouses specifically designates such income or growth as SP. IDAHO CODE § 32-906.	No. Divided on an equitable basis. IDAHO CODE § 32-712. However, unless there are compelling reasons otherwise, there shall be a substantially equal division in value, considering debts, between the spouses. IDAHO CODE § 32-712.	No. on divorce. Yes, on death. Yes, but Idaho only recognizes quasi-CP at death. See IDAHO CODE ANN. § 15-2-210(a). At divorce, Idaho determines division of property under the conflict of laws approach. *Berle v. Berle*, 97 Idaho 452, 546 P.2d. 407 (1976).

(Continued)

COMMUNITY PROPERTY AND COMMUNITY PROPERTY-TRUST STATES CHART *(Continued)*

Louisiana	Automatic. Spouses can opt out by marital property agreement.	Yes, a separate or community obligation may be satisfied during the CP regime from CP and from the SP of the spouse who incurred the obligation. LA. CIV. CODE Art. 2345. To balance this, the nondebtor-spouse has a right of reimbursement if community assets are used to pay the other spouse's separate debt. LA. CIV. CODE Art. 2364.	Yes, but a spouse may reserve them as his or her SP by a declaration made in an authentic act or in an act under private signature duly acknowledged. See LA. Art. 2339.	Yes. LA. Stat. §9:2801(4)(b). See also, *Rearden v. Rearden*, 568 So. 2d 1111 (La. App. 2d Cir. 1990).	Yes, on divorce. Yes, on death. Yes, Louisiana recognizes quasi-CP at both divorce and death. LA. CIV. CODE ANN. Art. 3526 (as to divorce and as to death).
Nevada	Automatic. Spouses can opt out by marital property agreement.	No, the creditor of only one spouse cannot generally reach all CP to satisfy the debt unless the debt qualifies as a community debt. *Norwest Fin. v. Lawver*, 849 P.2d 324 (Nev. 1993) (holding that creditor may not proceed against CP acquired post-petition by nonbankrupt spouse to satisfy community debt). Debts incurred during marriage are presumed to be community debts. *Dubler v. Moret*, 281 P.3d 1169 (Nev. 2009); *Morse v. USAA Fed. Sav. Bank*, No. 2:12-CV-00381-KJD, 2012 WL 6020090 (D. Nev. Dec. 3, 2012).	No. Income generated on SP generally retains its character as SP. But fruits of the community's expenditures of time, talent, and labor are CP. *Cord v. Neuhoff*, 573 P.2d 1170 (Nev. 1978). "It is now settled in [California and Nevada] that in such circumstance there must be an apportionment of any increment in value between the separate estate of the owner and the community, unless the increment is due solely to a natural enhancement of the property or the owner of the separate estate expended only minimal effort and there was no evidence presented attributing a value to his services." *Cord*, at p. 1173.	No. Divided on an equitable basis. See NV. STAT. § 125.150. The statute instructs the court to make an equal distribution of the CP of the parties, "to the extent practicable." But the statute gives the court broad discretion to make an unequal disposition of the CP "if the court finds a compelling reason to do so." NV. STAT. § 125.150(1)(b).	No, on divorce. No, on death. No, Nevada follows the conflict of laws approach for property characterization and division issues at both divorce and death. Braddock v. Braddock, 542 P.2d. 1061 (Nev. 1975).

COMMUNITY PROPERTY AND COMMUNITY PROPERTY-TRUST STATES CHART *(Continued)*

New Mexico	Automatic. Spouses can opt out by marital property agreement.	No, the creditor of only one spouse cannot generally reach all CP to satisfy the debt unless the debt qualifies as a community debt. NM Stat. §§ 40-3-9-40-3-11. Neither spouse's interest in CP or SP shall be liable for the separate debt of the other spouse. NM Stat. § 40-3-10.	No. The income and growth on SP are generally presumed to remain SP. NM. Stat. § 40-3-8; *Bayer v. Bayer*, 800 P.2d 216 (N.M. App. 1990). However, this presumption can be rebutted if there is direct and positive evidence that the increase was due to community funds or labor. *Id.*	Yes. *Bustos v. Bustos*, 673 P.2d 1289 (N.M. 1983) ("Although mathematic exactitude is not required in the division of community assets, it is the duty of the district courts, upon dissolution of a marriage, to divide as equally as possible the property of the community.")	Yes, on divorce. No, on death. Yes, New Mexico only recognizes quasi-CP at divorce. NM. Stat. § 40-3-8(C). At death, New Mexico determines the character and division of property under the conflict of laws approach. *Hughes v. Hughes*, 91 N.M. 339, 573 P.2d 1194 (1978).
Texas	Automatic. Spouses can opt out by marital property agreement.	Yes, in Texas a creditor of only one spouse can generally reach the CP to satisfy the debt, but the extent of this reach depends on the management and control of the property and the nature of the debt. TX Stat. § 3.202. CP Yes - But sole management, control, and disposition rule applies. *Id.* TX Stat. § 3.102 outlines what property is considered separately managed and what property is considered jointly managed.	Yes. Income produced from SP is considered CP, regardless of the nature of the SP generating the income, including stock, shares in a corporation, livestock, or other assets. *Richardson v. Richardson*, 424 S.W.3d 691 (Tex. App.–El Paso 2014).	No. Divided on an equitable basis. TX. Stat. § 7.001 ("just and right" standard). CP does not need to be divided equally, but the division must be equitable. *Chacon v. Chacon*, 222 S.W.3d 909 (Tex. App.–El Paso 2007).	Yes, on divorce. No, on death. Yes, but Texas only recognizes quasi-CP at divorce. Tex. Fam. Code. § 7.002. At death, Texas determines the character and division of property under the conflict of laws approach. *Estate of Hanau*, 730 S.W.2d. 663, 666 (1987).

(Continued)

COMMUNITY PROPERTY AND COMMUNITY PROPERTY-TRUST STATES CHART *(Continued)*

Washington	Automatic. Spouses can opt out by marital property agreement.	No, the creditor of only one spouse can generally only reach the debtor-spouse's one-half interest in the CP to satisfy the debt. *Haley v. Highland*, 12 P.3d 119 (2000) ("under this court's decisional law, CP is generally not available to satisfy the separate debts of either spouse," citing *Nichols Hills Bank v. McCool*, 104 Wash. 2d 78, 701 P.2d 1114 (1985). The Court in *Haley* further noted, "[T]he general provision of RCW 26.16.200 was not intended to protect CP, but rather was intended to protect one spouse from vicarious liability for the separate obligations of the other. . . . We affirm the Court of Appeals by holding that RCW 26.16.200 does not bar the use of Highland's CP to satisfy a judgment based on his premarital tort. We further hold that this case is governed by *deElche* and *Keene*, permitting the use of Highland's one-half interest in community personal property to satisfy his separate tort obligation if his separate property is insufficient to satisfy the claim," citing *deElche v. Jacobsen*, 95 Wash. 2d 237, 622 P.2d 835 (1980), and *Keene v. Edie*, 131 Wash. 2d 822, 935 P.2d 588 (1997).	No. Any increase in the value of SP remains SP, but this presumption may be rebutted by direct and positive evidence that the increase is attributable to community funds or labor. *Elam v. Elam*, 650 P.2d 213 (1982).	No. Divided on an equitable basis. WASH. REV. CODE § 26.09.080. No requirement that CP be divided equally at divorce. *In re Marriage of Rockwell*, 170 P.3d 572 (Wash. App. Div. 1 2007).	No, on divorce. Yes, on death. Yes, but Washington only recognizes quasi-CP at death. WASH. REV. CODE § 26.16.220 and § 26.16.230. At divorce, Washington determines the character and division of property under the "statutory" equitable distribution approach (i.e., statutes that grant a court authority to divide all, or nearly all, of the property acquired by the spouses, see *Kingma*, supra). WASH. REV. CODE § 26.09.080. See *Shanghai Com. Bank Ltd. v. Kung Da Chang*, 404 P.3d 62 (2017) for a recent Washington Supreme Court en banc opinion discussing the conflict of law issues.

COMMUNITY PROPERTY AND COMMUNITY PROPERTY-TRUST STATES CHART (*Continued*)

Wisconsin	Automatic. Spouses can opt out by marital property agreement.	No. The creditor of one spouse may reach only the debtor-spouses individual property and the debtor-spouse's one-half interest in the CP unless the obligation is (1) a support obligation or (2) an obligation incurred in the interest of the marriage/family, in which case all marital property is liable. An obligation is, however, presumed to be incurred in the interest of the marriage/family. Wis. Stat. § 766.55.	Income generated by SP is considered distinct from the property itself and is generally included in the marital estate. *Arneson v. Arneson*, 355 N.W.2d 16 (Wis. App. 1984). Appreciation in value of a separate asset will remain SP where the appreciation is due solely to general economic conditions (e.g., inflation, real estate value increases). However, where the appreciation in value of the SP is due to the efforts and abilities of the marital partnership, that appreciation becomes part of the marital estate. *Schorer v. Schorer*, 501 N.W.2d 916 (Wis. App. 1993).	No. Divided on an equitable basis, with a presumption of equal division. Wis. Stat. § 767.61.	No, on divorce. Yes, on death. Yes, but Wisconsin only recognizes quasi-CP at death. Wis. Stat. § 861.02 and § 861.03. At divorce, Wisconsin determines the character and division of property under the statutory equitable distribution approach. Wis. Stat. § 767.61.
Alaska	Elective by Agreement or Trust.	No. Only as to the debtor-spouse's one-half interest in the CP. AK Stat. § 34.77.070(j).	No. Except where the CP agreement provides that all property acquired by either or both spouses during the marriage is CP, § 34.77.030(d). The Alaska Community Property Act at least considers the issue, unlike the other CP trust states.	No. Divided on an equitable basis. AK. Stat. § 25.24.160. When dividing a marital estate, the trial court generally should begin with the presumption that an equal division of marital property is the most equitable. *Heustess v. Kelley-Heustess*, 158 P.3d 827, 833 (Alaska 2007).	No, on divorce. Yes, on death. Yes, Alaska has adopted the UDCPRDA; the act applies only at death. AK. Stat. § 13.41.005.

(*Continued*)

COMMUNITY PROPERTY AND COMMUNITY PROPERTY-TRUST STATES CHART *(Continued)*

Tennessee	Elective by Trust.	No. Only as to the debtor-spouse's one-half interest in the CP. TN STAT. § 35-17-106(a).	No. And the issue is not considered in the TN Community Property Trust Act.	No. Divided on an equitable basis. TN. STAT. § 36-4-121.	No, on divorce. No, on death. No, Tennessee does not have a Uniform Act applicable to the disposition of CP at death or divorce, and there is no known case law on this.
Kentucky	Elective by Trust.	No. Only as to the debtor-spouse's one-half interest in the CP. KY STAT. § 386.624(1).	No. And the issue is not considered in the FL Community Property Trust Act.	No. Marital property divided on an equitable basis. KY. STAT. § 403.190. "The law is clear that there is no presumption of a 50-50 division without regard to the evidence." *Gaskill v. Robbins*, 282 S.W.3d 306 (Ky. 2009).	No, on divorce. Yes, on death. Yes, Kentucky has adopted the UDCPRDA; the act applies only at death. KY. STAT. § 391.255.
Florida	Elective by Trust.	No. Only as to the debtor-spouse's one-half interest in the CP. FL STAT. § 736.1506(1) ("Unless a greater amount is otherwise provided by the CPT Agreement").	No. And the issue is not considered in the TN Community Property Trust Act.	No. Marital property divided on an equitable basis. FL. STAT. § 61.075. In distributing the marital assets and liabilities between the parties, the court must begin with the premise that the distribution should be equal, unless there is a justification for an unequal distribution based on all relevant factors. FL. STAT. § 61.075(1).	No, on divorce. Yes, on death. Yes, Florida has adopted the UDCPRDA; the act applies only at death. FL. STAT. § 732.216.

COMMUNITY PROPERTY AND COMMUNITY PROPERTY-TRUST STATES CHART *(Continued)*

South Dakota	Elective by Trust.	Only as to the debtor-spouse's one-half interest in the CP. SD STAT. § 55-17-11. But the South Dakota statutes are less clear.	No. And the issue is not considered in the SD Special Spousal Trust Act.	No. Marital property divided on an equitable basis. SD. STAT. § 25-4-44.	No, on divorce. No, on death. No, South Dakota does not have a Uniform Act applicable to the disposition of CP at death or divorce.

CP states that have enacted quasi-CP statutes are able to classify and divide all property under the law of the forum, which eliminates the administrative burden of classifying and dividing individual assets. Similarly, common law states that have enacted Uniform Acts have solved this issue as to death. But the UDCPRDA only applies at death, and there is not a similar fix for common law states at divorce other than the traditional conflict of laws approach or Restatement approach.

Index